D0984330

# Sermons
## of the
# Century

## Other books by Warren Wiersbe

*10 Power Principles for Christian Service*
*Be Myself*
*The Bumps Are What You Climb On*
*The Dynamics of Preaching*
*God Isn't in a Hurry*
*The Intercessory Prayer of Jesus*
*Living with the Giants*
*The Name of Jesus*
*On Being a Servant of God*
*Prayer, Praise and Promises*
*Preaching and Teaching with Imagination*
*Real Worship*
*So That's What a Christian Is!*
*Through the Year with Warren W. Wiersbe*
*Victorious Christians You Should Know*

# Sermons
## *of the*
# Century

**Inspiration from 100 Years
of Influential Preaching**

*Warren W. Wiersbe, editor*

**Baker Books**

A Division of Baker Book House Co
Grand Rapids, Michigan 49516

© 2000 by Warren W. Wiersbe

Published by Baker Books
a division of Baker Book House Company
P.O. Box 6287, Grand Rapids, MI 49516-6287

Printed in the United States of America

### Library of Congress Cataloging-in-Publication Data

Sermons of the century : inspiration from one hundred years of influential preaching / Warren W. Wiersbe, editor.
    p.    cm.
    Includes bibliographical references and index.
    ISBN 0-8010-9108-X (cloth)
    1. Sermons, American—20th century. 2. Sermons, English—20th century.
I. Wiersbe, Warren W.
    BV4241.S422    2000
    252'.00973'0904—dc21                      00-034285

For current information about all releases from Baker Book House, visit our web site:
http://www.bakerbooks.com

# Contents

6

# Introduction

This anthology brings together representative sermons of influential preachers of the twentieth century, all of whom would be identified with the Christian tradition. It begins with Dwight Lyman Moody, who almost made it into the twentieth century. Moody was undoubtedly the best-known evangelist of the latter half of the nineteenth century, so I think he belongs in the book. The anthology closes with William Franklin ("Billy") Graham, certainly the most famous evangelist of the twentieth century, if not in Christian church history.

Those two choices were easy, but it wasn't easy to select the rest of the preachers or identify their "representative" sermons. Philip Van Doren Stern defined an anthologist as "a person who uses scissors and taste," but we all don't have the same taste in preachers or in sermons. My aim was to compile a convenient volume that covered a broad spectrum of preachers, and I realize that not everybody will agree with my selections. If your favorite preacher is missing, or if one is included who you feel doesn't belong, perhaps you'll discover in these pages a preacher who is new to you, and this will compensate somewhat for your disappointment.

The presence of a preacher in this book doesn't mean that the compiler or the publisher agrees completely with his or her theological or political views, and the absence of a preacher doesn't mean that he or she didn't qualify. I make no claims to have chosen "the best of the best" because I lack the omniscience necessary for such a task. I selected those preachers who seemed to me to have influence beyond their own base of ministry and who left behind something to remind us that they had been among us.

Whatever else it may have been, the twentieth century was certainly a great century of preaching as far as the English-speaking world is concerned. The printing press, radio, and television, and more recently the Internet, have carried around the world sermons that might have had but a limited hearing. Perhaps not every sermon is worthy of such a wide hearing, but we never know how God will use his truth to change someone's life.

May the new century also be a time when God's Word will be proclaimed widely, with authority and compassion.

Warren W. Wiersbe

# Dwight Lyman Moody

*1837–1899*

Born in Northfield, Massachusetts, into a family marked by poverty and limited educational opportunities, D. L. Moody became the best-known evangelist of the nineteenth century, and his fame has not diminished. While working in his uncle's shoe store in Boston, he was led to faith in Christ by his Sunday school teacher, Edward Kimball, on April 21, 1855. Knowing he had a flair for business, Moody went to the booming city of Chicago in 1856 and there became a successful salesman.

In 1857 Moody became involved in Sunday school work and within two years had more than a thousand children attending his school. During the Civil War, he went to the front nine times to minister to the soldiers and there began to develop his approach to personal evangelism. He married Emma Revell, one of his Sunday school teachers, in 1862, and in 1865 founded the Illinois Street Church. Moody was busy in Christian work and traveled a good deal to promote both Sunday schools and the YMCA.

Moody lost almost everything in the Chicago fire (October 1871). He went to New York City to raise funds to rebuild his church, and while walking down Wall Street experienced a remarkable filling of the Holy Spirit that utterly transformed his ministry. The next year, while in Great Britain, he heard his friend Henry Varley say, "The world has yet to see what God will do

9

with and for and through and by a man fully and wholly consecrated to him." Moody's response was, "I will try my utmost to be that man," and from that time, he focused on mass evangelism.

From June 1873 to July 1875 Moody and soloist Ira Sankey held huge evangelistic campaigns in England and Scotland and saw thousands trust Christ. When Moody and Sankey returned to the United States, they found that they were famous and they conducted successful campaigns in many cities, including Philadelphia, New York City, Chicago, and Boston.

Though Moody lacked a formal education, he founded educational institutions: the Northfield Schools in 1879 and the Chicago Evangelistic Society in 1886, which in 1889 became the Moody Bible Institute. He also founded the Northfield Conference in 1880, a summer gathering of people to hear missionary reports, biblical exposition, and methods for reaching the lost. It was also a "convocation for prayer." The best-known preachers and missionaries of that day spoke at Northfield.

On November 12, 1899, Moody launched his Kansas City campaign but became so ill that he was unable to continue preaching. "Excused" was the last sermon he preached; it was one he often used in his campaigns. He died at home in Northfield on December 22 and was buried there on "Round Top" on December 26, with Dr. C. I. Scofield conducting the funeral service.

It is estimated that Moody traveled over a million miles during his ministry, preached the gospel to more than one hundred million people, and personally dealt with 750,000 inquirers. He was never ordained and throughout his ministry was known simply as "Mr. Moody."

The official biography is *The Life of D. L. Moody* by his son William R. Moody (Revell, 1900). There have been many biographies, but among the best are *Bush Aglow* by Richard Ellsworth Day (Judson, 1936); *They Called Him Mr. Moody* by Richard K. Curtis (Doubleday, 1962; Eerdmans paperback, 1967); and *Moody: A Biography* by John Pollock (Baker, 1997). The most insightful study of Moody's theology and methodology is *Love Them In: The Proclamation Theology of D. L. Moody* by Stanley Gundry (Moody Press, 1976).

# Excused

*I prayed thee have me excused.*
Luke 14:19

These three men that we read about to-night were not invited to hear some dry, stupid sermon or lecture, but they were invited to a feast. The gospel in this parable is represented as a feast, and there was an invitation extended to these three men to come to the feast. "And they all with one consent began to make excuse." It does not say that they had an excuse, but they made excuse—manufactured one for the occasion.

Now, excuses are as old as man. The first excuse that we hear of was in Eden. The first thing we hear after the fall of man was man making excuse. Instead of Adam confessing his guilt like a man, he began to excuse himself—to justify himself. That is what every man is trying to do—justify himself in his sins. Adam said, "It is the woman that thou gavest me." He hid behind her—a mean, cowardly act. And it was really charging it back on God. "It is the woman that thou gavest me." Blaming God for his sin. From that time that Adam fell from the summit of Eden to the present time, man has been guilty of that sin, charging it back on God, as if God was responsible for his sin and God was guilty.

Now, I venture to say that if I should go down among the congregation here tonight every man that has not accepted this invitation would be ready with an excuse. You have all got excuses. You would have one right on the end of your tongue. You would be ready to meet me the moment I got to you. If I met that excuse, then you would get another and you would hide behind that. Then, if I drove you out from behind that, you would get another. And so you would go on, hiding behind some excuse—making some excuse; and if you should get cornered up and could not think of one, Satan would be there to help you make one. That has been his business for the past six thousand years. He is very good to help men make excuses, and undoubtedly he helped these three men we read of here to-night. No sooner do we begin to preach the gospel of the Son of God than men begin to manufacture excuses. They begin to hunt around to see if they cannot find some reason to give for not accepting the invitation. Excuses are the cradle, in other words, that Satan rocks men off to sleep in. He gets them into that cradle of excuses that they may ease their consciences.

But let me say to you, my friends, there is no man or woman in this assembly to-night that can give an excuse that will stand the light of eternity. All these excuses that men are making are nothing but refuges of lies after all. We read in the prophecy of Isaiah that God shall sweep away these refuges of lies. When a man stands before God he will not be making excuses. His excuses will all be gone then, and he will be speechless.

We read of that man that got into the feast without a wedding garment, and when the lord of the feast came in he saw the man there. That man perhaps thought he could get in with the crowd. Some people say, "Oh, I will go with the crowd." He thought he could get in with the crowd, and he would not be noticed. But that eye was keen to detect one that had on not the wedding garment. Do not think for a moment that God's eye is not upon you. He knows how all the excuses are made. You cannot hide anything from Him. You may make excuses and put on a sort of garment, and that you are justifying yourself in living away from God and not accepting this invitation; but really it is nothing that will stand the light of eternity. Things look altogether different when you stand before Him.

Did you ever stop to think what would take place in a city like Cleveland if God should take every man and woman that wants to be excused at their word, and should say, "I will excuse you"? God took these three men that we read of at their word. He said, "Not one of them that were bidden shall taste of my supper." They spurned the invitation; they turned their backs upon it; and then God withdrew the invitation. "Not one of them that were bidden shall taste of my supper." Suppose that that should take place in Cleveland, and then by a stroke of Providence He should sweep every man and woman in Cleveland that wants to be excused from this feast into eternity. Suppose every man and woman that wanted to be excused from this feast should die inside of twenty-four hours. I think there would be plenty of room in this tabernacle tomorrow night for all that want to come. There would be a good many of your stores closed tomorrow. There would be no one to open them. Merchants, employees, clerks would all be gone. Every saloon in Cleveland would be closed up. Every rum seller wants to be excused from this feast. He can't get into the kingdom of God with a rum bottle in his hand. "Woe be to the man that putteth the bottle to his neighbor's lips." He knows very well that if he accepts this invitation he has got to give up his hellish traffic. Every blasphemer in Cleveland wants to be excused from this feast, because if he accepts this invitation he has got to give up his blasphemy. Every drunkard in Cleveland, every harlot, every thief, every dishonest man, every dishonest merchant would be gone. They want to be excused from this feast. Why? Because they have got to turn away from their sins if they accept of this invitation.

The longer I live, the more I am convinced that the reason men do not come to Christ is because they do not want to give up sin. That is the trouble. It is not their intellectual difficulties. It is quite popular for people to say that they have got intellectual difficulties; but if they would tell the honest truth it is some darling sin that they are holding on to. They are not willing to give up the harlot; they are not willing to give up gambling; they are not willing to give up drinking, the lust of the flesh, the lust of the eye, and the pride of life. That is the trouble. It is not their intellectual difficulties as much as it is their darling sin. The grass would soon be growing in your streets in Cleveland if God should take every man at his word and excuse him from this feast and take him away. Things would look altogether different in your city inside of a week if God should excuse you that want to be excused. And yet the moment that God sends out His invitation excuses just run right in. "I pray thee have me excused." That is the cry to-day. Man prepares his feast, and there is a great rush to get the best seats. God prepares His feast—and what a feast it is! Think of it! It is not often that common people like you and me get an invitation to a royal feast. There is many a man that has lived in Windsor Castle for fifty years, and has never got sight of Queen Victoria. There are men in London that stand high, men of wealth, men of position who never were invited into her palace. Men think it is a great honor to be invited into a king's palace or the palace of a queen. But here we are invited to the marriage of the Lamb. We are invited by the Lord of glory to come to the marriage of His only begotten son, and men begin to make excuses. "I pray thee, have me excused."

Now, let us look for a moment at the excuses these three men gave. The first man might have been very polite. Some men are very polite. Some are very gruff, and treat you with a great deal of scorn and contempt. The moment you begin to talk to them they say, "You attend to your business and I will attend to mine." But I can imagine this man was a very polite man and he said, "I wish you would take back this message to your Lord, that I would like to be at that feast. Tell him there is not a man in the kingdom that would rather be there than myself, but I am so situated that I can't come. Just tell him I have bought me a piece of ground, and that I must needs go and see it." Queer time to go and see to land, wasn't it? Just at that supper time. They were invited to supper, you see. But he must needs go and see it. He had not made a partial bargain and wanted to go and close the bargain. He did not have that good excuse. He had bought the land, and he must needs go and see it. Could he not go and see this land the next morning? Could he not have accepted this invitation and then gone and seen his land? If he had been a good business man, someone has said, he would have gone and looked at the land before he bought it. But the land was already bought, and the trade made. He did not say, "I want to get the deed on record, because I am afraid someone else will get a deed of it, and get it on record first, and I will lose it." He had not got that good an excuse. The only excuse he had was, "I have bought me a piece of ground and I must needs go and see it."

You will see it was a lie right on the face of it. It was just manufactured to ease that man's conscience. He did not want to go to the feast, and he had not the common honesty to come out with it and say, "I don't want to go to the feast, but just take back word that I have bought me a piece of ground and I must needs go and see it." And away he went. How many men are giving their business as an excuse for not accepting this invitation! You talk to them about things pertaining to the kingdom of God, and they tell you they have got to attend to business, that business is very pressing. It does not say that this was a bad man. He might have been as moral as any man in Cleveland. He might have held as high a position as any man in Cleveland. He might have ridden in his chariot. He might have been a very liberal man to the poor. He might have been a very benevolent man. He might have given his substance, but he neglected to accept this invitation, and Christ teaches us plainly that if we neglect this salvation how shall we escape the damnation of hell?

People say, "What have I done? I have not got drunk; I have not murdered; I have not lied; I have not stolen. What have I done?" I will take you on the ground that you have not done anything—I will not admit that for a moment, but suppose I take you on that ground. If a man neglects salvation he will be lost. You see a man in yonder river, his oars lying in the bottom of his boat, and he is out there in the current, his arms are folded, and the current is quietly drawing him toward the rapids. Some one warns him: "Say, friend, you are hastening toward the rapids." "No, I am doing nothing, sir. My arms are folded. What have I done?" "But you are drawing toward the rapids." "I tell you, sir, I am not; I am doing nothing." You may try to convince him but he will be blind. So indeed he is not doing anything, but that current is quietly drawing him toward the cataract, and in a few moments he will go over. Many a man is flattering himself that he is not doing anything, but let him neglect salvation and he is lost.

The next man's excuse was one manufactured for the occasion. It was not one whit better than the excuse of the first man: "Take back word to thy Lord that I cannot come. I have got pressing business. I have bought five yoke of oxen and I must needs go to prove them." As if he had to prove his oxen that night at supper time. He had plenty of time to prove his oxen. He had bought them. They were in his stall. But the fact was, he was like the first man: he did not want to go and had not the common honesty to say so, and so he says, "I have bought five yoke of oxen and I must needs go and prove them." He must go right off that night to prove them. That is his excuse. There is not a child five years old that cannot see that that excuse is just manufactured.

These men began to make excuse. They did not have one—they manufactured excuses to ease their consciences. It was nothing but a downright lie; that is what it was. Let us call things by their right names. People think if they can make a sort of plausible excuse they are justified. But these excuses are nothing but refuges of lies.

The third man's excuse is more absurd than the others: "I have married me a wife, and therefore I cannot come." Who likes to go to a feast better than a young bride? He might have taken his wife with him. He had no excuse. That was the excuse he was hiding behind, "I have married me a wife, and therefore I cannot come." If his wife would not go with him he could let her stay at home, and he could go. This has got to be a personal matter. We are not going to heaven in families, as I said last night. It is a thing between you and your God. The invitation was extended to that man as the head of his own house. He was priest over his own household, and he had no excuse; but he just made up that excuse.

Now, there is nothing on record, you might say, against those three men. You might say there were a good many things noble about those men. It does not say that they were licentious; it does not say that they were drunkards; it does not say that they were dishonest; it does not say that they were thieves, but they only made excuses so as not to be at that feast. They did not want to accept of the feast.

I notice some of you smile as I take up those three excuses; but I would like to ask this congregation this question: Have you a better one? Come! I see a young man laughing down there. Have you a better excuse yourself? Come! Eighteen hundred years have rolled away, and they tell us we are living in a very wise age, that we are living in a very intellectual age, that men are growing much wiser, and that we know a good deal more than our fathers did; but with all men's boasted knowledge, can you find a man to-day who has a better excuse than those three men had? During the last three years I have spent most of my time talking to people about their salvation—their individual difficulties—and I have yet to find the first man or the first woman that can give me a better excuse than those three men had. I tell you that man or that woman cannot be found to-day. I will defy any man to come forward to-night and give me a better excuse than those three men had. The excuses men are hiding behind to-day are fearful. There is not an excuse that you would dare to give to God. Things look altogether different when you come to stand before Him.

Take a piece of paper, if you have it in your pocket, and a pencil and write down, "Why should I serve the god of this world?" Second, "Why should I serve the God of the Bible?" Then put down your reasons why you should serve the god of this world, and your reasons why you should serve the God of the Bible, and see how it looks; because it is clearly taught that we either serve the god of this world or the God of heaven. We cannot be neutral. There is no neutrality about this matter. We are either for God or against Him. We cannot serve God and mammon. We are either serving the god of this world—that is, Satan—or we are serving the God of heaven. The line is drawn. You may not be able to see it, but God sees it. God knows the heart of every man and woman in this assembly. He knows all about us, and He sees right through the excuses we make. He looks at the heart. He does not look at the excuses you make. Those are only from the tongue. They are only manufactured in the head. He knows that the difficulty lies down in the heart. It is because you will not come unto Him. It is not because men cannot come; it is because men set their wills up against God's will, and are not willing to yield.

One of the popular excuses of the present day is this good old book, the Bible. It is amazing to hear some men talk. I have touched upon this a number of times since I have come to Cleveland, but I find as I come out West a good deal of infidelity; men profess to be infidels. It is astonishing to hear them talk about the Bible—something they do not know anything about. I can find scarcely one of them that has ever looked into it and read it, and who knows anything about it. They have heard some infidel lecture—some scoffing, sneering man come along caviling at the Bible, and they have heard some few things that man has said, and they bring them out on all occasions. They will not look into that Book and ask God to help them to understand it. If a man will be honest with God, God will be honest with him. There is no trouble about this Book; the trouble is with the life.

Wilmot, the great infidel, as he lay dying, putting his hand upon that Book said, "The only thing against that Book is a bad life." When a man has got a bad record against him, he wants to get that Book out of the way, because it condemns him; that is the trouble. The trouble is not with the Book; it is with your record and mine. Because that Book condemns sin we want to get it out of the way. Men do not like to be condemned; that is the trouble.

Then men say they cannot understand it. Well, you and the Bible agree exactly. A man was telling me some time ago that he could not understand the Bible. I said, "You and the Bible agree exactly." He said, "I don't agree with the Bible at all." "Well," I said, "you agree exactly," and I referred him to a passage in the prophecy of Daniel—"Many shall be purified and made white and tried; but the wicked shall do wickedly, and none of the wicked shall understand." That is what Scripture says. If a man is living in sin, God is not going to reveal to that man His secrets.

I would like to ask those men who are giving this Bible as an excuse for not becoming Christians, Who wrote that Book? Did bad men write it? It is a very singular thing that they should write their own condemnation, isn't it? How that book condemns bad men. Bad men would not write their own condemnation, would they? They do not do it nowadays, do they? They are the last ones to write their own condemnation. Well, if good men wrote a bad book, they could not be good, could they?

Now, it seems to me that if a man will stop to think a moment he will see that the trouble is not with the Book. The trouble is with himself. And when a man bows to the will of God that Book becomes food to his soul. He can feed on it then; there is something to feed on. He gets life from it; he gets power, and he gets something that tells him how he can get victory over himself. I consider that the greatest triumph a man can have in this world. A man that knows how to rule himself is greater than he that taketh a city. Look at the misery and woe that has come into the world through that one door—men and women that cannot control themselves, that cannot control their tempers, their lusts, their passions, and their appetites. That Book tells me how I can get victory over myself, and it is the only Book in the wide world that can tell a man how to get victory over himself. I haven't time to dwell upon that excuse any longer.

There is another very common excuse, and I have heard it in Cleveland as much as any: "Why," they say, "Mr. Moody, you know it is a very hard thing to be a Christian—a very hard thing." When they tell me that I like to ask them, "Which is the hardest master, the devil?"—for we will call him by his right name, because every man that serves not the Lord Jesus Christ, and will have nothing to do with the God of the Bible, is serving the god of this world. "Now, which is the easiest master?"

Christ says that His yoke is easy and His burden is light. Now, you go right along and say, "That is a lie." You don't say it right out in plain English, but we may as well talk plainly to-night. When you say it is hard to be a Christian you say that God is a liar, that it is an easier thing to serve the god of this world than it is the God of the Bible. Now, I want to say that I consider that one of the greatest lies that ever came out of the pit of hell, and how Satan can stand up in this nineteenth century and make men believe he is an easier master than the God of heaven is one of the greatest mysteries of the present day.

"The way of the transgressor is hard." Blot it out if you can. Close up that Book, and you will see the evidence of that fact all around you. There is not a day passes but you can read upon the pages of the daily papers, "The way of the transgressor is hard." I wish I could drive that lie back into the hell where it came from.

You go over to the Tombs in New York City and you will find a little iron bridge running from the police court where the men are tried right into the cell. I think the New York officials have not been noted for their piety in your time and mine; but they had put up there in iron letters on that bridge, "The way of the transgressor is hard." They know that is true. Blot it out if you can. God Almighty said it. It is true. "The way of the transgressor is hard." On the other side of that bridge they put these words: "A bridge of sighs." I said to one of the officers, "What did you put that up there for?" He said that most of the young men (for most of the criminals are young men. "The wicked don't live out their days"—put that in with it)—he said most of the young men as they passed over that iron bridge went over it weeping. So they called it the Bridge of Sighs. "What made you put that other there: 'The way of the transgressor is hard'?" "Well," he said, "it is hard. I think if you had anything to do with this prison you would believe that text, 'The way of the transgressor is hard.'"

If a man will just look around him and keep in mind this one truth, "The way of the transgressor is hard," he will be thoroughly convinced inside of twenty-four hours that that passage of Scripture is true. It is not that God's service is hard. The trouble with men is they are trying to serve God with the old Adam nature. They are trying to serve God before they are born of God. Now, to tell a man in the flesh to serve God in the spirit, who is a Spirit, I would just as soon tell a man to try to jump over the moon and expect him to do it. He cannot do it. The natural man is not subject to the law of God and neither, indeed, can be. You are not to try to serve God until you are born of God, until you are born again, born from above, until you are born of the spirit; and when a man is born of the spirit the yoke is easy and the burden is light. I have been in the service upwards of twenty years, and I want to testify to-night that my Master is not a hard Master. What say you ministers here to-night? Do you find him a hard Master? Speak out. I thought you would say so.

Ah, my friends, He is not a hard Master. I want to have you remember that. No, He is not a hard Master. That is one of the lies coming from the pit. "My yoke is easy and my burden light." When a man submits his heart and will to God—takes Christ into his heart and lives a life of faith, it is delightful.

Now, I will tell you a good way to get at this. Put you people into a jury box. Just imagine you are on a jury to-night. I will take the most faithful follower the Lord Jesus has got in Cleveland. I don't know who the person is, it may be a man or woman that the papers, perhaps, have no record of. God knows where His loved ones are. It may be some poor person off in some dark street, but it is one who has great faith and walks with God, whose life is as pure and spotless and blameless as any person that you can find; one that has been living with Jesus Christ, say, fifty years. Let that person come upon this platform to-night and speak out and testify. You will see in his face that he has not had a hard Master. There will be no wrinkles in that brow. There will be light in the eye, there will be peace stamped upon that brow, joy beaming from that countenance. He need not speak; let that person stand here and by his face he will show he has had a good Master and an easy Master.

Now, find the most faithful follower that the devil has got in Cleveland. Let him or her come up here. Ah! you need not speak. I think you would say, "That is enough." You can tell by the looks, for the devil puts his mark upon his own. He stamps the mark deep. Men may try to get rid of it, but they carry the mark. And the Lord Jesus puts His stamp upon His own. You take the two and draw the contrast and see if that lie that has come from Satan is not as great a lie as ever was told—that our Lord is a hard Master. When people say they would like to become a Christian, but it is a hard thing to be a Christian, they virtually say God is a hard Master and Satan is an easy one.

Now, do you think it easy to go against your own conscience? Because that is what men do. They have to stifle conscience to serve the god of this world and turn the back on the God of the Bible. Do you think it is an easy thing to go against your own judgment? For if a man will just stop and consult his judgment, his judgment will tell him that the safest, and wisest, and best thing he can do is to believe on the God of the Bible. Is it an easy thing to go against the advice and wishes of the best friends you have got? There is not a person in this congregation to-night that has got a true friend that would not advise him to serve the God of heaven. A man or woman that would advise you to serve the god of this world would be the worst enemy you could have. They would make the world dark and bitter. Is it an easy thing to trample a mother's prayer under your feet, to break a mother's heart and send her down to an untimely grave? That is easy, is it? Ah! many a man has done it. You call that easy. Is it easy to go against the very best counsel and advice you have from the best and most loved friends you have got? Hear what the Master said to Saul: "Saul, Saul, why persecutest thou me? It is hard for thee"—He did not talk about its being hard for the disciples that Saul was going to put in prison, and perhaps, have them stoned to death like Stephen. It was not as hard for Stephen to be stoned to death as it was for Saul to persecute him. "Saul, Saul, why persecutest thou me? It is hard for thee to kick against the pricks." It is hard for a man to contend with his Maker. It is hard for a man to fight against the God of the Bible. It is an unequal controversy. It is an unequal battle, and God is going to have the victory. It is folly for a man to attempt to fight against the God of that Bible.

Mr. Spurgeon uses this parable of a tyrant ordering a subject into his presence and saying to him, "What is your occupation?" "I am a black-smith." "Well," says he, "I want you to go and make a chain a certain length," and he gave him nothing to make it with, "and on a certain day I want you to bring it into my presence." That day came. The blacksmith appeared with his chain. The tyrant says: "Take that chain and make it twice the length." He made it twice the length and he had to get friends to help him get in the presence of the tyrant, and when he brought it back the tyrant says to his men standing around, "Take that man and bind him hand and foot and cast him into a dungeon," and says Mr. Spurgeon, "That is what every man that is serving the god of this world is doing—forging the chain that is going to bind him." A man goes into a saloon and takes a social glass. You step up and tell that man of his danger, that he is binding himself, and that by and by he will be bound hand and foot, and he will laugh you to scorn and mock you; but he goes on adding link after link to that chain. By and by, the tyrant has got him bound, and he says, "Now, let us see you assert your freedom." Men say they don't want to give up their freedom. There is no freedom until a man knows the Lord Jesus Christ. A man is a slave to sin, to his passions and lusts, until Christ snaps the fetters and sets him free.

There was a man I used to know in Chicago that I talked to a great many times about drinking. He was a business man. He used to say: "I can stop when I please." One night I went out, and my family heard a strange noise. We lived on the corner. They heard him coming down the side street and he made an unearthly noise, and my wife said to the servants, "Are the doors locked?" He came around to the front door and tried to burst the door open. My wife says, "What do you want?" "Oh," he says, "I want to see your husband." "Well, he has gone down to the meeting." Away he started. I was walking down to the church and he went by me. He was run-ning so fast he could not stop. He went on a rod or two and came back.

The poor fellow was nearly frightened out of his life. He says, "I have got to die to-night." "Oh, no, you are not going to die." "I have got to die to-night." "Why," says I, "what is the trouble?" and I found the man had drank so much that he was under the power of the enemy. I saw what his trouble was. "Why," he says, "Satan is coming to my house to-night to take me to hell," and says he, "I have got to go. I begged of him to let me stay until one o'clock. He told me at one o'clock he will be back after me." I said, "He will not come after you." "He will; there is no chance of my getting away from him. He is coming!" Well, I couldn't convince that man. Poor man! He had been serving the god of this world, and now he was reaping what he had been sowing. On that night I had six men come to that man's house and at one o'clock those six men could not hold him. "Look there! See him! There they are! They are after me! He is taking me! He is going to take me to hell! He is after me!" I thought that man would really die. Poor man! He is one of those men that thought God a hard master and the devil was one that was easy. That is the way the devil serves his subjects. Reaping time is coming. Poor man, he suffered untold agonies that night. Yet men, with all these witnesses around them, will go on drinking. A young man will go from this Tabernacle to-night, and go down to a saloon and order a glass and drink, and go on drinking, until by and by delirium seizes him and the snakes crawl around his body, and would seem as if death would lay right hold of him. I can't describe it. It would take some of these men that have been there to tell you about it. Oh, tell me that the devil is an easy master and that God is a hard one! Away with that lie; away with that excuse. My friends, never give it as long as you live. It is false.

When I was in Paris I saw a little oil painting, only about a foot square; it was at the Paris Exposition in 1867. I was going through the Art Gallery, and on that painting there was a little piece of white paper that attracted my attention. I went and looked at that white paper, and it said, "Sowing Tares," and there was the most hideous countenance I think I ever saw. A man was taking out a handful of seed, sowing tares all around him, and wherever a tare dropped there grew up some vile reptile, and they were crawling up his body and all around him. Off in the distance was a dark thicket, and prowling around the borders of that forest were wild beasts, and that hellish and fiendish look! What a fearful thing it is for a man to sow tares when he is going to reap them. And yet man goes on sowing with a liberal hand, and laughs and scoffs when we warn him and tell him what he is coming to by and by. The papers are full of it. I sometimes think these papers ought to preach the gospel to the people—ought to warn them to flee from the wrath to come.

Look at that case we have just had in a court in New Jersey. Look at that poor man. For four long days the jury has been out. I don't know when my heart has been more touched than when I read that scene in court, when those little children climbed up on their father's knee and said, "Papa, papa, come home. Mamma cries so much now you are away." The law had him. Poor man! He reaped what he sowed. He had an uncontrollable temper. He took his weapon and shot down a coachman because he got mad with him. He never will get over it. He never can step back into the place where he was. The jury may acquit him. Poor man; he has got to reap a bitter, bitter reaping; what an awful thing sin is; and yet men will stand up with all these facts around them and tell you God is a hard master and the devil an easy one.

Let us look at the scene in the court. A young man just coming into manhood, twenty-one, promising, talented, gifted, beautiful young man, an only son; but he has been out drinking, and in a drunken spree helped kill a man, and now he is on trial for his life. In that court sits his father and mother and three lovely sisters. That is the only brother they have got. That is the only son they have got. The jury bring in the verdict, guilty; the man is sentenced to the penitentiary for life.

And with all these facts people stand up and say God is a hard master and the devil is an easy one. Oh that the God of heaven may open our eyes to-night to show us how wicked it is to give these excuses, and that we will have to answer for them at the bar of God—for a person with an open Bible to say that God is a hard master and that Satan is an easy one.

I remember closing a young men's meeting in Chicago a few years ago, when a young man got up and said, "Mr. Moody, would you allow me to say a few words?" And I said, "Say on."

"Well," said he, "I want to say to these young men that if they have friends that care for them, and friends that love them, and that are praying for them— I want to say you had better treat them kindly, for you will not always have them. I want to tell you something in my own experience. I was an only son, and I had a very godly father and mother. No young man in Chicago had a better father and mother than I had; and because I was an only child, I suppose, they were very anxious for my salvation, and they used to plead with me to come to Christ. My father many a time at the family altar used to break down in his attempt to pray for his only boy. At last my father died, and after my father died my mother became more anxious than ever that I should become a Christian. Sometimes she would come and put her loving arms around my neck and say, 'My boy, if you were only a Christian I would be so happy. If you would take your father's place at the family worship, and help me worship God, it would cheer your mother!' I used to push her away and say, 'Mother, don't talk to me that way; I don't want to become a Christian yet, I want to see something of the world.' Sometimes I would wake up in the night and hear my mother praying, 'O God, save my boy!' and it used to trouble me, and at last I ran away to get away from my mother's influence, and away from her prayers. I became a wanderer. I did not let her know where I went. When I did hear from home indirectly, I heard that mother was sick. I knew what it meant. I knew it was my conduct that was crushing my mother and breaking her heart, and I thought I would go home and ask her forgiveness. Then the thought came that if I did I would have to become a Christian, and my proud heart would not yield. I would not go.

"Months went on, and I heard again indirectly. I believe that if my mother had known where I was she would have come to me. I believe she would have gone around the world to find her boy. And when I heard that she was worse, the thought came over me that she might not recover, and I thought I would go home and cheer her lonely heart. There was no railway in the town, and I had to take the stage. I got into town about dark. The moon had just begun to shine. My mother lived back about a mile and a half from the hotel, and I started back on foot, and on my way I had to go by the village graveyard. When I got to it I thought I would go and see if there was a new-made grave. I can't tell why, but my heart began to drop, and as I drew near that spot I trembled. By the light of the moon I saw a new-made grave. For the first time in my life this question came stealing over me, Who is going to pray for my lost soul now? Father has gone and mother is dead. They are the only two that ever cared for me, the only two that ever prayed for me. I took up the earth and saw that the grave was a new-made grave; I saw that my mother had just been laid away; and, young men, I spent that night by my mother's grave, I gave myself away to my mother's God, and then and there settled the great question of eternity, and I became a child of God. I will never forgive myself. I murdered that sainted mother."

Poor man! He was reaping what he sowed. Tell me that the way of the transgressor is easy! Tell me that God is a hard master, and that the devil is an easy one! Young men, take the God of your mother; take the God of the Bible to be your God. Set your faces like a flint towards heaven to-night, and it will be the best night of your life. I wish I could say something to induce you to come to Christ. I wish I could see souls pressing into the kingdom of God. May the God of all grace touch every heart here to-night.

# Reuben Archer Torrey

*1856–1928*

One of D. L. Moody's associates, R. A. Torrey was an effective evangelist in his own right. He conducted evangelistic campaigns throughout the United States and Canada, the United Kingdom, Europe, Australia and New Zealand, China, Japan, and India. Unlike Moody, who was self-taught, Torrey was a graduate of Yale, earning a B.A. from the university and a B.D. from the divinity school, and he also studied in Germany.

Emerging from a period of religious skepticism, Torrey was ordained into the Congregational ministry in 1883 and pastored churches in Ohio and Minnesota. From 1889 to 1908 he served as superintendent of what today is the Moody Bible Institute in Chicago and he also served as pastor of the Chicago Avenue Church. In 1912 Torrey moved to Los Angeles to become dean of the newly formed Bible Institute of Los Angeles, and in 1915 became pastor of the Church of the Open Door, which was associated with the institute.

Leaving the school and church in 1924, Torrey devoted himself to writing, evangelistic crusades, and lecturing at schools and Bible conferences. Because of his own personal experience with doubt, and his excellent education, he often preached sermons that defended the doctrines of the Christian faith, especially the inspiration and authority of the Bible. He frequently gave his address "Ten Reasons Why I Believe the Bible Is the Word of God." He wrote more than fifty books, many of which attacked the theological liberalism that was spreading rapidly at that time. Torrey is buried at the Montrose, Pennsylvania Bible Conference, which he helped to found.

*R. A. Torrey: Apostle of Certainty* by Roger Martin (Sword of the Lord Publishers, 1976) is the only book-length biography of Torrey I have found.

# The Only Gospel
# That Has Saving Power

For I am not ashamed of the Gospel: for it is the power of God unto salvation to every one that believeth: to the Jew first, and also to the Greek.

Romans 1:16

But though I, or an angel from heaven, should preach unto you any Gospel other than that which we preached unto you, let him be Anathema. As I have said before, so say I now again, If any man preacheth unto you another Gospel from that which ye received, let him be Anathema.

Galatians 1:8–9

My subject is "The Only Gospel That Has Saving Power." I have two texts: Romans 1:16: "For I am not ashamed of the Gospel: for it is the power of God unto salvation to every one that believeth." Galatians 1:8–9: "But though I, or an angel from heaven, preach unto you any Gospel other than that which we preached unto you, let him be Anathema. As I have said before, so say I now again, If any man preacheth unto you another Gospel from that which ye received, let him be Anathema."

We hear much in these days about various Gospels. Some extol the Gospel of Social Service, others talk of the Gospel of the Universal Fatherhood of God and the Universal Brotherhood of Man; and others of the Gospel of Work, others of the Social Gospel, and others of various other Gospels. But there is but one real Gospel, only one Gospel that in actual fact has saving power. That Gospel is "the Gospel of Christ," the Gospel which Paul preached, and of which he said that if any man, or even an angel from Heaven, should preach any other Gospel, he would be accursed of God. All these Gospels have one fatal fault; they don't save. These other Gospels may sound well, they may be described with entrancing rhetoric, they may be preached with great eloquence, with marvelous beauty of diction, with charming figures of speech, they may seem exceedingly alluring, *but they don't save.* For all their pretenses and prettiness, instead of saving, they darken, debase and damn. They do not enlighten, elevate and save.

### I. Man's Need of Salvation

What man needs is salvation, not mere social uplift nor mere moral improvement, not mere intellectual enlightenment. Man is lost. Every man is lost until he is definitely saved. The only thing that will save him is the Gospel that Paul preached.

1. *Every man needs salvation from the guilt of sin.* Every man and woman on this earth is a sinner. Every man and woman on this earth has been a great sinner. Every man and woman on this earth has broken the first and greatest of God's commandments, namely, "Thou shalt love the Lord thy God with all thy heart, and with all thy soul, and with all thy mind" (Matt. 22:37–38) and every one of us, therefore, is a guilty sinner in the sight of a Holy God, and we need salvation from the guilt of sin. That is the first need, the great need, the crying need, the fundamental need of every one of us.

2. But *every man also needs salvation from the power of sin.* Sin has a hold upon every one of us, a mastery over every one of us, that we cannot overcome in our own strength. We must find a deliverer from the power of sin. The one universal need is the need of salvation, the need of salvation from the guilt and power of sin.

3. *The Gospel has power to save.* As our text puts it, "the Gospel is the power of God unto salvation to every one that believeth: to the Jew first, and also to the Greek," and no other religion of philosophy has power to save, nothing else in all the world has power to save from the guilt and power of sin.

### II. What Is the Gospel?

We come now right to the question, *What is the Gospel that has power to save?* Gospel means, as I presume you all know, "Good news" or "Glad tidings." What is the good news, or the glad tidings, that has saving power in it? Paul himself tells us what this Gospel was which he preached, and of which he said, "It is the power of God unto salvation to every one that believeth."

We are not left to speculate about that for Paul himself defines in the simplest and most easily understood terms exactly what the Gospel was that he preached, the Gospel that had saving power and the only Gospel that has saving power. Paul's full, and at the same time very plain, description of the Gospel which he preached, you will find in 1 Corinthians 15:1–4: "Now I make known unto you, brethren, the Gospel which I preached unto you, which also ye received, wherein also ye stand, *by which also we are saved,* if ye hold fast the word which I preached unto you, except ye believed in vain," and now comes the description of the Gospel, "For I delivered unto you first of all that which I also received: *that Christ died for our sins* according to the Scriptures; and *that he was buried;* and *that he hath been raised* on the third day according to the Scriptures."

1. You notice first of all in regard to this Gospel that Paul preached, that *the good news* is *facts,* not theories, not speculations, not guesses, but solid, substantial, established, unmistakable, inescapable, absolutely sure facts. I am glad of that. Most of the gospels one hears nowadays are mere theories. The Gospel of Christ is facts.

2. The facts that constitute the good news were three:

(1) First, *"that Christ died for our sins."* That certainly is good news. You and I are sinners. Every one of us has sinned. If any one here to-night seeks to deny that he is a sinner, his denial that he is a sinner does not make him any less a sinner; indeed, it makes him all the more a sinner; for it makes him a liar, as well as a sinner in other respects. As we read in 1 John 1:8, 10, "If we say that we have no sin, we deceive ourselves, and the truth is not in us. . . . If we say that we have not sinned we make him (God) a liar, and his word is not in us." So, by the denial of our sin we do not make ourselves any less sinners, but we prove ourselves to be liars and make ourselves guilty of the enormous sin of making God a liar. That is what every Christian Scientist does, he makes God a liar, and that is what every one else who denies that he is a sinner does, he makes God a liar. God says that we are sinners and when we deny the fact we give the lie to God. Every man, therefore, who denies that he is a great sinner is a liar, and all liars, unless they repent, are bound for the eternal fire; for God says in Revelation 21:8, "The fearful, and the unbelieving, and the abominable, and murderers, and fornicators, and sorcerers, and idolaters, *and all liars,* their part shall be in the lake that burneth with fire and brimstone; which is the second death."

But not only are we sinners, but God is holy, infinitely holy, and cannot tolerate sin. God is "of purer eyes than to behold evil," and He can "not look on iniquity," and some day you and I must meet Him. We must either meet Him bearing our sin, with all our sin upon us, or else we must find some one else to bear our sin for us. If we should meet this

Holy God with our sin upon us then must we be forever banished from His presence, "be punished with everlasting destruction from the presence of God and from the glory of his power." But the Gospel tells us that some one else has borne our sin in our place. It tells us that a competent sin-bearer has been found. It tells us that "Christ died for our sins," that the Lord "Jesus paid our debt, all the debt we owe," that though "sin had left a crimson stain," "He washed it white as snow." Even Isaiah, seven hundred years before Christ, got a glimpse of this wonderful truth of the Gospel. Speaking in the Holy Spirit, he said, "All we like sheep have gone astray; we have turned every one to his own way; and the LORD hath laid on him the iniquity of us all" (Isa. 53:6). So if we accept the Lord Jesus who died for our sins as our substitute Saviour, then no matter how long we have sinned, no matter how greatly we have sinned, we can meet God with absolutely no sin upon us, for God Himself has put it upon Another. So the Lord Jesus, by His death, saves us completely from all the guilt of sin.

(2) The second fact that goes to make up the Gospel is that *the Lord Jesus "was buried."* At first sight, it is not clear how this is "good news," but it is good news; for *the fact of His burial shows the reality of His death and the actuality and literalness of His resurrection.* The burial of Jesus Christ shows that the death of Jesus Christ was no sham death, no mere "illusion," it was not merely "mortal thought," as the "Christian Scientists" would have us believe. It was a *real death* and therefore it was a *real atonement.* All that "Christian Science" and various other false systems offer us is a *sham atonement* for *imaginary sin,* and thus they offer us only *a sham salvation.* The Gospel of Christ, the Gospel that God makes known, the Gospel that Paul preached, the Gospel of a Saviour who not only died, but was buried, offers us a *real atonement for sins* that we know are *very real* and *very great* and *therefore* it offers us *a real salvation* from the guilt of sin. This true Gospel says to the vilest sinner in the world, "There is perfect pardon and justification for you, for the Son of God really died, He was really buried, and there is therefore a real and perfect salvation for you from all your guilt: 'The *blood* of Jesus his Son *cleanseth* us *from all sin*'" (1 John 1:7).

(3) The third fact in the good news is that *Jesus Christ rose again,* or as Paul puts it in his description of the Gospel in 1 Corinthians 15:4, "He hath been raised on the third day according to the Scriptures." That is certainly good news; it is great news. It is good news for many reasons, but especially good news from the standpoint of salvation, because it shows that Jesus Christ cannot only save from all the guilt of sin by His atoning death, but that He can also save from all the power of sin by His resurrection power. As it is put in that wonderful verse in Hebrews, "Where-

fore also he is able to save *to the uttermost* them that draw near unto God through him, seeing he ever liveth to make intercession for them" (Heb. 7:25). We need not only salvation from the guilt of sin, but we need just as much salvation from the power of sin. Supposing I were a great sinner and through faith in Christ crucified, should find salvation from all my guilt, and find perfect peace of conscience, and should go out of here to-night very happy in the thought that all my sins were blotted out. Then suppose that on the morrow the same old temptations that have overcome me in the past, for example the appetite for drink, or some form of lust or impurity, or an appetite for drugs, or an ungovernable temper, should confront me, and I had no power to resist the temptation, and down I go, how much would such a salvation be worth? But Jesus Christ not only died and was buried, He rose again, and to-night He lives and He has all power in heaven and on earth and so He can save me from my appetite for drink, or from the power of any evil desire, or from my temper, or whatever my sin may be; and however weak I may be I can begin here and now to live a clean and victorious life.

The following incident of a man who once called upon me in Chicago I have, I believe, related before. This man sought a private interview and when we had taken our seats alone in Mr. Moody's office the man said, "I want to tell you my story," and he went on as follows: "I am a Scotchman. When I was a child of seven over in Scotland I began to read the Bible through. One day I came to a passage in Deuteronomy that told me that if I should keep the law of God a hundred years and then broke it at one point after having kept it a hundred years, I would be under the curse of the broken law of God. Was that right?" "Yes," I replied, "the Bible doesn't put it in just that way, but the Bible does say, 'Cursed is every one that confirmeth not all things which are written in the book of the law to do them.'" "That's the passage," he said, "that I found and I knew that I had already broken the law of God and therefore I knew that I was under the curse of the broken law. Though I was only seven years of age, I was in deep distress. Night after night I went to bed and wept myself to sleep, thinking how I was under the curse of the broken law of God. But I went on reading my Bible and the next year when I was eight years old I came to John 3:16: 'For God so loved the world, that he gave his only begotten Son, that whosoever believeth in him should not perish, but have everlasting life,' and all my burden rolled away. Was I converted?"

"Well," I replied, "that sounds like a good, evangelical conversion."

"Let me tell you the rest of my story," he continued. "I grew up to manhood. I came to America, I came out here to Chicago, I found work down in the stockyards. I am living down in the stockyards. Now, the stockyards, as you know, are a hard place, and I got to drinking and every little while

I go off on a drunk. What I have come to ask you is if there is any way in which I can get victory over the drink?" "You have come just to the right place," I replied. "I can answer your question. There *is* a way in which you can get victory over the drink. You have only believed half the Gospel, and therefore you have only got half a salvation." I said, "Let me show you the whole Gospel," and I opened to the fifteenth chapter of First Corinthians and read, "'Moreover, brethren, I declare unto you the Gospel which I preached unto you, which also ye have received and wherein ye stand; by which also we are saved, if ye keep in memory what I have preached unto you, except ye believed in vain, for I delivered unto you first of all that which I also received, that Christ died for our sins according to the Scriptures; and that he was buried, and that he rose again the third day according to the Scriptures.'

"Now," I went on, "you have believed the first part of this Gospel, that Christ died and was buried, and through believing that you have found pardon and peace." "Yes." "But," I continued, "that is only half the Gospel. There is another half to it, and that is *that He rose again.* Do you believe that?" "I believe everything in the Bible," he replied. Again I asked, "Do you believe that Jesus rose again the third day?" "Yes, I do." "Very well, then, if He rose the third day, then He has all power in heaven and on earth." "Yes." "And He has power to keep you from the power of the drink, and from the power of sin. Do you believe that?" "Yes," he said, "I do." "Will you trust Him to do it?" "I will," he replied. "Let us kneel down and tell God so," I said. We knelt side by side. I prayed first and then he prayed. These were about the words he uttered. "O God, I have been believing half the Gospel and I have had half a salvation. I have believed that part of the Gospel that told me that Christ died for my sins according to the Scriptures and through believing that I have found pardon and peace; but now I have come to believe the other half of the Gospel, that Christ not only died, but that He rose again and that He has all power in heaven and on earth and that He has power to keep me from the power of the drink."

Then he changed his mode of address and commenced speaking directly to Jesus Christ. "Lord Jesus," he said, "I believe that Thou art risen from the dead and I believe that Thou hast all power in heaven and on earth, I believe that Thou hast power to save me from the drink. O Lord Jesus, save me from the power of drink right now. I ask it in Thine own name. Amen." As he still knelt there, his head bowed in prayer, I said, "Did you really trust Him to do it?" He replied, "I did." He rose, I gave him some instruction as to how to make a success of this life upon which he had entered, he left the office, and I didn't hear from him for some weeks. Then I received a brief letter, but the letter was very much to the point. It ran this way: "Dear Mr. Torrey, I am so glad I came to see you. *It works.*"

Yes, thank God, it *does* work. It works with any one who really believes it. The Gospel of a Saviour who died and was buried and rose again has power to save from the guilt of sin and it also has power to save from the power of sin. It has power "to save *to the uttermost*" those who come to God through Jesus Christ. And it is the only Gospel that can do it. The Gospel of Christian Science, with a sham death and a sham resurrection, cannot do it. The Gospel of New Thought cannot do it. The Gospel of Theosophy cannot do it. The Gospel of Social Service, of which we are hearing so much in our day, cannot do it. No Gospel but the Gospel of Jesus Christ, the Gospel of a Saviour who really died, who was really buried, and who really rose again, can do it. A short while ago a well known pastor in Los Angeles announced that he was going to preach a Gospel *"without an atonement of blood."* Well, if he does he will preach a Gospel that cannot save, he will preach a Gospel that will send men to hell and not a Gospel that will ever fit men for heaven. And any one who preaches a Gospel that Christ died, but not a Gospel that He rose again, will preach a Gospel that will not save from the power of sin. But the Gospel contained in this blessed Book of God, the Gospel that Jesus both died and rose again, will save. It will save from both the guilt and the power of sin, it will "save to the uttermost."

### III. Whom the Gospel Saves

But whom does the Gospel save? It does not save everybody. This Gospel has been proclaimed for more than eighteen hundred years, but it has not saved everybody yet, and it never will. There are many in these days who are saying, The Gospel is a failure because the great majority of men and women are not saved. They say, "Christianity is a failure, because after eighteen centuries our governments are not Christian, and wars and other damnable things are still possible." But herein lies their mistake. God never intended the Gospel to save everybody. He never gave it to save everybody. He never expected it to save everybody. He gave it to save those who would believe it and those only. It is not Christianity that has failed, but man that has failed, by rejecting this glorious Gospel. The Gospel has not failed because it has not saved everybody any more than a perfectly good medicine that will cure anybody who takes it fails where it doesn't cure those who don't take it. God has told us plainly from the beginning just who the Gospel would save. Who does it save? Listen: "The Gospel . . . is the power of God unto salvation to *every one that believeth*." This tells us whom the Gospel saves.

1. First of all, *it saves those who believe*. Not those who hear, but those who believe. The Gospel does not save every one who hears it. Millions of men have heard the Gospel all through their lives and died in their sins and

gone to hell. There are many who fancy that merely hearing the Gospel or living in a Christian land makes them Christians. One night I approached a very intelligent looking man in Duluth, Minnesota. I said to him, "Are you a Christian?" He replied, "Certainly; do you think I am a Mohammedan?" He thought that simply because he was born and brought up in a Christian land and heard the Gospel that made him a Christian; but it does not. It is *believing* the Gospel, not merely hearing the Gospel, that saves. It is believing the Gospel and not merely hearing it that makes one a Christian. The Gospel does not even save the one who merely admires it. A man may have a great admiration for the Gospel, for the profound philosophy of the Bible, and yet be an utterly unsaved man. THE GOSPEL SAVES THE ONE WHO BELIEVES IT AND HIM ALONE. The one who believes what? *The Gospel.* Really believes it, believes it with the heart. The one who has that kind of faith that leads to action, the faith that

(1) leads you to accept Christ as your atoning Saviour and to trust God to forgive you simply because Jesus Christ died in your place;

(2) the faith that leads you to accept Christ as your risen Saviour and to trust Him to deliver you from the power of sin;

(3) the faith that leads you, having accepted Him, to show the reality of your faith by an open confession of Him before the world, as it is written, "If thou shalt *confess with thy mouth Jesus as Lord,* and shalt *believe in thy heart* that God raised him from the dead, thou shalt be saved: for with the heart man believeth unto righteousness; and *with the mouth confession is made unto salvation*" (Rom. 10:9–10).

2. But it not only saves those who believe. It saves "*every one* that believeth." As it is put in our text, "The Gospel . . . is the power of God unto salvation to *every one that believeth.*" There is not a man or woman in this room to-night whom the Gospel cannot save. There is not a man or woman in the world so sunken in sin, so lost to all that is good and true and pure, that the Gospel cannot save, *if they will only believe.* There is not a man or woman so utterly weak and helpless in sin that the Gospel will not save them, *if they believe it.* Why then is there a man or woman in the world who is not saved? Why is there a man or woman in the world who is not saved from the guilt and power of sin? *Simply because you will not believe.* Let me illustrate. Here is a great Mogul engine on the track. It is coaled and has water in the boiler, there is fire underneath the boiler, the steam is up, there is a full head of steam, there is power in that locomotive to draw a heavily loaded freight train up the steepest grade, and now that locomotive backs down to the train and now the engineer reverses the lever and the locomotive starts up the grade, but not a car moves. Why not? Was it because there was not power in the locomotive to draw the train? No, there was plenty of power for that. What was the trouble? The brakeman

had not put in the coupling pin. And now the locomotive backs down again and backs up to the train of cars. The brakeman goes in between the tender of the locomotive and the train, and drops in a little coupling pin and now the engineer reverses the lever and the locomotive starts up the track again, and this time the train moves up the grade. Just so, the Gospel has power to save, *if you couple on*. The Gospel locomotive stands on the track, there is power in that locomotive to carry the train most heavily loaded with sin up the track, steam is up, it is starting up the grade to glory, it can pull you, no matter how heavily weighted you are with tons of sin, up the grade to glory. Fall in line. Couple on. Faith is the coupling pin. Just believe the Gospel. It rests with every man and woman here to-night to say whether you will be saved or not, saved right now from the guilt and power of sin. It all turns upon whether you will or will not believe the Gospel. "For I am not ashamed of the Gospel, for it is the power of God unto salvation to *every one that believeth*."

# William Ashley
# "Billy" Sunday

## 1862–1935

Between the ministries of D. L. Moody and Billy Graham, it was Billy Sunday who seemed to be God's anointed evangelist to the American people. However, unlike Moody and Graham, he didn't conduct campaigns outside the United States and he was much more flamboyant and dramatic in his style of preaching.

Born in Ames, Iowa, Billy Sunday never knew his father, a Union soldier who died in the Civil War. The fatherless family often relocated, and young Billy even spent time in an orphanage. When he was fourteen, he struck out on his own and in 1883 became a professional baseball player with the Chicago White Stockings.

Five years later Sunday was converted to faith in Christ at Chicago's Pacific Garden Mission, became active as a lay evangelist, and eventually quit baseball to work with evangelist J. Wilbur Chapman. When Chapman left the evangelistic field in 1895, Sunday launched his own crusades, putting into practice what he had learned from Chapman and on the baseball diamond.

In 1903 Sunday was ordained to the Presbyterian ministry. His direct and dramatic style of preaching attracted the masses who identified with his down-to-earth vocabulary and his heart-tugging stories. Music was important to his ministry, and just as

Moody had his Sankey, Billy Sunday had his Homer Rodeheaver. His enthusiastic crusade against "Mr. Booze" was an important emphasis in his crusades, and the passing of the Eighteenth Amendment in 1919 was a great victory for him and his followers. (The amendment was repealed in 1933.) During World War I, Sunday preached some of his largest crusades in key American cities, and huge tabernacles were constructed to house the large crowds.

Following the war, the mood of America changed and Sunday's popularity began to wane but he was still active in evangelistic efforts. From 1933 to 1935 he suffered three heart attacks and he died November 6, 1935. The funeral was held at the Moody Church in Chicago.

Billy Sunday was criticized by some for his "theatrical" approach to preaching, his friendships with moneyed people, and his opposition to modern "worldly amusements," but it is estimated that at least a million people came to faith in Christ through his ministry.

The earliest biography is *The Spectacular Career of Rev. Billy Sunday,* by T. T. Frankenberg (Columbus, Ohio: McClelland and Co., 1913). Homer Rodeheaver wrote his reminiscences in *Twenty Years with Billy Sunday* (Cokesbury, 1936). *Billy Sunday Was His Real Name* by William G. McLoughlin (University of Chicago Press, 1955) and *The Billy Sunday Story: The Life and Times of William Ashley Sunday* by Thomas Lee (Zondervan, 1961) describe and evaluate the life and work of this remarkable preacher.

# Wonderful

His name shall be called Wonderful.
Isaiah 9:6

In olden times all names meant something, and this is still the case among Indians and all other people who are living in a primitive way. Whenever you know an Indian's name and the meaning of it, you know something about the Indian. Such names as Kill Deer, Eagle Eye, Buffalo Face and Sitting Bull tell us something about the men who possessed them.

This tendency to use names that are expressive still crops out in camp life, and whenever men are thrown together in an unconventional way. In mining, military and lumber camps nearly every man has a nickname that indicates some peculiarity or trait of character. Usually a man's nickname is nearer the real man than his right name.

All of our family names to-day had their origin in something that meant something. All Bible names have a meaning, and when you read the Scriptures it will always help you to a better understanding of their meaning to look up the definition of all proper names.

There are two hundred and fifty-six names given in the Bible for the Lord Jesus Christ, and I suppose this was because He was infinitely beyond all that any one name could express.

Of the many names given to Christ it is my purpose at this time to briefly consider this one: "His name shall be called Wonderful." Let us look into it somewhat and see whether He was true to the name given Him in a prophecy eight hundred years before He was born. Does the name fit Him? Is it such a name as He ought to have?

Wonderful means something that is transcendently beyond the common; something that is away beyond the ordinary. It means something that is altogether unlike anything else. We say that Yellowstone Park, Niagara Falls and the Grand Canyon of the Colorado are wonderful because there is nothing else like them.

When David killed Goliath with his sling he did a wonderful thing, because nobody else ever did anything like it. It was wonderful that the Red Sea should open to make a highway for Israel, and wonderful that the sun should stand still for Joshua. Let us see whether Jesus was true to His name.

His birth was wonderful, for no other ever occurred that was like it. It was wonderful in that He had but one human parent, and so inherited the nature of man and the nature of God. He came to be the Prince of princes, and the King of kings, and yet His birth was not looked forward to in glad expectation, as the birth of a prince usually is in the royal palace, and celebrated with marked expressions of joy all over the country, as has repeatedly happened within the recollection of many who are here.

There was no room for Him at the inn, and He had to be born in a stable, and cradled in a manger, and yet angels proclaimed His birth with joy from the sky, to a few humble shepherds in sheepskin coats, who were watching their flocks by night.

Mark how He might have come with all the pomp and glory of the upper world. It would have been a great condescension for Him to have been born in a palace, rocked in a golden cradle and fed with golden spoons, and to have had the angels come down and be His nurses. But He gave up all the glory of that world, and was born of a poor woman, and His cradle was a manger.

Think what He had come for. He had come to bless, and not to curse; to lift up, and not to cast down. He had come to seek and to save that which was lost. To give sight to the blind; to open prison doors and set captives free; to reveal the Father's love; to give rest to the weary; to be a blessing to the whole world, and yet there was no room for Him. He came to do that, and yet many of you have no room for Him in your hearts.

His birth was also wonderful in this, that the wise men of the East were guided from far across the desert to His birthplace by a star. Nothing like this ever announced the coming of any one else into this world. As soon as His birth was known the king of the country sought His life, and ordered the slaughter of the Innocents at Bethlehem. The babies were the first Christian martyrs.

His character was wonderful, for no other has ever approached it in perfection. It is wonderful that the greatest character ever known should have come out of such obscurity, to become the most famous in all history. That such a time and such a country and such a people should have produced Jesus Christ can be accounted for on no other ground than His divinity. On his return from a trip to the Holy Land a minister was asked what had made the greatest impression upon him while there. "Nazareth," he answered, and for this reason:

"The same kind of people are living there to-day as in the time of Jesus, and they are about the worst specimens of humanity I have seen anywhere. Lazy, lustful, ignorant and unspeakably wicked, and to think of His coming out from such a people is to me a sure proof of His divinity. Had I not been a believer in His divinity before going there, I should have to believe in it now."

His life was wonderful. Wonderful for its unselfishness, its sinlessness and its usefulness. Even His enemies could not bring against Him any graver charge than that He claimed God for His Father, and that He would do good on the Sabbath day. Not the slightest evidence of selfishness or self-interest can be found in the story of His life. He was always helping others, but not once did He do anything to help Himself. He had the power to turn stones into bread, but went hungry forty days without doing it. While escaping from enemies who were determined to put Him to death He saw a man who had been blind from birth, and stopped to give him sight, doing so at the risk of His life. He never sought His own in any way, but lived for others everyday of His life. His first miracle was performed, not before a multitude to spread His own fame, but in a far-away hamlet, to save a peasant's wife from humiliation. He had compassion on the hungry multitude and wept over Jerusalem, but He never had any mercy on Himself.

His teaching was wonderful. It was wonderful for the way in which He taught; for its simplicity and clearness, and adaptation to the individual. Nowhere do you find Him seeking the multitude, but He never avoided the individual. And His teaching was always adapted to the comprehension of those whom He taught. It is said that the common people heard Him gladly, and this shows that they understood what He said. He put the cookies on the lower shelf. No man had to take a dictionary with him when he went to hear the Sermon on the Mount. He illustrated His thought and made plain His meaning by the most wonderful word-pictures. The preacher who would reach the people must have something to say, and know how to say it so that those who hear will know just what he means.

Jesus made His meaning clear by using plenty of illustrations. He didn't care a rap what the scribes and Pharisees thought about it, or said about it. He wanted the people to know what He meant, and that is why He was always so interesting. The preacher who can't make his preaching interesting has no business in the pulpit. If he can't talk over ten minutes without making people begin to snap their watches and go to yawning all over the house, he has misunderstood the Lord about his call to preach. Jesus was interesting because He could put the truth before people in an interesting way. We are told that without a parable He spake not to any man. He made people see things, and see them clearly. It is wonderful that this humble Galilean peasant, who may never have gone to school a day in His life, should have made Himself a Teacher of teachers for all time. The pedagogy of to-day is modeling after the manner of Christ closer and closer every day.

He was wonderful in His originality. The originality of Jesus is a proof of His divinity. The human mind cannot create anything in an absolute sense. It can build out of almost any kind of material, but it cannot create. There is no such thing as out-and-out originality belonging to man. You cannot imagine anything that does not resemble something you have previously seen or heard of.

I grant that you can take a cow and a horse and a dog and a sheep and from them make animals enough to fill Noah's ark, but you must have the cow and the horse and the dog and the sheep for a beginning. Everything you make will simply be a modification of the various forms and properties of them.

There is said to be nothing new under the sun, and there is a sense in which it is true. Everything is the outgrowth of something else. The first railway cars looked like the old stage-coaches, and the first automobiles looked like carriages. It is that way about everything. No man ever made a book, or even a story, that was altogether unlike all others.

The stories we hear to-day on the Irish and Dutch are older than the Irish and Dutch. You can find stories like them in the earliest literature, but you can't find any stories anywhere in any literature that even in the remotest way resemble the parables of Jesus. Such parables as the prodigal son and the Good Samaritan are absolutely new creations, and so proclaim Jesus as divine, because He could create.

His teaching was wonderful, not only in the way He taught, but in what He taught. He taught that He was greater than Moses. Think of the audacity of it! Making such claims as that to the Jews, who regarded Moses as being almost divine. Think of the audacity of some man of obscure and humble parentage standing before us Americans and trying to make us think he was greater than George Washington.

Jesus also declared that He fulfilled the prophecies and the law of Moses, and the only effort He ever made to prove His claim was to point to the works that He did. The first thing an impostor always does is to overprove his case. Jesus never turned His hand over to try to convince His enemies that He was the Christ. You have to explain a coal-oil lamp, but you don't need to waste any breath in giving information about the power of the sun. The springtime will do that by making all nature burst into bud, flower and leaf, and the power of Christ is shown just as convincingly in the changed lives of men and women who believe in Him.

Jesus taught that all would be lost who did not believe on Him. I have seen multitudes of saved people, but I have yet to see one who did not get his salvation by believing on Christ. Find the place in this world that comes the nearest to being like hell itself, and you will find it filled with those who are haters of Jesus Christ. You can't argue it. Go into saloons, gambling halls, and such places, and the people you find there are all haters of Jesus Christ, and the more of them you find the more the place in which you find them will be like hell itself.

Jesus taught that He was equal to God. He said, "He that hateth Me hateth My Father also" (John 15:23). Did you ever know of anybody else making such claims? He said, "Come unto Me, all ye that labor and are heavy laden, and I will give you rest." Offering to bear the burden of the whole world. Think of it! He said, "I am come that they might have life, and that they might have it more abundantly." And He said, "I am the resurrection and the life; and he that believeth in Me, though he were dead, yet shall he live. And whosoever liveth and believeth in Me shall never die." Surely He was wonderful in what He taught.

It is not surprising that He so stirred them in the Capernaum synagogue, where He taught them not as the scribes, but as one having authority. Is it any wonder that they were right after Him for heresy? Let any one to-day begin to teach in our churches something as entirely new as the teachings of Jesus were, and see what will happen.

He was wonderful in what He prophesied of Himself. He foretold how He would die, and when He would die. It was wonderful that He should have been betrayed into the hands of those who sought His life, by one of His own trusted disciples, and wonderful that He should have been sold for so low a price.

Wonderful, too, that He should have been condemned to death in the way in which He was, by both the religious and civil authorities, and on the testimony of false witnesses, in the name of God, when all the laws of God were defied in the trial. It was wonderful that He was tormented and tortured so cruelly before being sent to the cross, and that He should have been put to death in the brutal manner in which He was. The time of His death was also wonderful; on the day of the Passover, thus Himself becoming the real Passover, to which the passover lamb had so long pointed.

The great publicity of His death was also wonderful. It is doubtful if any other death was ever witnessed by so many people. Hundreds of thousands of people were in Jerusalem, who had come from everywhere to attend the Passover. The sky was darkened, and the sun hid his face from the awful scene. A great earthquake shook the city; the dead came out of their graves, and went into the city, appearing unto many, and the veil of the temple was rent from top to bottom. And remember that up to that time no eye had been allowed to look behind that veil, except that of the high priest, and then only once a year, on the great Day of Atonement.

His resurrection was wonderful. He had foretold it to His disciples, and had done so frequently, always saying, whenever He spoke of His death, that He would rise again on the third day, and yet every one of them appeared to forget all about it, and not one of them was expecting it. None of them thought of going to the sepulcher on the morning of the third day, except the women, and they only to prepare His body more fully for the grave. Womanhood has always been on the firing line.

This shows how fully they had abandoned all hope when they saw Him dead. Some left the city, for we are told of two who went to Emmaus. The manner of His resurrection was godlike. No human mind could ever have imagined such a scene. Had some man described it in the way in which he thought it should have occurred, he would have had earthquakes and thunders and a great commotion in the heavens. A sound like that of the last trump would have proclaimed to all the terrified inhabitants of Jerusalem that He was risen. But see how far different it was.

An angel rolled away the stone from the mouth of the sepulcher as quietly as the opening of the buds in May, and the women, who were early there, found no disorder in the grave, but the linen clothes with which they had tenderly robed His body were neatly folded and tidily placed.

And then how wonderful are the recorded appearances after the resurrection, again so different from what man would have had them. He appeared to every one of His friends, and to His best friends, but not a single one of His enemies got to see Him. I know that this story of the resurrection is true, because none but God would have had things happen in the order that they did, and in the way in which they occurred. Had the story been false the record would have made Jesus go to Pilate and the high priest, and to the others who had put Him to death, to prove that He was risen.

The effect of His teaching upon the world has been wonderful. Remember that He left no great colleges to promulgate His doctrines, but committed them to a few humble fishermen, whose names are now the most illustrious in all history. Looked at from the human side alone, how great was the probability that everything He had said would be forgotten within a few years. He never wrote a sermon. He published no books. Not a thing He said was engraved upon stone or scrolled upon brass, and yet His doctrines have endured for two thousand years. They have gone to the ends of the earth, and have wrought miracles wherever they have gone. They have lifted nations out of darkness and degradation and sin, and have made the wilderness to blossom as the rose.

When Jesus began His ministry Rome ruled the world, and her invincible legions were everywhere, but now through the teachings of the humble Galilean peasant, whom her minions put to death, her power and her religion are gone. The great temple of Diana of the Ephesians is in ruins, and no worshipper of her can be found.

When Jesus fed the five thousand with a few loaves and fishes, and healed the poor woman who touched the hem of His garment, there wasn't a church, or a hospital, or an insane asylum, or other eleemosynary institution in the world, and now they are nearly as countless as the sands upon the seashore. When the bright cloud hid Him from the gaze of those who loved Him with a devotion that took them to martyrdom, the only record of His sayings was graven upon their hearts, but now libraries are devoted to the consideration of them. No words were ever so weighty or so weighed as those of Him who was so poor that He had no where to lay His head. The scholarship of the world has sat at His feet with bared head, and has been compelled to say again and again, "Never man spake as He spake." His utterances have been translated into every known tongue, and have carried healing on their wings wherever they have gone. No other book has ever had a tithe of the circulation of that which contains His words, and not only that, but His thoughts and the story of His life are so interwoven in all literature that if a man should never read a line in the Bible, and yet be a reader at all he could not remain ignorant of the Christ.

He is true to His name because He is a wonderful Savior now. You have only to lift your eyes and look about you to see that His wonderful salvation is going on everywhere to-day. This vast audience throws the lie back into your teeth when you say the religion of Jesus Christ is dying out. There has never been a time when the love of Christ gripped the hearts of humanity as it does to-day.

When John the Baptist, in prison, sent two of his disciples to Jesus, saying: "Art thou He that should come, or do we look for another?" Jesus sent this answer to John: "The blind receive their sight; the lame walk, the lepers are cleansed, and the deaf hear; the dead are raised up, and the poor have the gospel preached unto them"; and that test of His power is as apparent in nearly every part of the world to-day as it was in Galilee. If you have eyes to see the works of God, you will always find them going on.

The heavens declare the glory of God, but there are people so blind they can't see anything but a spell of weather in the rainbow.

Jerry McAuley in prison, a man who had lived by crime, and who had never heard the name of God outside of profanity; as blind and dead to anything good as a stone, one Sunday in the prison chapel heard a verse of Scripture quoted that took hold of his attention. He thought he would like to see it and read it for himself. So he took the Bible in his cell and began to search for it. He didn't know but one sure way to find it, and that was to begin at the first verse in the Bible and read straight on until he came to it. The verse he wanted was in Hebrews, away over in the back part of the New Testament.

Jerry read on, chapter after chapter, and day after day, looking for that verse, but long before he found it he found Jesus Christ—just as some of you would do if you would only be honest with God, and give Him a chance at you by reading His word. From that time on everybody who came near Jerry McAuley knew that the eyes of the man born blind had been opened in him. He started the Water Street Mission in New York, where I don't believe a service was ever held in which somebody was not converted.

Any number of men who were headed straight for the devil are preaching the gospel to-day because they were stopped by the light of God and the voice of His Christ as suddenly as St. Paul was. Yes, He is a wonderful Savior because He is able to save to the uttermost now.

A man would be a great surgeon who could save ninety percent of those upon whom he operated, but mark this: Jesus Christ never lost a case. He never found a case that was too hard for Him. His disciples were continually finding cases they thought were hopeless, and this shows how little they knew Him while He was with them.

Jesus never sent anybody away who came honestly and earnestly seeking His help. They brought to Him all kinds of desperate cases, but at a word or a touch from Him their troubles were all gone. The hardest cases were no more difficult for Him than the easiest, and the same is true to-day, for there is no change in Him. He is the same yesterday, to-day and forever. He can save the scarlet sinner—the man who commits murder—as easily as He can the woman who cheats at cards.

He is a wonderful Savior, too, because He can save so quickly. Quicker than thought He can give you life. It is only, look and live. As quick as you can come He receives you, and as quickly as you could receive a present you had been wanting for years, you can have salvation. "Him that cometh to Me I will in nowise cast out." "To as many as received Him, to them gave He power to become the sons of God." No need of taking very much time about that.

In a meeting Thomas Harrison was holding, a railroad engineer came forward with his watch in his hand and said, "Mr. Harrison, can I be saved in ten minutes? I must leave here to take my train out then."

"Yes," replied Harrison, "you can be saved in ten seconds." The man dropped on his knees, was quickly saved and had seven minutes to spare. A conductor on a fast Pennsylvania train, in Ohio, was converted while crossing a bridge fifty feet long, when going at the rate of a mile a minute. Yes, indeed, He is a wonderful Savior because He can save so quickly.

Moody used to tell of a banker in San Francisco, who was awakened in the night by a burglar at his bedside. The robber held a revolver almost against his face, and said, "If you move I'll kill you!" The banker said, "God have mercy on my soul!" and knocked the burglar down before he could pull the trigger, and was soundly converted before the man struck the floor, as his life afterward proved.

And now I come to the last evidence I will give you that He is true to His name, and that is—

He is a wonderful Savior because He saved me. There is nothing that can be so convincing to a man as his own experience. I do not know that I am the son of my mother any more certainly that I know that I am a child of God, and I do not know that I have been born in a natural way any more convincingly than I know that I have been born of the Spirit.

And now let me ask you this: Has this wonderful Savior saved you? Do you know Him as your Savior? Have you ever given Him your case? When the proof is so overwhelming that He does save, and has been saving for centuries, and that none have ever been saved or ever can be saved except through Him, is it not wonderful that any one can be indifferent to the claims of Jesus Christ?

*4*

# George Washington Truett

*1867–1944*

George Washington Truett was born in North Carolina but moved with his family to Texas when he was twenty-two years old. His plan was to become a lawyer but in 1890 he felt a call to preach. That same year he became financial secretary for Baylor University in Waco, Texas, and raised sufficient funds to get the school out of debt. In 1893 he became a student at Baylor and also assumed the pastorate of the East Waco Baptist Church. He was widely recognized for his character, leadership ability, and devotion to the Lord, and when he graduated from Baylor, the board asked him to become president of the school. But the call to preach was too compelling, and in 1897 he accepted the pulpit of the First Baptist Church of Dallas, Texas, where he served faithfully for forty-seven years.

When Truett came to Dallas, the church had 715 members and was deeply in debt; but many people were converted, the church began to grow, and soon the debt was paid. During the forty-seven years of his pastorate, Truett baptized 5,350 people and saw more than 20,000 join the membership of the church. He was a strong denominational leader and was elected president of the Southern Baptist Convention in 1927, serving three terms.

One of Truett's unique ministries was his annual "Cowboy Roundup" evangelistic week in West Texas, where more than two thousand ranchers, farmers, and cowboys camped together and heard him preach. He preached at the "Roundup" for thirty-seven years.

In 1934 Truett was elected president of the Baptist World Alliance. On June 7, 1944, Truett was on his deathbed and sent a letter of resignation to the church. The minutes read, "The resignation of Dr. Truett as pastor was received and lovingly declined." He died as pastor of the church he dearly loved, pastor of the people who dearly loved him.

*Prince of the Pulpit* by Joe Wright Burton was published by Zondervan in 1946 and *George W. Truett: A Biography* by his son-in-law Powhatan W. James was published in 1939 by Macmillan, with a reprint edition by Broadman Press in 1953. Numerous editions of his sermon books have been issued.

# Trumpeting the Gospel

*An Anniversary Sermon*

From Paul's First Letter to the Thessalonians, the first chapter and eighth verse, this sentence is taken for our text: "From you sounded out the Word of the Lord, not only in Macedonia and Achaia, but also in every place your faith to God-ward is spread abroad; so that we need not speak anything."

Paul is here paying a most remarkable compliment to the church at Thessalonica. We shall search in vain in all the Scriptures for a more delicate and beautiful, and yet worthy compliment than this paid by Paul to that old-time church. Paul's compliments were worth having. He was no fulsome flatterer. He was discriminating and just, sincere and true; and therefore the more beautiful and significant stands out this compliment that Paul paid that church. "You are a dynamic force for the Gospel," said Paul; "you have made, and are making, an impression for it so wonderful that I do not need to say one word." Did you ever note a more desirable compliment?

Some time before this Paul had gone from Philippi, where he had been assaulted, maltreated, beaten, into this heathen city of Thessalonica. When he opened his lips to speak the wonderful words of life, there was a remarkable response right in the heart of that heathen capital. Men who served idols, men steeped in the lust of idolatry and in the basest forms of vice that enshrouded that city, heard this man tell about One who came from the Father's house to reveal the Father's love, and who gave Himself to break the shackles from men who would be disenthralled,

48

and who would walk in the sunlight of truth and righteousness. And they believed that message, and from that hour they voiced it with their noble living. From that hour their lives were fundamentally changed.

You have noted, haven't you, what an eye Paul had for strategic places? He was a seer. He had the forecast of the first statesman of the world. He knew that what was done in a city was a thing not done in a corner, but everybody would hear about it and know about it, and feel it, according to whether it should be good or bad. He knew that, and he put that great heart and hand and brain of his on the city. As goes the city so shall go the country and the whole land. The city is the nerve-center and the storm-center of civilization and of Christianity. If these cities are not saved, Christianity is lost and all is lost. If these cities are saved, the whole land shall be vocal with the songs of heaven. Paul knew that, and that statesman-like eye of his swept those cities of Europe and Asia, and his heart coveted those centers, those strongholds for God.

Let everybody keep his eye on the city. That little remote village yonder, far in the country place, away from the noise and confusion of the city, is vitally interested in what we do here in the city, and we must not forget this, nor must they. A road leads from that little village, or from that remote country schoolhouse to the city; and not only does the road lead here, but the boy out there is coming here, and we shall contaminate him and damn him, or we shall disenthral him and add to his strength and nobleness, and send him back a joy to the old folks that sent him away with so much concern. The little remote country community is vitally interested in the city, interested in its laws, interested in it in every respect. There is no drawing a line and saying, "The city shall stay on this side." It isn't going to do it. "And the country shall stay on that side." It isn't going to do it. We are neighbors, and ever becoming more so, mingling and intermingling. We are to plan our deeds of noblest strength right in the heart of the city. Paul did that in Thessalonica, and in the other cities of the time in which he lived, showing what an eye he had for strategic situations.

Did you notice this expressive word that Paul employed? We come upon it here for the first time, and I think the only time in the New Testament, in its description of the business of a church: "From you sounded out the word of life." The church is to be God's trumpet, "From you is trumpeted forth the word of life." From this trumpet the word of life is to be sounded forth. A church is God's agency supreme in the world through which His love is revealed and His grace made known. That is the business of a church, and here it is strikingly set forth.

Let us look at two or three vital truths that are enwrapped in this compliment Paul pays to the church at Thessalonica.

And, first, he tells us the kind of men that sounded out the word of life. The context gives us the description of such men. They were men who possessed the fundamental virtues of the Christian life, the cardinal virtues, the vital virtues—three of them. "Remembering," said Paul, "without ceasing, your work of faith, your labor of love, and your patience of hope in our Lord Jesus Christ." These are the fundamental, Christian virtues, and these Christians in Thessalonica possess them. "Your work of faith, your labor of love, your patience of hope." What a trio that, and how fond Paul was of such trios! In concluding that incomparable chapter on Love, the thirteenth chapter of First Corinthians, Paul said: "And now abideth faith, hope, love, these three; but the greatest of these is love." The abiding virtues, the cardinal virtues, the fundamental virtues in a Christian life, were possessed by these Thessalonian Christians, who sounded forth the word of life, about whom Paul spoke so glowingly.

And Paul further said: "You were possessed by these virtues; you did not receive the Gospel in word only, but also in power, and in the Holy Ghost, and in much assurance." "That is to say," said Paul: "You were absorbed by these great matters; you took your religion seriously; you accounted it the first thing in the world to be true followers of God, to be faithful imitators of Christ." And still further, said Paul: "You held constant, you were invariable in the midst of sorest trials." Go read again in the book of the Acts, and see how those early Christians in Thessalonica were assaulted by the mob, how their blood flowed down their backs from the scourgings laid on them by cruel persecutors. Mark how they were hunted like the wild beasts on the mountains, how they watched, and yet as they watched, mark how they sang their songs of praise and voiced their hymns of obedience to Jesus! Paul said to those Christians: "You were constant in the midst of sorest trials; you did not recant when the battle became fierce; you did not flee, cowardlike, when the stress of the storm was on you; you were true." Oh, what a tribute was that for Paul to pay a little group of Christians, that they were constant, that they were invariable, that they obeyed without wavering! What a tribute was that—to the dependable man!

I have had occasion to say it before, but I would say it again and again—I care less and less for what you are pleased to term your brilliant man. I care more and more for your dependable man—the man true in every storm, the man who, when folks discuss him in their little circles and cliques and caucuses, must say: "You may put that man down as on the side of right though the heavens fall." Your dependable man, your man who is not a weathervane, your man who does not try to ride two horses at the same time going in opposite directions, he is the salt of the earth, the life-blood of civilization. William Pitt made correct answer when one asked him one day: "Mr. Pitt, what would you pronounce the first qualification for a prime minister of Great Britain?" And he said: "The first qualification is patience." Said the questioner: "What would you pronounce the second qualification for a prime minister of Great Britain?" And Pitt replied: "The second qualification is patience." "Well, then," said the questioner, "what would you pronounce the third qualification?" And he said: "The third is patience." Wasn't it wisely said? We need patience to hold on, patience to plod, patience to persevere, patience to keep at our work without wavering or fainting. "Be thou faithful unto death"—not until death—that isn't what it says, that isn't what it means. "Be thou faithful unto death"—that is, die before being unfaithful. Any man ought to prefer any hour to die than to play the ignominious traitor and be unfaithful to the right thing. "Be thou faithful unto death"—die before being unfaithful—"and"—note the great promise—"I will give thee the crown of life." Now such were the men to whom Paul paid this incomparable compliment.

Notice here also the means that they employed for sounding out this word of God, this Gospel of life. The context explains that fully for us. First of all, the chief means for sounding out this conquering Gospel was that such Gospel produced in debauched lives the most marvelous transformations. There is nothing else in the world so moving, so startling, as for a man to be soundly converted by the Gospel of God. These men of Thessalonica were converted all over, they were fundamentally changed. They had long served idols, but when Paul's Gospel came in, breaking those idols into dust, presenting Jesus, the Way, the Truth, and the Life, the Emancipator of sin-driven men, the Life-Bringer, the Hope-Giver—when they heard that, they turned away from their idols to serve the living and true God, and to wait for His Son from heaven, whom He raised from the dead, even Jesus, who delivered us from the wrath to come.

There is nothing so wonderful as a true conversion, as for a man to be genuinely saved. We are hearing a great deal these days about all manner of prescriptions for advancing Christianity. They are telling us much, these days, about "socializing Christianity." I am shy of much of that kind of talk. The greatest thing in the world is for the individual man to be saved by the Gospel, for such man to have a Divine power to come into his life and turn him to God. That is the greatest thing in the world. The best advertisement for this Gospel which we love is a saved man, living his religion. That is the supreme advertisement. Paul said: "You men are my advertisement; you are such a good advertisement I do not need even to speak anything." Did you ever hear of a more wonderful compliment than that? Oh, this is to be our glory, our predominant passion, to see men saved, to see men converted divinely by this glorious Gospel, transformed, changed, saved!

I have told you before, I think, of the most remarkable conversion I ever saw. Will you bear with me while I tell you again about it? The occasion was several years ago, in a great outdoor Texas meeting. Conditions religiously were dreadfully hard and bad where such meeting was held. I think I never knew them worse. Men with white locks about their ears were lost, and even their grandchildren followed in forbidden and ruinous paths; and the few people of God in the community were down and beaten and defeated, it seemed. One of the causes for such conditions was that a group of men had had a series of little, pesky, religious debates, and the result was that conditions were hard and harsh and bad on every side.

All these things were recounted in the preacher's ears, as he began the meetings. I shall never forget the repeated story of the people there concerning one of their citizens, a man known for a radius of hundreds of miles. I could speak his name, but will not. He would not forbid it, for I could speak it to God's praise. They told me much about this same Big Jim. They said: "He will come to the meeting once this year; then he will curse you and the meeting out, and curse the churches, and then he will wait another year to come again. That is his style. You need not waste any preaching on him." They described him so that I could not mistake him—he was the largest man in all that section. One night I stood up to preach, and in came Big Jim. I shall never forget the emotions that then possessed me. Here was the chief of sinners, so the people said; what could be done for him?

That night I preached, and God's Spirit moved upon the audience mightily, and men with their white locks and stooped shoulders were, like little children, that night turned to the Saviour. Grandfathers that night came, who had walked the wrong way for well-nigh their threescore years and ten. And their grandchildren also came. The Spirit of the Lord was upon us in marvelous fashion that night.

Yonder sat Big Jim like a granite shaft. And when that service was concluded, a little group of people stayed behind and talked with one another about the hour just past, as men are wont to talk over such an occasion. Ever and anon they would refer to Big Jim. They said: "He was here to-night, but he won't be back." One said: "I believe he will return; I never saw him look as he looked to-night." Another said, "No"; another said, "Yes." Presently after I had left the tabernacle to find the cottage where I slept, as I went along through the quiet woods, I heard some one talking in the darkness of the night. I did not mean to be an eavesdropper. There were two of them talking, oh, so earnestly. They were talking to God. This is what they were saying: "Mighty God, the people are saying that Big Jim is too much for Thee. Oh, break to pieces our unbelief, and let all this country know that God is Master of the situation, that He can save even the chief sinner here!" They said: "Master, we plead Thy promise to Thy disciples about two who may agree, and if agreeing concerning anything they should ask, Thou wilt hear. We agree that we want Big Jim saved for the glory of God, and to stop the mouths of gainsayers once and forever in all this section."

I quietly went my way, leaving them thus on their knees. They did not know that I had heard them, nor do I know who they were. The next day came and wore to evening, and again I stood up to preach, and in came Big Jim again. Yonder he sat at the rear of the tabernacle; and then I said, "Father, give me the word of life for this brother man."

I told the story of the prodigal son, that restless, wayward lad, who went away from home against the protest of love and wisdom's voice, and who went from bad to worse, and down and down, until yonder he is in the swine fields eating of the husks wherewith he fed the swine. One day the prodigal became homesick and soulsick and he said: "I have missed it all; my whole life's course is a grim sarcasm; I have missed it all. I can do better than this as a servant in my father's house; and worst of all, worst of all, I have sinned against my best friend, I have sinned against my father who loved me, and I have sinned against my father's God. I will go back and I will tell him all." You know the rest. You know how the father, whose heart ached forever with an aching that would not stop because the boy was gone, looked one day and saw him coming, and while he was yet a great way off, that father ran to meet him and to fold that thing of rags and shame to his heart, while the boy wept and said: "Father, I did not come back to ask to be your boy, but to tell you that I have sinned against you and heaven, and that I am not worthy to be called your son, but ask only to have a servant's place." And the father said: "Kill the fatted calf for the boy returned; bring him the best robe; put on his finger the ring—emblem of love that never dies." That was what I preached. And then I said: "I bring you a Gospel to which I have anchored my very soul; I am willing to die by it, and I am trying to live by it; I am going to meet God with it when I stand before Him in the judgment. I came one day and surrendered to that Saviour whom God the Father sent. Is there a man here who will surrender to Him now?"

Big Jim started towards the preacher, and in a moment half a thousand men were seeing him and all these rose to their feet. Were they dreaming? Was it too good to be true? They were on their feet, looking, listening, sobbing. Down that long aisle came Big Jim, and when he reached me he caught my hand and said: "I put you on your sacred honor—will Jesus Christ save me if I give up to Him?" I said: "On my sacred honor, I answer that He will." And then he looked at me again while the men, who stood all about us now, were begging him to yield to Christ. He spoke again: "But you must remember that I am the worst man out of hell." I answered back: "My Saviour died for the worst man out of hell, and He is able to save him now." Once more he looked at me and said: "When would He save me if I were to surrender myself to Him right now?" I said: "On the authority of Jesus Christ, on which I have rested my soul for time and eternity, I declare that He will save you right now, and you yourself may be the judge, if you will fully surrender to Him now."

Then he turned that great, bronzed face, pitiful in its anguish, up towards the heavens, and gasped this prayer: "Lord Jesus, the worst man in the world gives up to You right now!"

I cannot tell you all the rest. I don't know that the angels could tell it all. But God unloosed his tongue, and Big Jim witnessed for Jesus then and there as I never heard Him witnessed for before nor since. Old grizzled men came and kissed Big Jim; and old women came and kissed him; and little children kissed him, for the chief of sinners was saved. And then the word went to and fro as fast as the winds could carry it that God was in the midst of the people forgiving sin.

Gentlemen, one such apologetic as that for Christianity sounds out the gospel word both far and near as can nothing else in all the earth. We will stay by the simple, old-fashioned, supreme vocation of Christ's church, and that is to win men to God. That is the biggest thing in all the world. And when that is done, light will spread and darkness will flee, and righteousness will follow. That was the way the Gospel of old was made victorious. Men were converted to God and others soon heard the gladsome news, and themselves were led to ask the way of life.

Then, again, these Thessalonians, by their lives, attested their profession. Their profession was vindicated by their lives. Paul said: "Your life has been so glorious, you have been such an inspiration, such a blessing, such an example to all the people throughout all Greece, north and south, that I do not even need to say a word in defense of the Gospel. You are the Gospel embodied, you are the Gospel incarnated in lives, you are the Gospel lighting up a house that was once inhabited by black evil things, and now shines to the praise of God." Their lives attested their profession.

Here is the best argument for Christianity: The right kind of a Christian—mark you, the right kind of a Christian. He is the one unanswerable, invulnerable argument for Christianity in this world—the right kind of a Christian. These men said, wherever they went throughout Greece, north and south, all through Macedonia, all through Achaia, wherever they went, they said: "We were debauched, we were bad, we were enslaved, we were handicapped by sin, we were depraved. We accepted Christ, and He changed our natures; we are now new men." And their lives said it much louder than anything their lips could say. That is the power of the Gospel.

Oh, my fellow Christians, that is its irresistible power. You can feel some men, the Christian element in them is so strong. That was the glory of Phillips Brooks. You could not analyze his preaching, it is often said, but you could feel him. That was the glory of Robert E. Lee, that matchless man of Southern history. That was the glory of William Pitt, Prime Minister of Great Britain. That was the glory of Washington, Father of His Country. That is the glory of many a little modest man, and many a little shrinking woman, whose life is radiant with the sunlight of sincerity, and with a glorious enduement of God's goodness and truth and grace. These men of old thus lived their religion.

There was another thing that was conquering in their Christian character, and that was their faith was as clear as the sunlight, and as enduring as a granite mountain. Their faith—what a vital word is that! What a vital word that is for these times, with all the theological millinery we have about us, and all the fads and fancies, the cults and innovations! Their faith was as clear as the sunlight, as unshakable as Gibraltar. These men knew what they believed, and why, and they were able to give to every man they met an answer for that marvelous hope that illumined their way, and transformed their lives.

I would summon you to-day, my fellow Christians, to be clear in your faith. Know what you believe concerning the things of religion, and why. The man who speaks with the accent of sincerity and definiteness is the man of power. Remember the apostle's question: "If the trumpet give an uncertain sound"—(and remember we are trumpets for Christ)—"if the trumpet give an uncertain sound, who shall prepare himself to the battle?" Your testimony for God is to be clear and unhesitating and certain. Alas! that some Christians in their faith are like Reuben of old, unstable as water, and like him, too, it may be said of each of them: "Thou shalt not excel." Be clear in your faith. Don't be religious mugwumps. Jesus was the very Prince of dogmatists, and His apostles after Him were to the last degree dogmatic in their faith. Listen to Peter: "Neither is there salvation in any other; for there is none other name under heaven given among men, whereby we must be saved." That is dogmatic. Listen to John, that disciple of love and gentleness. "Who is the liar, but he that denieth that Jesus is the Christ? This is the anti-Christ, even he that denieth the Father and the Son." Listen to Paul: "But though we, or an angel from heaven, preach any other gospel unto you than that we have preached unto you, let him be accursed." And to increase the emphasis, he repeats it in the next verse. Oh, my fellow Christians, on this tremendous matter of religious faith we want to be as clear as the sunlight, and as unshakable as the everlasting hills. "'Tis conviction that convinces."

Take Karl Marx. He is the most dogmatic and pronounced personality that Germany has produced in a hundred years—that noted Socialist leader. Mighty passions and convictions and beliefs have surged in his life, and he has put the stamp of his forceful personality throughout all Germany and Europe, and the world. Certainly you do not agree and I do not agree with many of his teachings; but when a man with the passion and the conviction and the personality and the power of Karl Marx goes across the world, men will feel him. And there are ten thousand fires burning in human hearts to-day because Karl Marx believed something. And the world is studying this hour, in a way never before, the teachings of Socialism, because Karl Marx believed something.

Take the Roman Catholic Church. She has two special dogmas, which, both in season, and out of season, she proclaims: The dogma of the church, and the dogma of the mass. We cannot in the remotest degree accept her teachings concerning the church and concerning the mass; and yet that great body concerning which I would not willingly say one improper or unjust word—that great body goes through the earth proclaiming that the church should be supreme in the regulation of all human conduct, in the home, in society, in things political, everywhere. You stand amazed, as do I, that such dogma should have advocates. And you are the more amazed at their other dogma that simple bread and wine are actually changed into the very body and blood of Jesus, their doctrine of transubstantiation, after the blessing of such bread and wine, by the proper ecclesiastic. And yet that mighty ecclesiasticism, through the centuries, has boldly taught these two dogmas, and has put the impress of such teachings in every land beneath the stars. They believe something—that explains it. I honor them, while utterly differing from them, for persisting evermore in urging those amazing dogmas, because they believe them.

And in the other days, when Martin Luther, that immortal Protestant, who before was a Catholic priest, came to believe that God-honoring doctrine that men are not justified by human works, nor by human righteousness of any sort, but that they are justified by faith in Jesus Christ, Luther went out and—aforetime a devout Romanist—Luther went out and proclaimed the doctrine of justification by faith in such a way that he wrested Germany from the hands of the Pope, and thrilled the world with his mighty pronouncement of Protestantism. He believed something, and he avowed it. When he had determined to go to the Diet of Worms, and men tried to keep him from going because he would go in the face of probable death, together with every threatened punishment, he answered them back: "If there were as many devils as there are tiles on every roof in Wurtemberg, I can but go and say what my soul knows to be true." He believed something.

My fellow men, let us have a faith that does not change with every change of the moon. John Knox put his marvelous personality on Scotland and on every other land beneath the sun because he believed something. He rescued Scotland from the grip of unbelief because he believed something. And John Knox's daughter, Jane Welch, when they offered her her husband's freedom if he would recant, answered like this: "I would sooner have my husband's severed head brought me in a charger than for him to deny the things he has taught and believed." Oh, for a generation of great believers!

But there was another all important thing about these early Christians. They attested their faith by their deeds. They proved their religion by their works. They vindicated their hope by their deeds. That is the apologetic that we must have—just that. All my time could be spent on that one simple point. But I leave it after referring to just one incident in the life of David Brainerd. That Christly missionary to the Indians, when he became so old and weak and crippled with rheumatism that it seemed that there was nothing else that he could do but wait there in his little hut and die, was found one day kneeling on the floor, too feeble to sit in his chair, teaching a little Indian girl her A B Cs. And men said: "What! Has it come to this? The great David Brainerd down on the floor teaching a little Indian girl her A B Cs!" And he said: "Happy if with my latest breath I may but be permitted even to teach a little Indian girl her ABCs."

You will make the application, won't you, of this old-time text? Every church, I remarked in the beginning, is to be a trumpet for Jesus Christ—to voice the word and love of Jesus Christ. My beloved people here of this flock, you will make the application. The church at Thessalonica was inevitably situated to influence many people. How like your own! Thessalonica was a city of telling commerce. How like your own city here! The roads were many that came and went to Thessalonica. How like your own! And the blows struck for Jesus Christ yonder in Thessalonica sounded out throughout all the province of Macedonia. Even so, a light here properly given will send its rays far and near. A testimony here properly given will go far beyond your own circles. Like Paul, who was a patriot, as every man ought to be, you can say to-day: "I am a citizen of no mean city." And by reason of that very position that you have, you are called upon to sound out the word of life, of righteousness and truth in every blessed and glorious way.

God has providentially thrust you into an exceedingly responsible place. Do not shrink from it. Oh, certainly there are times when you want to flee to the woods never to come back, but you can't. God has providentially thrust you into the gaze of the people, far and near, and you are called upon all the more to witness worthily for Jesus Christ. Here in Dallas are several of our denominational Boards. Here is your State Mission Board doing the largest state mission work in all the world. Here also is your Woman's Work, in its official organization. Here also is your Young People's Board. Here is your denominational paper. Here is your great Sanitarium. Then God has given us this noble church, with her more than two thousand members. What a host of people! And your fear sometimes is as mine, that this church will be a hospital of people not active, instead of a barrack of soldiers aggressive for God.

And then think of the army of strangers within our gates. I have often wondered if our ministry to the strangers is not broader than our ministry to our own homes and firesides; for scarcely a day passes that some stranger near or far does not write to give grateful testimony to the blessing brought him in this worship with us here. By all these facts we are called upon to be the right kind of men and women. Then see our various church agencies of this one church. See the Sunday-school, the supreme opportunity of the church. To save a boy is an incomparably bigger thing than to save a man. To save a girl is more important than to save a woman, for you save a life as well as a soul when you save a child. Here too are our organizations for our hosts of young people. Here too are the multitudes of women with their many and mighty forces. There is nothing more pitiful than for a woman saved through the blood of Christ to have her energies diverted into some little, narrow shallow channel of selfishness, to gratify some small, passing impulse. Some time ago a cultured woman came to her pastor, not in Dallas, I am glad to remark, to say there was a Buddhist lecturer in the city, and to ask if the pastor would not let the Buddhist lecturer have the pulpit from which to exploit Buddhism. The pastor was amazed beyond all speech, and said so, that a woman, given her position in this country, of happiness and honor—given such position by Jesus Christ—would wish her pastor to offer his pulpit for the exploitation of Buddhism, when a woman in Buddhist countries slavishly waits on her husband, is not worthy to eat at the same table with him, gets such crumbs only as he chooses to give, and is taught that she does not have any soul at all. What a tragedy it is when a woman, whose chief charm is her religion, is diverted from her church life into little, shallow, narrow channels of thought and activity. What a tragedy when her life is taken up with religious cults and fads and isms, and the deep practical things of Christianity are forgotten.

I summon the Christian women who are here to-day, given their incomparable position by the blood of the Son of God—I summon them to give their best to Jesus Christ and to His church. And these men, these saved men, I summon them to give their best to Jesus and His church. My fellow men, if Jesus Christ loved the church enough to die for it, you and I surely ought to love it enough to live for it. There are two great organizations in the world—there are not many that are worth a great deal; there are two that are absolutely invaluable, the home and the church. If you and I are to plant our labors in life where they will count for the most, then let us consecrate our best labors for the home and for the church. The home has been wretchedly neglected. I might mention a host of agencies at work for the redemption of children that would have been made unnecessary by the right kind of homes. The church also has been sadly neglected.

It is a day of organizations now. Sometimes I have wondered if some men could find enough space on their coats to put all the buttons of the various organizations to which they belong. I have not a word of railing to say against such organizations, but I would say, my fellow Christian men, that in these short lives that you and I are to live, we ought to link our lives with those organizations that will count the most, and with the organizations that are of most vital value to a needy world. Let us invest our lives, our love, our money, our service, not so that the fruits and influences therefrom shall be evanescent like some passing cloud of the morning, but so that they may abide through all the coming years and forevermore. I summon you to give your best to Christ, your best to Christ to-day and always.

I have been with you many years. Oh, I know the stress and the travail of the preacher's life. I have gone to my room a thousand times and asked God if I might be released from it all; and then the instant the words escaped my lips I have hastened to say: "Nay, Lord, nay, only give me grace to be the preacher I ought to be!" Every waking hour I sing:

> Happy if with my latest breath,
> I may but speak Thy name;
> Preach Christ to all, and gasp in death,
> Behold, behold the Lamb.

My grandfather was a preacher through the long, long years. In his last illness his affliction was such that he could not lie on his bed for one moment for many days. But people came to him for a region of forty or fifty miles, and there sitting in his chair, with his last expiring breath, he preached Christ Jesus, the world's one and only, but all-sufficient Saviour. I should like to go like that to the last, to the last, witnessing for Jesus. O my fellow Christians, I summon you to give Christ your best of love, of service, of life. His is the most virile, the most masculine, the most heroic, the sublimest business on earth—the making of His Gospel victorious everywhere. Give Him your best, your best, your best, forevermore.

O my fellow Christians of this church, a church dearer to me than my heart's blood, God knows—my fellow Christians of this church, I summon you anew to-day to give your best to Christ; to be done with all playing at your religion; to be done with all lukewarmness. I summon you to come with the red rich blood of human sympathy for all mankind, for good and bad, for high and low, for rich and poor, and give your best to win this city and state and world to Jesus, so that you may hear that plaudit which it were worth worlds at last to hear, "Well done, thou good and faithful servant."

# George Campbell Morgan

*1863-1945*

Known as the "Prince of Expositors," Campbell Morgan had no formal theological education and yet taught on several college faculties, served as president of a college, and wrote more than sixty books that are studied today by ministers of all denominations. The ten volumes of *The Westminster Pulpit* contain the best of his sermons from a long life of ministry.

Refused ordination in the Methodist church because he failed his "trial sermon," Morgan identified with the British Congregationalists and served churches in Stone, Rugeley, Birmingham, and London (New Court) before going to the United States to direct the extension ministry of D. L. Moody's Northfield Conference. He ministered widely in the United States and Canada and it can honestly be said that he was discovered in the United States before being discovered in England.

From 1904 to 1917 Morgan pastored the Westminster Chapel, Buckingham Gate, London, and made it a center for Bible study and expository preaching. His Friday evening Bible school attracted serious Bible students from all over the United Kingdom. From 1919 to 1933 he ministered throughout the United States as an itinerant Bible teacher and also served two brief pastorates, first in Cincinnati and then in Philadelphia. In 1933 he returned to a second ministry at Westminster Chapel and five years later took D. Martyn Lloyd-Jones as his associate. Morgan resigned from the church in 1943 and died May 16, 1945.

62

*A Man of the Word* by his daughter-in-law Jill Morgan is the official biography (Pickering and Inglis, 1951; Baker reprint, 1972). Revell published *G. Campbell Morgan* by John Harries (1930) and also *This Was His Faith: The Expository Letters of G. Campbell Morgan,* compiled and edited by Jill Morgan (1952). For the "Morgan approach" to Bible study, see his *The Ministry of the Word* (Revell, 1919) and *The Study and Teaching of the English Bible* (James Clarke), as well as *The Expository Method of G. Campbell Morgan* by Don M. Wagner (Revell, 1957).

# Understanding,
# or Bit and Bridle

Be ye not as the horse or as the mule, which have no understanding; whose trappings must be bit and bridle to hold them
in, else they will not come near unto thee.

Psalm 32:9

Be ye not foolish, but understand what the will of the Lord is.

Ephesians 5:17

The similarity between these two texts is self-evident. The
Hebrew Psalmist, and the Christian Apostle say the same thing.
The method of the former is illustrative and pictorial; that of the
latter is more direct and interpretive. Each of these men, separated from each other by centuries, saw two ways of living. The
one was described by the Hebrew Psalmist in the figure of the
horse and the mule, which must be held in with bit and bridle.
That same way was described by the Apostle in a word that really
is vibrant with sarcasm—"foolish!" This word, being literally
translated, means: having no mind. That is one way of life. The
Psalmist describes the method to be adopted with that state of
mindlessness; the Apostle simply refers to it. The other way of
life is described by Psalmist and Apostle by words which we have
translated by the same word "understanding." The Hebrew word
translated "understanding" means to separate mentally; or, as
we say, to distinguish. The Greek word translated "understanding" means to bring together or, as we say, to conclude.

The distinction between the two statements is that the first
illustrates one method, while the second interprets the other

63

method. So these texts complement each other while moving in the same realm and uttering the same injunction. The first declares what has to be done with the mindless horse or mule, or man. Such must be held in with bit and bridle. The second shows what the understanding mind takes hold of. It apprehends the will of the Lord.

In these injunctions a central idea of life is implicated, two methods of life are revealed, and in each case an appeal is made to choose the higher and the nobler. These, then, are the lines of our consideration.

We shall perhaps see the central idea of life most clearly by considering the illustration of the Hebrew Psalmist. What, then, are the functions of bit and bridle in the case of the horse and the mule? Let me say at once, and that for my own soul's comfort, that many of you may know a good deal more about horses and mules than I do. However, I am not proposing to deal with the characteristics of these animals, but rather to take the simplest things, which are perfectly patent to the ordinary person. In the case of horse and mule, the bit and the bridle mean, first, *restraint,* and second, *realization under restraint.* The restraint is preliminary; the realization is final. The restraint of bit and bridle is the indication to the will of the animal of the fact of a superior will. If the Psalmist said, and he did say, and that with inspired accuracy, that these animals have no understanding, he did not mean that they have no intelligence. *Understanding is something far more than intelligence. Horses and mules have intelligence; they have emotion; they have will.* These are the elements of human personality, but in a lower degree and yet very definitely, we find them in what we call the lower animals. No man knows anything about a horse who says that it has no intelligence. And that a mule has will none will deny who has attempted to manage one! The purpose of bit and bridle is to indicate to whatever there may be of intelligence in the animal that it has to do with a superior will.

Thus it becomes the method of *compulsion by the superior will, that which keeps all the forces represented in the life of the animal near to the master and under control.* That is what the Psalmist says: "Be ye not as the horse or as the mule, which have no understanding; whose trappings must be bit and bridle to hold them in else, they will not come near unto thee." The Revised Version has greatly helped us there. The text is somewhat obscure, but the Authorized rendering: "In order that they may not come near unto thee," is entirely misleading. We put bit and bridle on horse or mule in order to indicate to whatever intelligence they may have that they have to do with a superior will and in order to compel their will to yield to that superior will.

But there is a reason for such restraint; it is always in order to teach realization. In the horse and the mule there are forces of strength, of energy, of swiftness. The purpose of the bit and bridle is that these forces may be controlled and exercised, that they may become useful, that they may realize something.

For the sake of illustration let us exercise our imaginations and put ourselves in the place of the mule—*some of us have not far to travel*. The first sense of bit and bridle is simply that of something *curbing, hurting, checking, mastering*. As to mules I do not know, but I do know that after a while a horse will come to know the very touch of your hand on the bridle. You have but to make your own peculiar movement of the bridle, and it will turn to the right or left, it will halt, trot, gallop, or canter, as you desire. By restraint you have realized its powers, and you have given to the animal itself the sense of power. By the imposition of your superior will, curbing, checking, reining, mastering, you have made its life useful.

Now, what are the implications of that very beautiful illustration from the old Hebrew who loved a horse and a mule I verily believe, or he never would have written this psalm? The first is that life is power, energy, force, having values beyond its mere being. If life be energy, power, force merely, having no value beyond being, then it does not need bit and bridle, it does not need control, it does not need method or direction. In that case, let us merely live. But when a religious singer of the long ago and an apostle of the Christian era charge us not to be mulish, implicated in the charge is the idea that life is power and energy and force, having values beyond being; in other words, that life is purposeful. No human life has come to its realization when it is simply lived. It comes to realization only when it is being lived for purpose.

Again, the figure implies the truth that *life lacks direction within itself for the realization of this purpose*. It can exist, but it cannot achieve. The horse and the mule can live in the wilderness and the prairies, but they will not achieve. Lasso them, corral them, break them in, put the bit and the bridle on them; then they will achieve. The bit and the bridle are the means necessary to achievement. Man can live without any control external to himself. He can answer all the impulses of his own being, he can let them have full sway and run riot. He can live, but he cannot achieve. Unless the forces in his being are under some kind of controlling power that will direct and energize, life is nothing more than a putting forth of effort, which is without value.

And so, finally, this figure of the bit and the bridle teaches us that life needs restraint in order to be realized, it needs impulse in order to achieve, and that such restraint and impulse come, not out of the forces of the life, but from without.

Now let us look at the two methods of life suggested. Neither of these methods is godless. The man who is entirely godless is not in view. Neither writer was thinking of such a man. The Hebrew Psalmist was singing for the people of God, and the whole point of his charge is its application to the people of God. He was appealing to those who had heard the voice of God saying to them: "I will instruct thee and teach thee in the way which thou shalt go; I will counsel thee with Mine eye upon thee."

It was that sense of the Divine relation to the soul, and the soul's relation to the Divine, which led him immediately to say what he did. Because of that, because God is pledged to your guidance, "Be ye not as the horse or as the mule, which have no understanding." So also when Paul wrote this injunction in the Ephesian letter, "Be not foolish." Therefore I say again that neither of these ways is godless. They rather reveal two methods of God with men; which method He adopts always depends on the man. Whether God shall adopt with me the method of the bit or the bridle, or the higher method, depends on me. But to that we will return in conclusion.

Now, what are these methods? The first is the method of *compelling pressure;* the second is the method of *impelling motive.* In the first we see life controlled by pressure from the outside; in the second, we see life impelled by the mystic motive of understanding, which is within. The first is the method of conflict; the second is the method of communion. Be not like the horse and the mule, which have no understanding, and must be kept under control with bit and bridle. The necessity for getting near, and being under control, is admitted; but because there is no understanding, the bit and the bridle, the compelling pressure, the conflict ending in victory for the superior will, are necessary. Be not like that, said the Psalmist; have understanding. More bluntly, the Christian Apostle said, Be not foolish, but understand what the will of the Lord is. Get the deep profound inner secret of your life so related to God that you will understand by the communion of love rather than by conflict the restraint which is necessary for realization. We are offered the choice between the restraint of compelling pressure and the restraint of impelling motive, the restraint of bit and bridle and the restraint of understanding. Bit and bridle mean the fight between two wills, and ultimately the mastery of the weaker by the stronger. Bit and bridle are the symbols of intermediary methods, made necessary because the soul is not consciously near to God, because it has no understanding. Horse and mule must be held in with bit and bridle, for they have no understanding. They are not near to their master in spirit, in thought, in mind. They cannot help it. They are not to be pitied. But when a man is in that state he is to be pitied, nay, he is to be blamed. In the case of a man, the bit and the bridle mean God's employment of compelling pressure to force the will to higher purpose in harmony with His own will. God's method with most of us has had to be that of the bit and the bridle, of adverse circumstances, personal affliction, chastisement; and all because we have not been near enough to God to understand Him.

The method of understanding, the method of communion, the method of impelling motive, is the method, not of conflict between two wills, but of co-operation between the will of man and that which Paul, in another of his letters, so gloriously and adequately described as the good and accept-able and perfect will of God.

The method of understanding is based on the comprehension of these very facts concerning the Divine will, that it is good and acceptable and perfect. To understand the will of the Lord is to love the Lord. Under-standing is infinitely more than knowing. *It is the comprehension, not merely of what the Lord commands, but of why the Lord commands.* Understanding does not mean that we always know immediately the reason of what the Lord commands, but we know the One Who commands so well as to be perfectly at rest, even when we cannot understand the immediate reason of the command. It is good, it is perfect, it is acceptable. If we would finally apprehend the meaning of the word "understand," we may remind our-selves of another great psalm in which the Singer declared: "Thou under-standest my thought afar off." That is infinitely more than knowing it. God understands the thought, He knows the reason of it, the genesis of it, how it came to be. Understanding the will of the Lord is the response of the soul of man to God's understanding of the soul. God's understanding is ultimate and final and perfect, and there is no darkness in it. As the soul of man knows these things about God, that soul understands. What it does not know of God's immediate reason or purpose it does understand to be perfectly right, since it is His will. Is there any finer word in the language to express what friendship is than the word "understanding"? Leave all your acquaintances, and think in the narrow circle of your friends. I am not speaking disparagingly of acquaintances; they are very valuable. *But no soul has many friends.* Fasten your attention on one. The greatest thing you can say to that friend is, "You understand." That does not mean that your friend can explain to you the mystery of the thing you are thinking, but it does mean that your friend understands this mystic call of the soul. Under-standing goes out beyond intelligence, beyond emotion, and beyond will. It is a spiritual apprehension. To understand what the will of the Lord is, is to apprehend His motive. It is not always to know what the motive is, but it is to know that the motive is mastered by His infinite and unfailing love.

Now we see why I read that passage in Isaiah 11 for our lesson, which, in some senses, seems to have little connection with the line of our medi-tation. I read it for its remarkable suggestions concerning Jesus. The prophet of the olden time, having climbed a great height, having dived into a great deep of understanding, described God's perfect Servant, and in that passage we see Him first as Man, and then immediately as God. The merging of the human and the divine is wonderfully indicated, and in both cases we have this thought of understanding. "He shall be quick of understanding in the fear of the Lord." That is the final glorious word about the Messiah in His ideal humanity. The Spirit of the Lord shall rest upon Him, the spirit of wisdom and understanding, the spirit of counsel and might, the spirit of knowledge and of the fear of the Lord. The Revisers have rendered it: "His delight shall be in the fear of the Lord." The Authorized Version had, and it was a better rendering: "He shall be quick of understanding." Sir George Adam Smith translated it: "He shall be keen of scent in the fear of the Lord." That is understanding! That is the story of the life of Jesus on the manward side, understanding. To my risen and glorified and exalted Lord I render apology for saying the thing I am going to say. There was no need for bit or bridle in the case of Jesus. No compelling circumstances crowded Him into obedience. He went through circumstances that were to His soul as the burning of fire, but not to compel His obedience. He was quick of understanding in the fear of the Lord.

The very next sentence in Isaiah reveals Him on the other side, as God dealing with man. He shall not judge after the sight of His eyes, neither reprove after the hearing of His ears; but He shall judge righteous judgment. In other words, when the Messiah exercises the judgment of Deity His judgment is not based on the only things that human judgment can be based on; neither according to the seeing of the eye nor the hearing of the ear. His judgment shall be based on understanding, on perfect knowledge, and perfect sympathy. So the light of the great passage comes to help us. This is the higher way of life, understanding. He who understands, yields, not to the pressure of bit and bridle, but to the sweet constraint of the eternal love. Be ye not as the horse or as the mule, which have no understanding. Be not foolish, but understanding what the will of the Lord is.

Both texts make exactly the same appeal. That appeal is based on human capacity. That is the Biblical distinguishing conception of man. He is ever presented as capable of knowing, and of communing with God. Outside the Biblical revelation men have not yet reached that conclusion. They are approaching it. In the days of my youth the physical scientists were telling us that God was unknowable. Science is now beginning to admit that there may be the possibility of communication with a spirit world. That statement, however ignorant it is in some of its applications, is a step towards the ultimate truth that man is fashioned for having communion with God directly and immediately. That is the Biblical revelation. Think hurriedly of its outstanding figures. What are they? The first is that of a man in a garden. It is the story of Adam, the first man. What is the peculiar fact about him which the Bible insists on? That he could talk with God. What is the story of a man who came out from a great civilization that was entirely pagan and became the father and founder of a race that stands to this age in the world for the great monotheistic idea? It is the story of a man called Abram, who heard God speak, who was capable of communion with God. What is the story of a man who was a great lawgiver, and so great a lawgiver that his national code remains to this day the final court of high national morality? It is the story of a man, Moses, who spoke face to face with God as a man talks with his friend. What is the story of all those prophecies of Isaiah, Ezekiel, Jeremiah, Hosea, Amos, Habakkuk? They are all stories of men who heard God, who spoke to God, and in whose very bones the fire of the divine word burned.

Finally and centrally, there is the story of Jesus, and it is the story of a Man Who walked over dusty highways and over our fields, and in the midst of our temptations, enduring our toil, living by trust as we live by trust, but all the while talking with God. The Bible says to every man that he may know God and understand God. *The highest function of the human soul is the function of adoration.* That goes far out beyond intercession, is greater than thanksgiving, is far more magnificent even than praise which is uttered. It is the function of speechless consciousness of God. For that man is made.

The Biblical idea of man is that out of that exercise of adoration there shall come human inspiration for the carpenter's shop, the commonplaces of life, the doing of the next duty that comes, the taking of the next turning. That is the deepest meaning of Christianity.

The conception of Jesus concerning man is found in the words which John records for us in His final prayer, words perpetually quoted and never exhausted by quotation: "This is age abiding life, to know Thee, the only true God."

The letters of Paul's imprisonment, those to the Ephesians, the Colossians, and the Philippians, breathe his consuming passion that Christian people should come to the full knowledge of God. Again and again we find him expressing his thankfulness for their faith, their hope, their love; and when we read this we are inclined to say: What more could be needed? These people had faith and hope and love. Yet Paul said: I am praying always earnestly for you. To what end? That you may come to the knowledge, *epignosis*, the full knowledge of God. And there is the Biblical conception. In man is the light of life. In his new birth that light is rekindled. First, it is daybreak; then it groweth more and more unto the perfect day; and so at last it becomes high noon in the life of the soul. If a man will walk by that light, if he will answer that light, he lives by understanding, and the bit and the bridle are not necessary.

The appeal of the text expresses a divine purpose, and the divine purpose fundamentally is that of restraining and realizing life; and the divine desire is that this shall be done by understanding. The divine love, however, says: If you will not walk in the light by understanding, then you must learn by bit and bridle.

So, finally, the appeal of the text offers a great alternative, revealing to the life two methods of God with the soul, urging the higher, that of understanding, but definitely declaring that if the higher is not answered, then God will employ the other, and that for very love.

Now are we saying we have indeed been foolish, we have been as the horse and as the mule, and so we know the bit and bridle? If so, and I speak not to you now, but with you, let us learn to yield to the bit and the bridle, and if we do, because God has created us as He has, we shall come to understanding. Is not that the more common experience of life? Am I not touching the realm of experience when I say that almost all of us pass into the realm of understanding by the way of the bit and the bridle? With the majority of us it has been bit and bridle.

The young I would urge to choose the understanding way at once. This urging comes from one who has known much of bit and bridle through his own folly, through his own lack of spiritual mindedness. Choose the way of understanding. Cultivate your fellowship with God. Make time for the secret place, for the quiet hour, for getting near to God without pressure, that you may know, that you may understand. For the doing of this the great Lord Christ, our Saviour and our King, is ever at our disposal. Take advantage of His comradeship. Watch the glance of the eye, listen to the sound of the voice, observe the activity of the hand. Such contemplation brings the soul nearer to God, to more accurate understanding, and so makes less necessary the bit and the bridle.

# Aimee Semple Mcpherson

*1890-1944*

Aimee Elizabeth Kennedy was born on October 9 near Ingersol, Ontario, to parents who were connected with the local Salvation Army corps. She was converted to Christ in 1907 under the ministry of a Pentecostal preacher named Robert Semple, whom she married in 1908 and who helped Aimee discover and develop her gifts.

In 1910 they sailed to China to serve as missionaries, but after ten weeks there her husband died. A month later their daughter Roberta Star was born, and Aimee returned to the United States to live with her mother in New York City. It was there she met Harold McPherson, and they were married February 5, 1912.

In 1918 she established her base of ministry in Los Angeles, California, where in 1923 the 5000 seat Angelus Temple was dedicated. It became a center for evangelism, revival, healing, and benevolent ministries. That same year she founded the International Church of the Foursquare Gospel, proclaiming that Jesus Christ is Savior, Healer, Baptizer, and King. A year later she opened radio station KFSG ("Kall Foursquare Gospel"), which is still in operation. She was a pioneer religious broadcaster and was the first woman to receive a radio license from the FCC. During the Great Depression, she provided hot meals from the Angelus Temple for more than a million and a half people. She was a master of using contemporary communications

71

methods to carry her message. The International Church of the Foursquare Gospel today has more than nineteen hundred churches in the United States and Canada and over twenty-six thousand churches and 4 million members in ninety-nine countries worldwide. Aimee Semple McPherson died in 1944 while conducting a crusade in Oakland, California.

*Sister Aimee: The Life of Aimee Semple McPherson* by Daniel Mark Epstein (Harcourt Brace and Co., 1993) is an objective and accurate biography.

# Come—If—But

Come now, and let us reason together, saith the LORD; though your sins be as scarlet, they shall be as white as snow; though they be red like crimson, they shall be as wool.

If ye be willing and obedient, ye shall eat the good of the land.

But if ye refuse and rebel, ye shall be devoured with the sword, for the mouth of the LORD hath spoken it.

Isaiah 1:18–20

C-O-M-E; I-F; B-U-T; How much is expressed in the three opening words of the three above verses. The whole Gospel is embodied and expressed through these concise, plain statements of God. First of all let us take the word

## C-O-M-E

Dear sinner, Jesus loves you. His arms are outstretched toward you, His voice is calling you, He has prepared a glorious Salvation for your body, soul and spirit, and His great heart and love and life are composed of one great, loving c-o-m-e! c-o-m-e! c-o-m-e!

No matter how deep you may have fallen into sin, Jesus says, "Come, I will forgive you and wash you whiter than the driven snow."

No matter how black and vile your heart may be, no matter how evil your mind and filthy your appetites, or how strong your sinful habits, COME, and I will take away your sin-filled heart and give you a new heart—a clean heart filled with pure, holy thoughts; I will fill your mind with thoughts that are in heavenly places, and your mouth with praises; I will break the fetters of every evil habit and cause you to walk forth a free creature in Christ Jesus.

"No matter if you have been a moral professor, striving to live well in your own way you must come to Me just as you are," says Jesus. "You must be born again; nothing but the blood can save. All your righteousness is as filthy rags."

Let the little children come, the aged with their white heads and mis-spent years, the colored and the white, the yellow and the brown—*come unto Me, all ye ends of the earth, and be ye saved. COME! COME!! COME!!!* The call goes forth to the Queen upon her throne and to the poorest wretch in the convict's cell alike; all have sinned and come short of the glory of God; all have need of His great salvation.

Come, let the weeping tears be dried and the discouraged, hopeless soul take new courage, and find new hope, for Jesus is the hope of the hopeless. Plunge beneath the crimson flood that flowed from His wounded side, and thou shalt know that there is indeed balm in Gilead, and gladness in the house of the Lord.

Let the giddy, laughing, thoughtless sinner, dancing on the brink of Hell, be sobered and come to Jesus in repentance, confessing his sins, or he will be eternally lost in that land where laughing and dancing are never known. The invitation is extended to all mankind, irrespective of race, creed, color or age; all alike need Jesus, and without Him are undone; it will avail nothing to gain the whole world and lose one's own soul. *"Come, now, and let us reason together,"* saith the Lord, *"though your sins be as scarlet, they shall be as white as snow; though they be red like crimson, they shall be as wool."* No matter how great or how small your sins may be, Jesus will forgive and pardon you, and, better still, He will remember them against you no more if you will turn to Him today whilst there is yet time.

### I-F

*"If ye be willing and obedient, ye shall eat the good of the land."* I-F—dear sinner, Jesus has done His part, He has sent forth the great call, "Come," throughout the world; He has laid down His life and shed His blood to redeem you; He has prepared a great and glorious feast and builded a glorious, heavenly city for you to live in. But now we come to the great, middle word of our test, "I-F." It does not look like a very big word to read it, yet it is of such gigantic proportions and looms up such a mountain that your whole soul's eternal salvation or damnation depends upon that one little word—"IF."

God has left you a free-will, moral agent; He will plead with you to come; He will endeavor to win you to His salvation and love, but He will never force you to accept it. There must be a willingness upon your part to accept this Saviour as your Lord and King, a willingness to let Him give you a new heart, and shape your life and pattern it after our great example, Jesus. Here, then, is the whole key to the situation:

*"If ye be willing, and obedient, ye shall eat the good of the land."* First—Willing; Second—Obedient, then *ye shall eat the good of the land;* there is nothing too good for the Lord's children. Has He not told us that *"All that I have is thine"?* and that *"no good thing will He withhold from them that walk uprightly"?* The good of the land, with its joy, its peace that flows like a river, its heaven for evermore, are yours *IF ye be willing and obedient* to the calling and commands of the Lord. And O, His yoke is easy and His burden light. Hallelujah!

### B-U-T

But, then we come to the only other alternative, the solemn, dark, grim punishment of the wicked. *"But if ye refuse and rebel, ye shall be devoured with the sword; for the mouth of the Lord hath spoken it."* There are only two paths: one leads to life, the other to endless death; one leads to hope and joy, the other to despair and utter darkness.

God *hath no pleasure in the death of the wicked,* but longs that all should turn from the error of their ways, hearken to His great, eternal invitation, expressed in the word C-O-M-E, be willing and obedient, and inherit life everlasting. But, if you refuse His invitation, and rebel instead of obeying, you choose your own path, and thereby seal your own doom, signing your own death warrant, and shall surely be overtaken with God's sword of judgment, which will fall upon all who have rejected Jesus the Christ.

If ye be willing and obedient, and become a child of King Jesus by being born again and accepting His salvation, you will dwell in the courts of His glory forever.

*But if ye refuse and rebel,* and choose rather to remain in sin, and continue to walk on as the devil's child, you will, of course, share in the devil's home and reward, and *be devoured with the sword. The mouth of the Lord hath spoken it,* and no matter who has tried to tell you destruction will not come, nor sorrow overtake those who refuse and rebel, they cannot change the true facts of the case, *for the mouth of the Lord hath spoken it.*

O, dear sinner, heed this simple message today. Come to Jesus as you are. Will you not kneel down just where you are this moment, and cry out—"O, Jesus, You have invited us to come, poor, wretched, sinful, vile. O Lamb of God, I come. Forgive my sins, create in me a new heart, make me obedient and true to You forever. Take all desire for the world, the flesh and the devil from my life, and create a right Spirit within me, and I will follow You wherever You may lead me, dear Saviour." You will feel His cleansing blood applied and His Spirit will bear witness with your spirit that you are a child of God, and with His great, eternal arms about you, a new life will open out before you, and you will find your feet in the path that leads on through the gates of pearl and the streets that are paved with gold.

May God bless you, and help you to accept this great invitation at once, for today is the day of salvation. O, harden not your heart.

*7*

# Peter Marshall

*1902–1949*

When Peter Marshall was pastor of the New York Avenue Presbyterian Church in Washington, D.C. (1937–1949), many visitors to the nation's capital considered it as important to hear him preach as to see any of the city's historic monuments.

Marshall was born in Scotland and immigrated to the United States in 1927. He graduated from Columbia Theological Seminary in Decatur, Georgia, in 1931, and that same year began his pastoral ministry at the Covington Presbyterian Church in Covington, Alabama. Two years later he moved to the Westminster Presbyterian Church in Atlanta and while there married Catherine Wood. In 1937 he was called to the prestigious New York Avenue Church and the next year he became a United States citizen.

In 1947 Marshall was named chaplain of the United States Senate. It was his responsibility to open the sessions with prayer, and his prayers were so unique that everybody wanted to be on hand to hear them. The senators confessed that they didn't know if he was praying for them or preaching at them!

When he preached, he took a manuscript into the pulpit; the words were arranged as if the sermon were a poem. In true Scottish fashion, he preached to paint pictures and stir hearts, not just to share religious information, and he had a way with similes and metaphors that was the envy of other preachers. He also had a sense of humor and a tender heart, but sentimental Christianity found no place in his pulpit. He was a man's man who saw the Christian life as a robust enterprise that demanded the very best a person had to give. Marshall died of a heart attack on January 26, 1949, at the age of forty-six.

Catherine wrote her husband's biography, *A Man Called Peter* (McGraw-Hill, 1951), which was later made into a movie. She also compiled two books of his sermons, *Mr. Jones, Meet the Master* (Revell, 1949) and *John Doe, Disciple* (McGraw-Hill, 1963), as well as *The Prayers of Peter Marshall* (McGraw-Hill, 1954), a collection of his pastoral and senatorial prayers. The United States Government Printing Office also publishes a complete collection of the prayers he delivered as chaplain of the Senate.

# The Rock That Moved

There are not many cities in the heart of which you may suddenly hear the crowing of a cock.
That is one sound that is not likely to arouse the guests in any of Washington's downtown hotels.

One will never hear it in Times Square
                    at Broad and Market
                at Five Points
            at Woodward and Michigan
        or along Michigan Boulevard.
Yet even to this day you may hear it in Jerusalem, for Jerusalem is different.

One who was visiting the Holy City was enjoying the quiet of his room when suddenly the silence was pierced by the shrill crowing of a cock, and he immediately thought of a man named Peter, for whom the trumpet of the dawn opened the floodgates of memory.

What would it do for some lonely, homesick young woman in Washington, if, before the city has yawned itself into action, she were to hear the familiar bugle of the farmyard?

In a tide of sudden nostalgia she would be back home again
        on the plains of Kansas
            in the mountains of western North Carolina
                among the red barns of a farm in Ohio
                    on the rolling green countryside of Pennsylvania
                        or among the red clay hills of Georgia.

There is many a young man in the city, bright in the nighttime like day, his pulses racing with the throb of jungle drums and the moan of the saxophone, intoxicated with the lure of the city and in strong temptation, who could be saved were he to hear once again on the heavy night air the lowing of homeward-driven cattle and the calls of the old farmyards.

It is in mysterious and different ways that God comes to the rescue. He has a hundred ways of plucking at a man's sleeve.
He nudges some.
Others He taps on the shoulder.
To some it comes in music, to some in a picture, a story or a chance meeting on the street.
All these are used by God Who keeps watch over His own.

One St. Andrew's Day—a date all Scotsmen remember, I attended the annual banquet and had an emotional experience I shall not soon forget.

The Irish flaunt the shamrock in March, and the English remember Saint George and the dragon in June.
But to the Scot the 30th of November is one time when he throws aside his accustomed modesty and forgets he has always been outnumbered by the English eight to one, for this night is his own.
It is the night of the tartan and the haggis
the night for thoughts of home . . . a night for memories.

The hotel was filled with bagpipe music.
The skirl of the pipes, indescribably thrilling to the Scot, came dancing into every conversation, and must have made them wonder who had no Scottish blood.
There was a full pipe band—and a good one it was.

There were the old Scottish songs, and the Doric—the broad Scots tongue, soft and kindly and warm.
There were the kilts and the glengaries, the Balmorals and the honest faces of the sons of the land of the mountain and the mist.

My, what memories came back, as the drumsticks twirled above the drum, and the kettledrums rolled . . .
and our feet tapped out the time to Cock o' the North
The Forty-Second
and Hieland Laddie.

In memory I saw a battalion of the Gordon Highlanders, swinging down from Edinburgh Castle on to Princes Street when I was last in Scotland—
the pipes skirling
        and the kilts swinging
with the pride that only Scotsmen fully know.

I thought of the Fifty-first Division at El Alamein going through the German mine-fields to the blood-tingling call of the bagpipes.

I thought of home . . . and long ago . . . and choked back many a lump in my throat.
We sang the old songs . . . the songs my mither sang . . . and many an eye was misty.
We didn't say very much. Words were useless.
We just averted our eyes and blinked a bit and swallowed hard.

Memories . . . they come surging back into the heart to make it clean again . . . or to accuse it.

Yes . . . to some it is music . . . or a song.
        To others it is a picture or the face of a friend
*but to Simon Peter it was the crowing of a cock.*

He had seen the last flickering torch disappear round the turn of the path that wound down hill.
Only once in a while could the lights of the procession be seen through the trees—like giant fireflies.

The murmur of voices died away
        the crackling of twigs
        and the rustling of dislodged stones through the grass.
There swept over Peter the realization that his Master had at last been captured and was marching away to die.

The icy fear that gripped his heart was a startling contrast to the flaming courage with which he drew his short sword a few minutes before, for this was a different Peter.

He realized that he had blundered, and that he had been rebuked.
Disappointed and puzzled, he could not understand the calm submission with which Christ permitted them to bind His hands and march Him off, as a butcher would lead an animal to the slaughter.

82

Realizing that he stood alone in the deserted garden, Peter stumbled blindly down the trail, heedless of the twigs that lashed his face and tore at his robes.

Stumbling on down hill, instinctively hurrying to catch up with the others, and yet not anxious to get too close, he followed down to the foot of the Mount of Olives, across the brook Kedron, and back up the hill to old Jerusalem, still asleep and quiet.

The procession made first for the house of Annas, into which they escorted Jesus. The heavy door creaked shut behind Him, and when Peter approached timidly, it was to find John standing there.

John persuaded the girl stationed at the door to let them in, and as they slipped past her, she scrutinized Peter and said to him:
        "Art not thou also one of this man's disciples?"
He said: "I am not."

Perhaps she felt that she could speak to Peter.
Perhaps she felt sorry for him, seeing the hurt, wounded look in his eyes and the pain in his face.

Who knows what was in her mind?

Perhaps she had seen the Master as they led Him in, and felt the irresistible attraction of the Great Galilean.

Perhaps in that brief moment, as they had crowded past her, *He had looked at her.*
If He had—then something may have happened to her, within her own heart.
Her faith might have been born,
a fire kindled by the spark the winds of strange circumstance had blown from the altar fires in the heart of the Son of God.

Perhaps she wanted to ask Peter more about the Master.
Perhaps she would have said—had Peter acknowledged Him:

        "Tell me the sound of His voice.
                Is it low and sweet, vibrant?
        Tell me of some of His miracles.
                Tell me how you are sure He is the Messiah.

What is this salvation He speaks about?
How can we live forever?"

Maybe these questions would have come tumbling in a torrent from her
lips . . . who knows?

But whatever she meant, whatever her motive for asking the question, "Art
not thou also one of this man's disciples?" Peter denied his Lord and said:
"I am not."

We can only stand aghast at Peter and wonder if the strain and the shock
have destroyed his memory.

Simon, surely you remember the first day you saw Him.

Andrew and yourself floating the folded net . . . His shadow falling across
you as you worked.
Don't you remember His command, His beckoning finger,
        the light in His eyes as He said: "Follow Me, and
        *I will make you fishers of men*"?

Peter, don't you remember?

And that night when Nicodemus came into the garden looking for the
Master, don't you remember how he crept in with his cloak pulled up over
his face?

Don't you remember how he frightened you, and how the Lord and
Nicodemus talked for hours about the promises?

Don't you remember the wedding in Cana where He turned the water into
wine?
Do you remember the music of His laugh
        and the Samaritan woman at Sychar?
Don't you remember these things, Simon?

And now, they brought the Lord from Annas to Caiaphas, and the soldiers
and the temple guards mingled with the servants in the courtyard.

Because the night was cold, they had kindled a fire in the brazier, and Peter
joined himself to the group, and stretching out his hands warmed himself
at their fire.

84

Peter was glad to join the hangers-on huddled round the blaze, for the morning air bit sharply,
      and he found himself shivering. . . .
It was a kindly glow of warmth.

Coarse laughter greeted every joke and they discussed the things such people talk about:
      the coming cock-fight in Jerusalem
         the new dancing girl in the court of Herod
           the prowess of the garrison's drivers
              the gambling losses of their friends
              the latest news from Rome.

Peter was not paying much attention to their conversation until one of the soldiers nudged him and said:
      "Thou art also of them."
And Peter said, for the second time: "Man, *I am not.*"

Peter, you must remember . . . surely . . . it must be that you are afraid.

Your brave heart must have turned to water.
Surely you cannot have forgotten . . .
many a time . . . crossing the lake in boats like your own,
      with its worn seats
         its patched sails, slanting in the sun
           and its high rudder?

Remember the night He came walking on the water, and you tried it, and were walking, like the Master, until your courage left you . . . your faith gave way?

Simon, has your courage left you again?

Have you forgotten the pool at Bethesda and how you laughed when the impotent man rose up . . . rolled up his bed
         threw it over his shoulder
        and went away leaping in the air and shouting?

Ah, Simon, you spoke so bravely . . . and now here you are.

For the next hour or so they merely waited.

What was keeping them so long? They little knew the difficulty of getting witnesses to agree.
They little knew that sleepless men, with tempers raw and irritated, were trying to find some reason that they could submit to Pilate that would justify their demands for the death of Jesus.

After an hour had passed, there joined the group a soldier who had come out of the palace.

As he greeted his friends in the circle, his eye fell on Peter. He scrutinized him very carefully, and Peter, feeling the examination of the newcomer, looked round as the soldier asked: "Did not I see thee in the garden with Him?"

One of his friends joined in:
        "Certainly—he's one of the Galileans.
        Just listen to his accent."
And the soldier stubbornly went on: "I am sure I saw him in the garden, for my kinsman, Malchus, was wounded by one of them—who drew a sword,
and if I am not mistaken—it was this fellow here."

Then Peter, beginning to curse and to swear, said:
        *"I know not the man."*

He used language he had not used for years.
It was vile. . . . Even the soldiers were shocked.
They all looked at him in amazement.

They did not appear to notice the shuffling of feet, as soldiers led Christ from Caiaphas to Pilate.
Perhaps they did not make much noise. They were tired,
        worn with argument and talk
    so they were very quiet.

The group standing round the fire was silent, shocked at the vehemence and the profanity of Peter's denial.
It was a torrent of foulness, but it was his face that startled them.
It was livid
        distorted
        eyes blazing
    mouth snarling like a cornered animal.

It was not a pleasant sight, and they kept silent.
It was a silence so intense that the crowing of a distant cock was like a bugle call . . .

Immediately, Peter remembered the Lord's prophecy:
    "Before the cock crow twice, thou shalt deny Me thrice."
Like a wave there swept over him the realization of what he had done. All of a sudden he remembered what Jesus had said, and with tears streaming down his face, he turned away from the fire.

Through a mist of tears he saw ahead of him the stairway that led to Pilate's palace . . .
and by a terrible Providence, it was just at that moment that Christ was being led up the stairs to appear before Pilate.

The Lord had heard!
    The Lord had heard every hot searing word . . .
        The Lord had heard the blistering denial . . .
            the foul, fisherman's oaths . . .
He—He had heard it all!

Christ paused on the stair, and looked down over the rail—looked right into the very soul of Peter.
The eyes of the two met . . . at that awful moment.

Through his tears all else was a blur to Peter,
but that one face shone through the tears . . .
    that lovely face
        that terrible face
            those eyes—sad
                reproachful
                    tender . . . as if they understood and forgave.
Ah, how well he knew Him, and how much he loved Him.

The world seemed to stand still, as for that terrible moment, Peter looked at the One he denied.

We shall never know what passed between them.
Christ seemed to say again:
        "But I have prayed for thee, Simon.
        Satan hath desired to have thee.
        But I have prayed for thee."

His tears now overflowed and ran down his cheeks—
  hot and scalding tears they were—
and with great sobs shaking his strong frame, Peter spun round and rushed
out to have the cool morning air fan his burning cheeks.

He fled with his heart pounding in his breast, while the Nazarene walked
steadily to meet the Roman governor.

Something died within the heart of Peter that night.
Something was killed. That's why his heart was broken.

In fact, *the Simon in him was killed*
  the old arrogant boasting bravado of Simon
    the cocksure confidence of the strong fisherman
      the impetuous stubbornness
        the impulsive thoughtlessness of Simon . . .
these all died in that moment.

*Simon had ceased to be. Peter was being born.*

Nothing more is heard of Peter for two days.
Christ has been crucified.

The hammer blows seem to be re-echoing still among the temple domes,
and in the very heart of Peter he feels the thud of the hammer and hears
the screaming of the impenitent thief.

But we must follow Peter further. It is not fair to leave him a sinner, a swear-
ing traitor, a fugitive from the heart of love.
This apprentice apostle is still in the making.
And he is running true to form.

Only last night the Master had spoken a personal word of warning when
He said:
    "Simon, Simon, behold Satan hath desired to have thee that he
may sift you as wheat—"
and it had come true.

But he remembered that word of hope added by Jesus:
    "But I have prayed for thee that thy faith fail not."

His Lord had prayed that somehow he should not fail.
That prayer must be—would be answered—but how?

88

Never again would his Master trust him.

And what of the other disciples? What would they think of him?
What could he do?

Ah, but Jesus had said even more:
"And when thou art converted"—that is, turned around—
when you have got new bearings
when you turn your face once more toward Me—
"strengthen thy brethren."
What did He mean?

"Black Saturday passed.
A new day dawned . . . a new week . . .
aye, indeed, a new age . . . though they knew it not."

There came the strange story gasped out by breathless women who had
come running from the tomb.
Then a race with John and the discovery of the empty grave . . .
Then the strange tale of the two disciples who came back from Emmaus.

Something had happened.
Life could never be the same again.
The dead had come to life.

The Christ who had been crucified was alive, but still Simon could only
nurse his deep and bitter shame.
He was a changed man, still smarting with the searing of the iron that had
eaten into his very soul.

There came that night when, having gone back to their boats and their
nets, they had worked hard and in comparative silence. Now as they came
back, discouraged and sad, they saw Someone standing on the beach in
the early light of morning. The sea was calm—calm as a millpond—and
the light, early morning mist still clung to the surface of the water.

They saw the flames leaping from a fire, and this mysterious figure waiting while their boat drew nearer to the shore.

"It is the Lord," said John, and that was enough for Simon.
Here was the opportunity for which he had longed—to tell the Lord that
he loved Him—to show how well he knew Him.

Without a moment's hesitation, he jumped overboard and waded ashore.
And then comes the loveliest record of God dealing with a penitent sinner . . .
Its tenderness and understanding come stealing into our own hearts like
the perfume of crushed flowers.

For every denial, Jesus asked a pledge of love.
Three times the question: "Simon, . . . lovest thou Me?"
Three times the answer—and then the restoration,
    "Feed my lambs. . . . Feed my sheep. . . . Feed my sheep."

    And when he had spoken this, he saith unto him, "Follow me."

When next we see Simon, he is Simon no more—
    but Peter—the Rock.

We see him fearless and eloquent
    fire in his eyes
        and his voice vibrant with conviction
            melodious with good news.
His own will has gone; his Master's will has taken its place.
Peter stands up and preaches the gospel of his crucified and risen Lord.

Is this Simon preaching a sermon?
    No, this is Peter.

Simon which was—the rock which had moved, but now is firmly established in the gospel.
The sinner-saint has become a witness
    a pillar of strength to the brethren
        an apostle to the ages.

The same Jesus, who called Simon, is calling you.
The same Jesus, who saved Simon, can save you.
The same mighty hand will hold you up.

The denials that you have made were made by Simon.
Yet he was restored; so may you be restored.

Christ changed Simon into Peter,
    the sinner into the saint.

He can change your life, if you are willing!

# Henry Allan
# "Harry" Ironside

*1876–1951*

H. A. Ironside was born in Toronto, Canada, and like D. L. Moody and Billy Sunday, he was left fatherless as a child. The family moved to Los Angeles where his godly mother taught her children the Bible, encouraged them to memorize it, and prayed that all of them would grow up to serve the Lord. When he was twelve, Ironside heard the preaching of D. L. Moody and prayed that one day he might also be privileged to preach the Word to great crowds. God answered that prayer. He was converted to Christ at fourteen and by then he had read the Bible through fourteen times. During his lifetime, he read the Bible through each year and memorized large portions of it.

Ironside's early ministry was with the Salvation Army but in 1895 he resigned his commission for doctrinal reasons. He then identified with the Plymouth Brethren and was in fellowship with them for the rest of his life. He was in demand as a speaker at Brethren assemblies and Bible conferences.

In 1930 Ironside became pastor of the Moody Church in Chicago, remaining there for eighteen years and preaching to four thousand people week after week. He also taught at the Moody Bible Institute. His preaching style was conversational and his approach was to teach verse-by-verse through an entire book of the Bible, explaining and applying the Scriptures as he went along, always with telling illustrations.

Ironside wrote more than sixty books on various biblical topics. His commentaries consist of edited versions of his messages and cover selected Old Testament books, including all of the prophets, as well as the entire New Testament. While in conference ministry in New Zealand, Ironside died—January 15, 1951. He is buried there.

*H. A. Ironside: Ordained of the Lord* by E. Schuyler English was published by Zondervan in 1946, and Loizeaux published a revised and updated edition in 1976. The nearest thing we have to an autobiography is his *Random Reminiscences,* published by Loizeaux in 1939.

# The Heart of the Gospel

For God so loved the world, that He gave His only begotten Son, that whosoever believeth in Him should not perish, but have everlasting life. For God sent not His Son into the world to condemn the world; but that the world through Him might be saved. He that believeth on Him is not condemned: but he that believeth not is condemned already, because he hath not believed in the name of the only begotten Son of God. And this is the condemnation, that light is come into the world, and men loved darkness rather than light, because their deeds were evil. For every one that doeth evil hateth the light, neither cometh to the light, lest his deeds should be reproved. But he that doeth truth cometh to the light, that his deeds may be made manifest, that they are wrought in God.

John 3:16–21

Martin Luther called this sixteenth verse the "Miniature Gospel," because there is a sense in which the whole story of the Bible is told out in it. "For God so loved the world, that He gave His only begotten Son, that whosoever believeth in Him should not perish, but have everlasting life." The verse negatives the idea that a great many persons seem to have; that God is represented in Scriptures as a stern, angry Judge waiting to destroy men because of their sins, but that Jesus Christ, in some way or other, has made it possible for God to come out in love to sinners; in other words, that Christ loved us enough to die for us and, having atoned for our sins, God can now love us and be merciful to us. But that is an utter perversion of the gospel. Jesus Christ did not die to enable God to love sinners, but "God so loved the world, that He gave His only begotten Son." This same precious truth is set forth in similar words in the fourth chapter of the First Epistle of John, "In this was manifested the love of God toward us, because that God sent His only begotten Son into the world, that we might live through Him. Herein is love, not that we loved God, but that He loved us, and sent His Son to be the propitiation for our sins." So the coming to this world of our Lord Jesus Christ and His going to the cross, there to settle the sin question and thus meet every claim of the divine righteousness against the sinner, is the proof of the infinite love of God toward a world of guilty men. How we ought to thank and praise Him that He gave His Son for our redemption! "God commendeth His love toward us, in that, while we were yet sinners, Christ died for us." It could not be otherwise, because He is love. We are taught that in 1 John 4:8, 16. "God is love." That is His very nature. We can say that God is gracious, but we cannot say that God is grace. We can say that God is compassionate, but we cannot say that God is compassion. God is kind, but God is not kindness. But we can say, God is love. That is His nature, and love had to manifest itself, and although men had forfeited every claim that they might have upon God, still He loved us and sent His only Son to become the propitiation for our sins—"God so loved the world that He gave His only begotten Son, that whosoever believeth in Him should not perish, but have everlasting life."

Our Lord Jesus Christ is spoken of five times as the "only begotten" in the New Testament: twice in the first chapter of this Gospel. In verse fourteen we read, "The Word was made flesh, and dwelt among us, (and we beheld His glory, the glory as of the only begotten of the Father,) full of grace and truth." Also in verse eighteen, "No man hath seen God at any time; the only begotten Son, which is the bosom of the Father, He hath declared Him." Then here is this sixteenth verse of the third chapter, "God so loved . . . that He gave His only begotten . . ." Again in verse eighteen, "He that believeth not is condemned already, because he hath not believed in the name of the only begotten Son of God." The only other place where this term is used is in 1 John 4:9, "God sent His only begotten Son into the world, that we might live through Him." It is a singular fact, and shows how wonderfully Scripture is constructed, that that term is not only used five times in the New Testament, but He is also called the "first begotten" or "the first born" exactly five times in the same book.

Now "only begotten" refers to His eternal Sonship. The term, "the first begotten," tells what He became, in grace, as Man, for our redemption. When He came into the world God owned that blessed Man as His first begotten, saying, "Thou art My beloved Son, this day have I begotten Thee." The term "only begotten" does not carry in it any thought of generation, but that of uniqueness—Son by special relationship. The word is used in connection with Isaac. We read that Abraham "offered up his only begotten." Now Isaac was not his only son. Ishmael was born some years before Isaac, so in the sense of generation you would not speak of Isaac as the only begotten son. He is called the "only begotten" because he was born in a miraculous manner, when it seemed impossible that Abraham and Sarah could ever be the parents of a child. In the Spanish translation we read that "God so loved the world that He gave His unique Son"; that is, our Lord Jesus Christ is the Son of God in a sense that no one else can ever be the Son of God—His eternal Son—His unique Son. Oh, how dear to the heart of the Father! And when God gave Him, He not only became incarnate to bear hardship and weariness and thirst and hunger, but God gave Him up to the death of the cross that there He might be the propitiation for our sins. Could there be any greater manifestation of divine love than this?

You remember the story of the little girl in Martin Luther's day, when the first edition of the Bible came out. She had a terrible fear of God. God had been presented in such a way that it filled her heart with dread when she thought of Him. She brooded over the awfulness of the character of God and of some day having to meet this angry Judge. But one day she came running to her mother, holding a scrap of paper in her hand. She cried out, "Mother! Mother! I am not afraid of God any more." Her mother said, "Why are you not?" "Why, look, Mother," she said, "this bit of paper I found in the print shop, and it is torn out of the Bible." It was so torn as to be almost illegible except about two lines. On the one line it said, "God so loved," and on the other line it said, "that He gave." "See, Mother," she said, "that makes it all right." Her mother read it and said, "God so loved that He gave." "But," she said, "it does not say what He gave." "Oh, Mother," exclaimed the child, "if He loved us enough to give anything, it is all right." Then the mother said, "But, let me tell you what He gave." She read, "God so loved the world, that He gave His only begotten Son, that whosoever believeth in Him should not perish, but have everlasting life." Then she told how we can have peace and eternal life through trusting Him.

Am I speaking to anyone today who dreads the thought of meeting God? Do you think of your sins and say with David of old, "I remembered God and was troubled"? Let me call your attention to this word: The love of God has been manifest in Christ. If you will but come as a needy sinner He will wash your sins away. "But," you say, "how can I be sure that it is for me? I can understand that God could love some people. I can understand how He can invite certain ones to trust Him. Their lives have been so much better than mine, but I cannot believe that this salvation is for me." Well, what else can you make from that word, "whosoever"? "God so loved . . . that He gave . . . that whosoever believeth in Him should not perish, but have everlasting life." He could not find another more all-embracing word than that. It takes you in. It takes me in. You have many another "whosoever" in the Bible. There is a "whosoever" of judgment: "Whosoever was not found written in the book of life was cast into the lake of fire." "Whosoever" there includes all who did not come to God while He waited, in grace, to save. If they had recognized that they were included in the "Whosoever" of John 3:16, they would not be found in that of Rev. 20:15.

Somebody wrote me the other day and said, "A man has come to our community who is preaching a limited atonement. He says it is a wonderful truth that has been only recently revealed to him." Well, I could only write back that the term "limited atonement" has an uncanny sound to me. I do not read anything like that in my Bible. I read that "He tasted death for every man." I read that "He is the propitiation for our sins, and not for our sins only, but for the whole world." I read that "All we like sheep have gone astray; we have turned every one to his own way; and the Lord hath laid on Him the iniquity of us all." And here I read that "Whosoever believeth in Him should not perish, but have everlasting life." I say to you, as I said to the writer of that letter, that there is enough value in the atoning work of the Lord Jesus Christ to save every member of the human race, if they would but repent and turn to God; and then if they were all saved, there still remains value enough to save the members of a million worlds like this, if they are lost in sin and needing a Saviour. Yes, the sacrifice of Christ is an infinite sacrifice. Do not let the enemy of your soul tell you there is no hope for you. Do not let him tell you you have sinned away your day of grace; that you have gone so far that God is no longer merciful. There is life abundant for you if you will but look up into the face of the One who died on Calvary's cross and trust Him for yourself. Let me repeat it again, "Whosoever believeth in Him should not perish, but have everlasting life."

"Whosoever believeth." What is it to believe? It is to trust in Him; to confide in Him; to commit yourself and your affairs to Him. He is saying to you, poor needy sinner, "You cannot save yourself. All your efforts to redeem yourself can only end in failure, but I have given My Son to die for you. Trust in Him. Confide in Him!" "Whosoever believeth in Him should not perish."

A lady was reading her Greek Testament one day. She was studying the Greek language and she liked to read in the Greek Testament. She had no assurance of salvation. While pondering over these words, "whosoever believeth," she said to herself as she looked at the Greek word for *believeth,* "I saw this a few verses back." She went back in the chapter, and then back into the last verse of chapter two, and she read, "Many believed in His name when they saw the miracles which He did. But Jesus did not commit Himself unto them, because He knew all men." "Oh," she said, "there it is!" "Jesus did not commit Himself unto them," and she stopped and thought a moment, and light from heaven flashed into her soul. She saw that to believe in Jesus was to commit herself unto Jesus. Have you done that? Have you said,

> Jesus, I will trust Thee, trust Thee with my soul,
> Weary, worn and helpless, Thou canst make me whole.
> There is none in heaven, or on earth like Thee;
> Thou hast died for sinners; therefore, Lord, for me.

Now, "whosoever believeth in Him should not perish." As you turn the pages of Holy Scripture you get a marked picture of those who refused this grace. To perish means to go out into the darkness; to be forever under judgment; to exist in awful torment. He wants to save you from that. "Whosoever believeth in Him should not perish, but have everlasting life."

"Have," that suggests present possession. He does not say, "*hope* to have everlasting life." You will have everlasting life right here and now when you believe in Jesus, when you trust Him. Somebody pondered about this one day and then he looked up and said, "God loved—God gave—I believe—and I have—everlasting life." Everlasting life, remember, is far more than life throughout eternity. It is far more than endless existence. It is the very life of God communicated to the soul in order that we may enjoy fellowship with Him. "This is life eternal, that they might know Thee, the only true God, and Jesus Christ, whom Thou hast sent."

In verse 17, as though to encourage the guiltiest to come to Him, He says, "For God sent not His Son into the world to condemn the world; but that the world through Him might be saved."

I remember, years ago, a dear old man behind the counter in a big department store in Los Angeles, where I worked as a lad. The old man was very kind to me. He saw that I was very green and knew not what was expected of me. He took me under his wing and cared for me. I soon got interested in finding out whether he was saved or not. My dear mother was never with anybody very long before she asked them the question, "Are you saved? Are you born again?" I became so used to hearing her ask that question that I thought I ought to ask it of people too. I went to him one day and said, "Mr. Walsh, are you saved?" He looked at me and said, "My dear boy, no one will ever know that until the day of judgment." "Oh," I replied, "there must be some mistake; my mother knows she is saved." "Well, she has made a mistake," he said; "for no one can know that." "But the Bible says, 'He that believeth on Him . . . hath everlasting life.'" "Oh, well," he said, "we can't be sure down here unless we become great saints; but we must just do the best we can and pray to the Lord and the blessed Virgin and the saints to help, and hope that in the day of judgment it may turn out well and we will be saved." "But," I said, "why do you pray to the blessed Virgin? Why not go direct to Jesus?" "My dear boy, the Lord is so great and mighty and holy that it is not befitting that a poor sinner such as I should go to Him, and there is no other who has such influence as His mother." I did not know how to answer him then. But as I studied my Bible through the years, I could see what the answer was. Jesus unapproachable! Jesus hard to be contacted! Why, it was said of Him, "This Man receiveth sinners," and though high in heavenly glory, He still says to sinners, "Come unto Me all ye that labor and are heavy laden." Yes, you can go directly to Him and when you trust Him He gives you eternal life. He did not come to condemn the world. He came with a heart of love to win poor sinners to Himself.

And then the eighteenth verse is so plain and simple. Oh, if you are an anxious soul and seeking light, remember that these are the very words of the living God, "He that believeth on Him is not condemned: but he that believeth not is condemned already, because he hath not believed in the name of the only begotten Son of God." Now, do you see this? There are just two classes of people in that verse. All men in the world who have heard the message are divided into these two classes. What are they? First, "He that believeth." There are those who believe in Jesus. They stand by themselves. Now the other class, "He that believeth not." Every person who has ever heard of Jesus is in one of those two classes. You are either among those who believe in Jesus or among those who do not believe. It is not a question of believing *about* Him; it is a question of believing *in* Him. It is not holding mental conceptions about Him, mere facts of history; but it is trusting Him, committing yourself to Him. Those who trust Him and those who do not trust Him—in which of the two groups do you find yourself? "He that believeth in Him:" are you there? "He that believeth not:" are you there? Oh, if you are, you should be in a hurry to get out of that group into the other, and you pass out of the one and into the other by trusting in Jesus.

Are you in the first group? "He that believeth in Him is not condemned." Do you believe that? Jesus said that. "He that believeth in Him is not condemned."

I was in Kilmarnock three years ago and gave an address one night in the Grant Hall, and a number of people had come into the inquiry room and I went in afterwards to see how they were getting along. A minister called me over and said, "Will you have a word with this lad?" I sat down beside him and said, "What is the trouble?" He looked up and said, "I canna see it. I canna see it. I am so burdened, and canna find deliverance." I said,

"Have you been brought up in a Christian home?" He told me he had. "Do you know the way of salvation?" He answered, "Well, in a way, I do; but I canna see it." I said, "Let me show you something." First I prayed with him and asked God, by the Holy Spirit, to open his heart. Then I pointed him to this verse and said, "Do you see those two classes of people? What is the first class? What is the second class? He answered clearly. "Now," I said, "which class are you in?" Then he looked at me and said, "Why, I am in the first class. I do believe in Him, but it is all dark. I canna see." "Now look again," said I. "What does it say about the first class?" He did look again and I could see the cloud lift, and he turned to me and exclaimed, "Man, I see it! I am not condemned." I asked, "How do you know?" He replied, "God said so." The minister said, "Well, lad are you now willing to go home and tell your parents? Tomorrow when you go to work, will you be willing to tell your mates?" "Oh," he said, "I can hardly wait to get there."

Now, suppose you are in the other group. Listen, "He that believeth not is condemned already." You do not need to wait till the day of judgment to find that out. Condemned! Why? Because you have been dishonest? Because you have lied? Because you have been unclean and unholy? Is it that? That is not what it says *here*. What does it say? "He that *believeth not* is condemned already because he hath not believed in the name of the only begotten Son of God." That is the condemnation. All those sins you have been guilty of, Christ took into account when He died. "He was wounded for our transgressions, He was bruised for our iniquities: the chastisement of our peace was upon Him; and with His stripes we are healed." So, if you are condemned, it is not simply because of the many sins you have committed through your lifetime. It is because of spurning the revelation of the Saviour that God has provided. If you turn away from God and continue rejecting Jesus, you are committing the worst sin there is. He came, a light, into the world to lighten the darkness. If you turn away from Him, you are responsible for the darkness in which you will live and die.

"And this is the condemnation, that light is come into the world, and men loved darkness rather than light, because their deeds were evil." Is it not strange that men would rather continue in darkness than turn to Him, who is the light of life, and find deliverance. "For every one that doeth evil hateth the light, neither cometh to the light, lest his deeds should be reproved. But he that doeth truth (*i.e.,* he that is absolutely honest with God) cometh to the light, that his deeds may be made manifest, that they are wrought in God." Are you going to turn away from the light today or are you coming into the light? Will you trust the blessed One who is the light of the world, and thus rejoice in the salvation which He so freely offers you?

# Walter Arthur Maier

*1893–1950*

*I*f ever preacher, scholar, and astute businessman were combined in one person, that person was Walter A. Maier, founder of *The Lutheran Hour* and its speaker for twenty years (1930–1950). A graduate of Boston College and Concordia Seminary, with a Ph.D. from Harvard (1929), he was an ordained minister of the Lutheran Church Missouri Synod (1917).

Maier served briefly as an army chaplain during World War I and for two years was head of the Walther League, the LCMS youth ministry. In 1922 he was appointed professor of Old Testament and Hebrew at Concordia Seminary in St. Louis. Fascinated by the possibility of the new medium of radio, he convinced the seminary to start a radio station, and KFUO was born in 1924, with Maier preaching regularly. He went on to enlist the Lutheran Laymen's League to sponsor a national broadcast, and in 1930 *The Lutheran Hour* went on the air. Eventually *The Lutheran Hour* was broadcast on over twelve hundred stations weekly in fifty-five countries, with an estimated twenty million listeners.

Maier received more than half a million letters a year in response to his messages. The first year's sermons are compiled in *The Lutheran Hour* (Concordia, 1931), and the program issued regular volumes with titles like *Christ for Every Crisis* (1933), *Winged Words for Christ* (1937), *Peace through Christ* (1940), *America, Turn to Christ* (1944), and *For Christ and*

*Country* (1942). Maier's sermons were biblical and their titles were usually dramatic: "I Pledge Allegiance to the Crucified Christ" (John 19:25–26), "More Important Than the Election—Your Decision Concerning Christ" (1 Kings 18:21), "Christ's Challenge to Seventy Million American Unbelievers" (John 18:22–23), and "The Call for This Crisis—Come and See Jesus" (John 1:38–39).

Along with the sermon books, Maier wrote *For Better, Not for Worse* (Concordia, 1935), a series of Lenten devotional books, and a scholarly commentary on Nahum (Concordia, 1959). The official biography is *A Man Spoke, A World Listened: The Story of Walter A. Maier,* written by his son Paul L. Maier (McGraw-Hill, 1963).

# Awake! Watch! Pray!

He cometh unto the disciples, and findeth them asleep, and saith unto Peter, What, could ye not watch with Me one hour? Watch and pray, that ye enter not into temptation.

Matthew 26:40–41

Christ, who didst Suffer Agony in the Garden for Us: Give us the penitent faith which recognizes that, when the weight of human sin crushed Thy soul almost into death at Gethsemane, Thou didst endure such anguish for us! Abide in us, O strengthening Savior, to reenforce the faith by which we may overcome the slumber of carnal security and, watching prayerfully, resist evil forces which would keep us from Thee! Contritely do we confess that the sleep of sin has often overtaken us when, instead of arousing ourselves to faithful vigilance, we rested unconcerned, while enemies of Thy grace sought to restrain the Kingdom's course. Pardon us for every refusal to follow the appeal of Thy love with unwavering devotion! Continue to look down mercifully on a world that has forgotten and betrayed Thee! If it be Thy will, restrict the horrors of further war! Grant us, although we have not deserved it, a beneficial, building peace! O Jesus, without Thee we can do nothing. Bless us, then, and enrich our souls by the grace of Thy Cross and the cleansing power of Thy blood! Amen.

Crucial days have dawned for America. Perhaps even before I speak to you again momentous decisions will have been reached by Congress. Whether we realize it or not, the nation's destiny is being shaped not only for this crisis year but for decades to come.

Little doubt remains that we are close to war. Every day on the Senate floor the assertion is emphatically repeated that the United States must take an active part in European military operations. Confidential reports released by financial experts regard our part in the struggle as practically inevitable. After the first World War we said, "It must not happen again!" Now we fear, "It will happen again." Only a miracle can save this country from war.

Even if the miracle should occur and we be spared actual participation in bloodshed; if, despite its unworthiness, the world be granted an honorable, constructive peace, for which I still ask you to work and pray in this eleventh hour, we nevertheless stare into a problem-filled future. We shall experience financial hardship; for even though we hardly glance a second time at head-lines reporting multibillion-dollar appropriations, these staggering expenditures *must* finally be paid by the people. War or peace, active belligerency or passive, long-drawn hostilities or quick armistice, we should prepare to counteract the immoralities which flourish in days of easy money and lavish spending like these. The most alarming upswing in American crime began after the last war. Have we any reason to suppose that with the far greater proportion of our present-day difficulties the revolt against God's Law and man's will decrease during the years before us?

Dwarfing these social and moral perplexities, however, is the increase of opposition to Christ which the churches will soon meet. In this national emergency every American Christian should understand clearly and personally that our faith will be tried as never before. Recent reports from Britain tell us that through constant war strain the Church of England has been paralyzed. What reason have we to suppose that the Savior's cause in the United States will not suffer appalling setbacks? If the late war put Karl Marx and his atheism over Jesus Christ and His Gospel in Russia, placed the State over the Church in Germany and Italy, helped to enthrone reason more solidly over revelation in Britain, France, and our own country, let us put on our spiritual armor to defend ourselves, before it is too late, against a large-scale assault on Jesus within our borders.

Although circumstances which have brought about this crisis are now out of our control, we have a command by Christ, our Savior, that marks our path of duty and promises peace, courage, confidence, to all who love Him and follow His instructions. I thank God that in this first Lenten message I can give you as the crisis cry for inward and outward struggle, the battle-call for the Church in its conflicts, this motto of militant Christianity: Awake! Watch! Pray! a plea which takes us back to the beginning of our Savior's Passion in these words of Saint Matthew (chapter twenty-six, verses forty and forty-one), *"He cometh unto the disciples, and findeth them asleep, and saith unto Peter, What, could ye not watch with Me one hour? Watch and pray, that ye enter not into temptation."*

## I. Awake!

This command by Jesus broke the nocturnal stillness in the Garden of Gethsemane, one of the few Palestinian localities, hallowed by our Savior's suffering, that can be identified with some certainty. If it was of the same size as the present site, this enclosure, which Saint John alone calls the "garden," was a small plot, only about fifty yards square; but the whole world would not be large enough to contain adequate descriptions of the agony which Christ experienced there. Only eight gnarled olive-trees today mark the place, but the most magnificent and costly monument that wealth and art could erect would never begin to commemorate worthily the convulsive agony which there almost crushed Jesus into death.

Gethsemane was only half a mile from the Jerusalem city walls; and the pathway which crossed that distance could have been traversed leisurely in fifteen minutes. Yet what startling difference a half mile and a quarter hour produced in our Lord! Before that last walk we hear Him in His high-priestly prayer, confident, joy-filled, triumphant, concerned chiefly about the preservation and deliverance of His disciples; but now, after this short span of space and time, rejoicing has given way to relentless anguish. His thoughts are riveted on the impending ordeal. Until this hour the disciples depended on the Master, but in Gethsemane, Jesus needs His followers with the deepest urgency. He selects three, perhaps those of whom sympathy and perseverance may best be expected: Peter, James, John; and taking them with Him to a secluded spot, He engages in the most penetrating prayer earth and heaven have ever heard. As the Passover moon sends its beams on Christ, we can witness terror and soul-searing pain, such as human eye will never otherwise see. The Scriptures themselves can hardly find adequate words to picture that agony. They state that Jesus was *"sorrowful," "sore amazed," "very heavy," "full of sorrows."* Neither these four terms nor four hundred more can plumb the abyss of His grief. Jesus falls on His knees to plead with His Father, only to find that the torment of His soul casts Him prostrate on the damp ground. Had it not been for the preordained plan of our redemption, Christ would have died then and there. And He almost did, for He moaned, *"My soul is exceeding sorrowful, even unto death."* No human agency could save Him. An angel had to come from heaven to revive Him for the climax on the cross.

The voice which the three selected disciples had heard defeat the grave when Jesus, gripping the cold hand of a lifeless corpse, cried, *"Maid, arise!"*

now pleads for help. Thrice that never-to-be-forgotten cry rings out through the night, *"O My Father, if it be possible, let this cup pass from Me!"* The countenance which these favored followers had seen glorified on the Mount of Transfiguration, where the Savior's face shone as the sun, is now pale and covered with bloody sweat!

As you ask God ever to keep this glimpse of the Savior's unparalleled agony before your mind's eye, stop to learn why Jesus was stretched out on Gethsemane's soil! It was not merely fear that almost took His life, a cringing before His crucifixion, a dread of death, as modern enemies of the Cross declare. Our Lord knew how to overcome such terror. See Him a few hours after this ordeal in the Garden, when, calm and composed, He endures one cruelty after the other by His Jewish countrymen and the Roman authorities. Behold Him on the way to Calvary stopping to preach to the women who fringed that road! Picture Him on the cross as He promises a penitent thief the immediate glories of Paradise. Confidently He cries, *"It is finished!"* and commends Himself into His Father's hands. You need not be a Christian to know that there is nothing fearful and cowardly in the Christ of Gethsemane.

The only true explanation of this mystery in the Garden is that there the Savior's suffering for all human transgressions begins. We sometimes limit Christ's agony to the physical pain He endured throughout the various hours of torture that culminated in His death on the cross; but we should not exclude Gethsemane's soul-grief which Jesus sustained (not for His own sins, since He had none; and even His enemies' perjury could invent no true charge against Him) for my iniquities and yours. Here, by God's eternal plan for our redemption, the Guiltless languished for the guilty, the Faultless for the fault-filled, the Lawgiver for the law-breaker, the eternal God for His death-marked creatures!

What a terrifying curse Jesus assumes as He prepares to die by man, yet for man! A single sin in your life can open the flood-gates of unspeakable misery for the rest of your days. The one misstep that some of you young folks take can torment you as long as you live. An isolated transgression can visit its disastrous consequences on the third and fourth generation. How immeasurable, then, must be the penalty for the wrong committed! But how horrifying the retribution which God's outraged justice must demand for the total of all sins committed by mankind throughout every century of mankind's sordid history! Yet nothing less than that appalling aggregate was laid upon Christ in the Garden. There His soul was afflicted for social outcasts, prostitutes, degenerates, murderers, war-profiteers, white-slavers, debauchers of youth, as well as for you, the self-righteous and self-satisfied. You brought Him to Gethsemane. You made Him cry, *"Let this cup pass from Me!"* You, no matter how good you think you are or try to show yourself, regardless of the esteem in which you are publicly held; you, whoever, wherever, whatever, you are, made Him fall to the ground and require the strengthening angel. Admit that now! Declare before your God that Jesus bears the brunt of this indescribable pain for you!

Then you will not wonder why Christ in that last conflict craved the companionship of His own followers. He was so truly human that even their presence would have brought Him assurance in His anguish. So He asks His three trusted disciples, the inner circle, we may say, of the Twelve, *"Tarry ye here and watch with Me!"* What a modest request that was! We gladly keep long night-vigils at the bedside of our beloved ones. A true Christian pastor will gladly forego sleep to pray with any one in his charge who is besieged by heavy sorrows. Even the Government grants a convicted murderer the sustaining counsel of a spiritual adviser in the final hours before the electric chair. Yet small as was this last service which Peter, James, and John were asked to render the Lord, it was too great. What depth of human weakness we see in these words, *"He cometh unto the disciples and findeth them asleep."* Their cruel slumber seems too much even for the gentle Christ; and beholding Peter, who only a few minutes before had loudly boasted that he would readily die for Him, now relaxed in heavy slumber, the agonized Savior cries, *"What, could ye not watch with Me one hour?"*

We seek an explanation for this heartless sleep, and the Scriptures give two reasons: The disciples were weary, and they were heavy with sorrow. Yet, before we pour out our scorn on these men who could not stay awake for a single hour during the one crisis for which Jesus asked their companionship, let us be honest enough to admit that the best among us fall asleep when Christ's cause suffers attack and we should be awake to the danger. Jesus has just as little help from many a professing Christian today as He had from that slumbering trio. If Saint Paul had to tell first-century believers, *"Now it is high time to awake out of sleep,"* the cry that should shake twentieth-century church-members from their lethargy asks, "Christians of America, awake! Our faith is being assaulted! Wake up to the truth that the Savior is being assailed by indifference, compromise, and denial within the churches! Wake up to the peril that modernist unbelief is often capturing your pulpits, divinity schools, church-papers! Wake up to the realization that many churches are spiritually dead, without the living Christ in their sermons, without missionary zeal in their members' lives! Wake up to the dangers of this hour, when atheism, materialism, sensualism, are arrayed against the Church in the strongest force ever mobilized in this country! Wake up, churches of America, to the conviction that in this crisis only Christ can solve our difficulties!"

The Savior's appeal for wakeful followers, however, is an individual plea to every one of you. May it reach some who are slumbering securely in the carnal sleep of sin! Too many of you are in a constant coma of spiritual carelessness, as unconcerned about your soul as a sleeping man is about his body. You think your life without Jesus is satisfying. You don't want Christ because you claim that you do not need Him! Or do you? Before long the sins you serve will find you out. Before long you will face eternity, when death, which this week summoned king and commoner, comes to you. How terrifying, then, this spiritual encephalitis, the sleeping-sickness of the soul! Before it is too late, wake up! See Christ convulsed in the Garden and say, "O Jesus, all this agony was for me! Forgive me! Make me Yours! Keep me awake!" And that plea will be answered.

## II. Watch!

Christ demanded more than mere wakefulness. *"Watch,"* He told the disciples, *"that ye enter not into temptation!"* Encircled, as He was, by sorrows without number, He is now concerned with His followers' welfare. Satan, He knows, will assault them with redoubled force; temptations will multiply. In His betrayal, capture, and arrest their human weakness will need support. So He pleads, *" 'Watch!'* Be on your guard! Be prepared!"

The same trials which tested these disciples surround us day and night. The enemies of the Cross have increased, and it is still true even of the most loyal among Jesus' followers that *"the spirit indeed is willing, but the flesh is weak."* Ten thousand forces of evil, each one a crafty, superhuman power of hell, line up against us; and daily do we need the Savior's warning *"Watch . . . that ye enter not into temptation!"*

*" 'Watch,'* Christian youth of America," His Word commands; "guard against the evil which appeals to your baser nature, asks you to reject the sacred statues of purity and to run along with the world!" *" 'Watch,'* Christian parents of America! Resist the dark forces which seek to destroy Christian home-life, belittle parenthood, childhood, and the sacred marriage vow!"

"Christian citizens of America," Christ would say, *" 'Watch!'* Take steps to guard the religious liberties, the separation of Church and State, the right of assembly, the freedom of worship that is constitutionally ours!" War emergencies may seek to restrict or destroy this heritage. Last week the people of Germany were told that they were not primarily Protestants or Catholics. First of all, their *Fuehrer* commanded, they were to be Germans. Let us hope that in our own country, as the times become more critical, no false nationalism will demand that we give Christ a second place. No conflict ever need arise between our Christian creed and our love for country; but if the time should ever come (and in view of present tendencies, who will say that it cannot?) when we are told, "You are Americans first and Christians second," may the Holy Spirit strengthen us to declare,

*"We ought to obey God rather than men,"* and give Jesus uncontested supremacy in our hearts!

"'*Watch,*' Christian churches of America," the Savior cries to us from the Garden. Prepare for the darker day! Get ready now for the new conditions that will follow the war, by bringing the Gospel to the masses! Let American people know that this Christ in Gethsemane is the Savior of the common people, too! When Millais' picture of Jesus in the carpenter shop was exhibited throughout England, great throngs of working-men flocked to inspect the canvas, because, they said, "This is our Comrade." American labor should repeat their acclaim of our Lord. You men in the factories, as welcome letters assure me, are passing the word from one worker to the other that this broadcast is for the masses and not reserved for a few, just as Christ is the universal, not the restricted Savior. The churches should *"watch"* by fortifying our children against the temptations of these coming years, giving the rising generation daily Christian instruction in church-supported schools. With the mandate from God Himself *"Comfort ye, comfort ye, My people, saith your God!"* ringing in our ears, we who are Christ's must *"watch,"* so that churches do not waste their efforts in political or cultural discussions which leave souls untouched. Instead, they must bring the pure message of Christ's saving, sustaining Gospel to the distressed multitudes. The poor, the dispossessed, the unemployed, may be won for any future revolutionary upheaval unless churches show a more concerted desire to help the destitute and avoid slanting their favoritism toward the rich. Remember what happened in Russia, Spain, and Mexico! Let us preach Christ's Gospel with greater force and frequency, pointing overburdened souls to the grief-gripped Christ in Gethsemane, with this message, "He suffered for you so that you might be spared eternal agony"; directing the forsaken to that solitary Sufferer with the assurance, "He was abandoned, deserted, so that you need never be alone in life or death."

Despite that pleading, warning, repeated *"Watch!"* the disciples failed. Sleep continued to weight their eyes. Yet Christ mercifully forgave them! And He can pardon us! We are moved by the story which tells how Abraham Lincoln extended clemency to a soldier sentenced to death for having fallen asleep at his post. Today, in this glimpse of sacred Gethsemane, Christ offers you complete acquittal for every failure to keep awake and watch, for each instance in which Christ's enemies have triumphed because you have fallen asleep on duty. As Lincoln's commutation of sentence called forth inexpressible gratitude in the sentry saved from the firing-squad, so may the Savior's pardoning love make both us and the angels of God above rejoice when we, unfaithful soldiers of Christ, are restored and saved!

### *III. Pray!*

The Savior's command to the drowsy disciples also asked them to *"pray,"* to implore God for strength that they might resist the temptations to disloyalty which would soon confront them. Jesus Himself knew and practiced the power of such petition. This was doubtless not the first time He knelt in the Garden. The Gospels tell us that He customarily retreated to its shade and protection. Our Christian life would be stronger and the number of soul-tragedies reduced, were prayer a holy habit with us! If Christ, the sinless Son of God, found refuge and strength in prayer, how eagerly should we follow the appeal *"Ask, and it shall be given you"*!

Have you ever recognized that His pleading in the Garden, as a sort of final but unspoken instruction, summarizes everything we need to know about prayer? Jesus, kneeling in Gethsemane, shows us to whom our petitions must be addressed as He cries, *"O My Father!"* the only recorded instance He uses the word *"My"* in addressing His Father; and it is only when we address the Triune God, whom Jesus clearly revealed, only when we, too, call God "our Father" through Christ, that we can have assurance of answer.

Jesus, pleading in Gethsemane, also teaches us how to approach the holy God despite the unholiness in our sinful lives. Pointing to Christ, we say, "Father, that Savior whose soul was *'exceeding sorrowful, even unto death'* has made me Thy child." Jesus Himself promises, *"If ye shall ask the Father anything in My name, He will give it you."* What a clear-cut rejection of all Christless prayers! What a sacred promise for Christ-grounded petitions!

We must likewise be impressed by our Lord's earnestness. Can we read the story of Gethsemane without being moved by the truth that this prayer, far from being mere routine, was the outpouring of the Savior's innermost soul? Blessed are we, too, if we speak our petitions with the fervor of faith! Jesus falls on His knees; if God's Son could thus humble Himself, who are we to forget that posture of lowliness?

The suffering Savior prayed alone, in solitude with His Father; and while we need prayer in the churches, prayer in the family, we must also cultivate the private, personal pleading, which brings its rich reward in stronger faith and intensified courage. Select some spot in your home or, as the Savior did, in the realm of nature and learn what a privilege it is to speak confidently with your God, without any distraction whatever!

Note that Jesus pleaded three times, *"Let this cup pass from Me!"* The last night of His early life reminds us how necessary protracted prayer often is. Do not expect the Almighty to hear you immediately when Jesus had to repeat His petition! Our omniscient Father sometimes delays in answering because postponement makes us realize more keenly how completely we depend on Him. Wood used in carving must be seasoned to prevent warping; and if God wants to fashion your life into a masterpiece of His mercy that will not lose its symmetry, do not complain when the process takes time! Keep on praying, and you continue to store strength!

Particularly, however, let us learn of Jesus how to plead submissively, in accordance with God's gracious will. In His soul torture, bearing the total of human transgressions, suffering as our Substitute, Jesus begs that the cup of sorrows might be taken from Him; yet He adds, *"If it be possible,"* and *"Nevertheless, not as I will, but as Thou wilt."* How contrarily our requests specify their answer! We even dictate to God the time, place, manner, of His response, and we are so short-sighted that, if He were to follow our petulant demands and give us everything we ask, we should ruin ourselves. For your spiritual advancement and for the glorious triumph of faith learn to follow Jesus when you implore God in the Third Petition, *"Thy will be done in earth as it is in heaven"!* With the Spirit's help, overcome stubborn self-will and acquire the calm composure of a life completely surrendered to God!

The cup did not pass from our Lord. He had to drink it to its bitter dregs. Yet His crucifixion was not the end, death not the final chapter. After Calvary came the resurrection; after the cross, the crown of heaven. Similarly in our lives it often may seem that God is deaf to our entreaties; yet all the while His loving heart has planned to give us something far better than we have requested. If He keeps us poor on earth that we may be unspeakably rich in heaven; if He checks our ambitions and we remain unnoticed during this life that during the next we may experience how blessed is the fulfilment of His promise, *"the last shall be first,"* why should we dare to think unworthy thoughts of our Father when He gives us gold instead of glitter?

May the Holy Spirit touch you so that this sincere wish will form itself in your contrite heart, "I want to pray as Jesus did"!

Do not be discouraged by the tragedy that we have so little Christ-centered prayer today! During difficult times, men think that they themselves can build defense against the approach of every evil, individual and nation; but you cannot build a life, a home, a church, a community, a country without God and expect that it will prosper. As I look into the future, I fail to see a single ray of purely human hope which can guarantee peace and blessing. Yet come war, with its wounds and death; come inflation, repudiation, bankruptcy; come the restriction of our religious liberty, persecution for the churches; come a totalitarian America—if we behold the Christ of Gethsemane, hear Him plead, "Awake! Watch! Pray!" and ask God, "O Father, keep me wakeful, watchful, prayerful, with my Savior!"; if at the cry: "On your knees, America!" "Prayer in the homes!" "Prayer in true churches!" we humble ourselves penitently before the Almighty, then just as Gethsemane gave way to the resurrection glory, so we, too, shall meet our nation-wide perplexities and emerge from our personal afflictions stronger and better than ever before. May God thus graciously show every one of us that the Savior's grief in the Garden becomes our sacred pledge of spiritual peace on earth, our assurance of redemption in heaven! May we learn, if necessary in heart-trying experience, that the pathway to Christian power is marked by obedience to our Redeemer's repeated request, "Awake! Watch! Pray!" We ask this in Jesus' name! Amen.

# Thomas Todhunter Shields

*1873–1955*

Thomas Todhunter Shields was born in England and converted to Christ in 1891 under the ministry of his father, who was a Primitive Methodist preacher. When the family moved to Canada, they united with the Baptists. Shields had no formal ministerial training yet he pastored five different churches before going to the Jarvis Street Baptist Church in Toronto in 1910, where he served until 1954 and was used of God to make it one of the most significant evangelical pulpits in Canada.

Like his hero Charles Spurgeon, Shields was largely self-taught, was a devoted Calvinist, and boldly proclaimed Reformation theology while churches across Canada were turning to theological liberalism. He opposed the theological erosion in the divinity school at McMaster University and eventually helped to found the Toronto Baptist Seminary.

In 1922 he began publishing *The Gospel Witness,* a biweekly newspaper that defended the faith, opposed modernism, and promoted the principles of Protestantism. Shields was also active in the fundamentalist movement in the United States and helped to found the Baptist Bible Union in Kansas City in 1923 and served as its first president. However, after 1929 he had a tenuous relationship with his American fundamentalist friends, mainly because they were promoting premillennial dispensationalism and Shields was amillennial. He even attacked the popular

111

Scofield Bible in his newspaper. At the dissolution of the Baptist Bible Union in 1932, the General Association of Regular Baptist Churches was formed, but Shields did not join. In 1948 he began to associate with Carl McIntire and the International Council of Christian Churches, and McIntire preached the sermon at Shields's funeral on April 7, 1955.

The official biography is *Shields of Canada* by Leslie K. Tarr (Baker, 1967), and the Jarvis Street Baptist Church has published several volumes of sermons by Dr. Shields.

# The Doctrine of Election

In the second verse of the first chapter of Peter's first epistle are these words, "Elect according to the foreknowledge of God the Father, through sanctification of the Spirit, unto obedience and sprinkling of the blood of Jesus Christ: Grace unto you, and peace, be multiplied."

It is not difficult to view a segment of life in our day and to compare it with a correspondingly limited view of life in another day, and to become very pessimistic. One can always find a bright spot here and a black spot somewhere else, while, of course, the reverse of that is true. It is possible thus to pour contempt upon what some people call "the good old days," and to show that we live in days which are much to be preferred to the days that have gone before us. It is therefore necessary to view life as a whole, and estimate its values relatively.

While there is much in this present day of which we have reason to be proud, and for which we may well be thankful, in the material realm, I seriously question whether the world has ever known a more superficial age than this when we look at the religious aspect of things. People are accustomed nowadays to get their religion at a delicatessen store, already made up in packages, duly labelled—and they take it, asking no questions for conscience' sake! It is surprising what people can be persuaded to believe, and still more surprising what people believe without any persuasion at all.

The gospel puts no premium upon ignorance, nor does it require any man to stultify himself. We ought to exercise our God-given powers, endeavouring to prove all things, and "to hold fast that which is good."

In the chapter from which I have read we are exhorted to "gird up the loins of our minds." We are not to be false Christians; we are not to be careless or superficial in our religious life, but virile and vigorous people, who know what they believe, and why they believe it. Yet I fear that the majority of religious people to-day reflect the opinions of the last person who has spoken to them. There seems to be a want of conviction, of a thorough and proportionate knowledge of the gospel. Comparatively few seem to have learned to think relatively, to relate one principle of the gospel to another.

I heard a very distinguished and popular preacher preach in this city some years ago, and it was, I think, one of the most illogical utterances I ever heard in my life. I refer to Dr. R. J. Campbell, when he was Pastor of the City Temple, London. He built up house after house only to knock them down again. When he had completed a lecture he said, "Now that is my strange work. I should like to preach to you. We shall therefore dismiss this service, and to as many of you as would like to hear a sermon, I will preach a sermon if you will stay." The first service was dismissed, but nobody left. We all stayed, and he built up a little house and knocked it down, and built up another, and knocked it down, all the way through. His preaching was like little children building houses of cards, and knocking them down again.

When I got home that night the editor of a certain paper called me up and said, "I think I noticed you in the service to-night?" I replied that I was there. Then he said, "You enjoyed Dr. Campbell?" I answered, "Yes, indeed. It was a very interesting service." He said, "I wish you would write me an appreciative article of the service." "You mean," I said, "that you want an article approving of the service?" "Why, certainly," was the reply. Yet this man was one who was frequently chairman at evangelistic services. When prominent evangelists came to the city he would be sure to be on the platform. I said, "I enjoyed both the lecture and the sermon, but I could not agree with either." "What was wrong with them?" he enquired. I said, "Did you agree with what he said?" "Absolutely," he replied. "Well now," I said, "let me review it a moment." It was fresh in my mind at the moment, as it was only an hour or so after the service. I said, "Dr. Campbell said so-and-so?" "Yes, he did." "Did you agree with that?" "Well, not exactly." "And he said so-and-so, didn't he?" "Yes." "Can you say Amen to that?" "Well, no; I cannot." I called his attention to one thing after another, and he said, "Well, I declare, I had no idea he was so inconsistent." He contradicted himself every five minutes of his speech.

I knew a preacher when I was in Hamilton, a very popular preacher. One day we had a discussion in a ministerial association (before Modernism had become as rampant as it is now), and there was one man who read an essay on the divine spark in man, and the development of the best that is in us—of course, entirely repudiating the doctrine of total depravity; and this popular brother took him to task. He did not agree with the speaker at all. The popular preacher was thoroughly orthodox, as I thought. He said that we are a bad lot, as Moody did, and he quoted Scripture to show that every faculty of the mind was biased, and that we were really totally depraved. Somebody suggested, "Perhaps Mr. So-and-So will give us a paper on the other side of this question. At the next meeting I suggest that Mr. So-and-So address us on the subject of Total Depravity." This was agreed, and the brother accepted the task.

Now this man who preached the doctrine of total depravity was an Arminian in theology. He shrank from the doctrine of election, and could not agree with it at all. He was great on free will, but not very strong on divine sovereignty.

The next time the brethren met, there was a good attendance, and this brother read his paper—he went all the way from A to Z. Calvin himself could not have outdone him. We were a bad lot beyond all peradventure. When he had finished the paper he said he hoped the brethren would excuse him, because he had an appointment and would not be able to remain for the discussion. But we had one man there who was as keen as a razor, but who was a Modernist. He would be called a Conservative now, but we thought he was pretty far gone then. He said, "Just a moment. I should like to ask Mr. So-and-So a question before he leaves."

Turning to the brother who had delivered the address he said, "I should like to ask you whether there is anything in man in his natural state which can respond to the appeal of the Spirit of God from without?" He thought a moment, and then said, "Certainly there is." "Well," said the Professor, "is that thing that can respond to the Holy Spirit good or is it evil?" He said, "If it responds to the Holy Spirit it cannot be evil." "I should think not," said the Professor, "then it is good?" "I suppose it must be." "Then your whole argument fails, sir, and we are not totally depraved."

You see, that brother had not learned to think relatively. He had not learned that if one certain doctrine be true, another cannot be true. There cannot be an upper without a lower, an east without a west, nor a north without a south.

Now if man is totally depraved (more of that in another lecture), there is nothing in him that can possibly respond to the Divine Spirit. If he is dead in trespasses and sins, he has no power of himself to deliver himself, or even to assist to deliver himself, out of his natural state. If he be altogether evil then he must remain for ever altogether evil unless God in sovereign mercy touches him into life. And if that be true, we must have the principle of election.

Two weeks ago I spoke to you on the subject of the Divine Sovereignty. I endeavoured to show that God is absolute in all the qualities of His being.

All perfections reside in Him. You can never go beyond God. He is the highest; He is the ultimate; He is the absolute in everything.

If God be thus Sovereign, it means that there is no power in the spiritual world among principalities or powers or the rulers of the darkness of this world; or in any human society, whatever it may be; or in an individual human life—there can be no power anywhere that is not subject to divine control. If there were a spot anywhere in the universe where any power could challenge the supremacy of God, then God must cease to be sovereign, and, as such, must cease to be God!

Last Thursday I tried to show you that God has shown His sovereign power by the revelation of Himself in grace through Jesus Christ our Lord. The scheme of redemption originated in the divine mind, and the outworking of it, the coming of Christ to this earth, and all the details of His earthly career, His ultimate Sacrifice at the Cross, and His resurrection and ascension to the right hand of God—from beginning to end it is of God, and man had not an infinitesimal part in it.

The question before us to-night is, How are the benefits of that salvation sovereignly provided to be mediated to us, to be applied to the people for whom that salvation is provided? Is God as sovereign in the application of redemption as He is in its provision? You have only to ask that question to answer it, if you have any adequate idea of sovereignty at all. If His sovereignty be absolute, He must be as sovereign in the application of redemption as in the provision of it. Otherwise, it would be a limited sovereignty, and, as applied to God, it would be no sovereignty at all.

The apostle here, addressing believers in certain places, describes them as "elect according to the foreknowledge of God the Father, through sanctification of the Spirit, unto obedience and sprinkling of the blood of Jesus Christ." I am aware that against the principle of election, the principle of the divine choice and foreordination, of the supremacy of the divine will, the natural man rebels, for that is the very essence of sin, to lift the human will against the divine, and to object to the universal, absolute, dominion of God Himself.

That was the first temptation: "Ye shall be as gods; ye shall share in the divine prerogatives; ye shall be equal with Him Who is the absolute Ruler." And from then until now natural men have been unwilling to admit the supremacy of God in anything. You see it in a little child who very soon wants to declare his independence. Even while learning to walk, he is soon ready to throw off all restraint; and almost before he can talk, says in effect, "Let me have my own way, I can walk. I do not need anybody's help."

Have you not seen it? Have you not seen that passion for independence, for self-will, even in the youngest children? And it is common also to maturer years.

Consider a moment the general principle of election as it operates in the physical world. We recognize it everywhere. In a month or so we shall be putting our clocks back—but the sun will not go back an hour. All the legislators of earth could not change the sun. The sun will rise at the appointed time, and drop below the horizon to the fraction of a second at the time appointed. You cannot change the clock in the heavens by any plan of human devising. That is impossible. You can build four walls and say, "I will live within that space"; you can then raise the temperature of the house in which you live and say, "I will have a bit of summer in the midst of winter"—but you cannot prevent the coming of frost: "By the breath of God frost is given." The man at the weather bureau can estimate only the weather probabilities for the next twenty-four hours, but he cannot affect or change them one whit. There are natural forces operating everywhere which are sovereignly independent of human control. There are forces to which we must conform whether we like it or not. That stairway to the gallery is a recognition of the principle. Downtown in one of the tall buildings you cannot say, "I think I will go up to the thirtieth floor—good-bye, up I go." No, you cannot! You must have some contrivance to overcome the law of gravitation. That law compels the erection of stairways and elevators, and governs the construction of the whole building. You cannot change God's law. "Which of you by taking thought can add one cubit unto his stature?" You cannot make yourself longer—nor can you make yourself shorter—without disastrous results.

If you review your life you will find that you have been made what you are physically by forces and circumstances that were entirely beyond your control. "Thou canst not make one hair white or black." We are subject, I say, in the physical world, to forces beyond our control; and we are what we are because those forces operate in spite of us. However we may object to it, the principle of election is there.

Why do you live in Toronto instead of living in Africa? Why were you born under the full light of the gospel where you had opportunity of hearing it from your earliest infancy when millions of people have not yet heard that Jesus was born in Bethlehem of Judaea? Why have you two good eyes while some people are blind? Why are you able to walk while some people are cripples? "Who maketh Thee to differ from another? and what hast thou that thou didst not receive? Now if thou didst receive it, why dost thou glory as if thou hadst not received?" I am not speaking now of spiritual matters: I am speaking only of our physical status. There is not a thing we have for which we are deserving of credit. A strong man ought to be the humblest man in the world. A beautiful woman ought to be the most modest. We ought to praise Somebody, whoever He is, for every good thing we have, because we have done nothing either to merit it or to secure it ourselves.

Let us now apply that principle to our spiritual state. Why are you a Christian? Because you were chosen so to be, my dear friend. Because you were "elect according to the foreknowledge of God the Father."

I have known some would-be theologians to try to get over what they seem to regard as a difficulty by saying that, of course, inasmuch as God has infinite knowledge. His foreknowledge enabled Him to see who would believe in Christ, and that is what election means. It cannot mean anything of the kind, for God is not absolute in one quality of His being only, but in all; and it is inconceivable that God should know a thing, and that in the light of that knowledge His will should be inactive. The fact that we are elect means not only that God knew and saw in advance, but that He chose us. We are chosen "according to the foreknowledge of God the Father."

The truth is, dear friends, we are Christians because God willed that we should be. I will show you presently that that principle lays a better foundation for your faith to rest upon than were it to be said that we are Christians because we willed to be. But that is the principle of Scripture. A little Scottish boy was once asked by the elders when he wanted to come into the church how he had been saved, and what he had done toward his own salvation. He replied, "I kicked against it all I could, and God did the rest." And that is about true,—

> 'Twas the same love that spread the feast
> That sweetly forced us in;
> Else we had still refused to taste,
> And perished in our sin.

There was a place, and there was a time, and there were means, ordained of God by which we were made children of God and heirs of glory. We are "elect according to the foreknowledge of God the Father." Look back over your Christian experience step by step and ask yourself, "How did I become a Christian? What instrumentalities were employed in my enlightenment? How did I at last apprehend the truth? How at last did I see the light and enter gladly into fellowship with God?" And you will find that there is not a spot anywhere where you can take any credit to yourself. It is "not of works lest any man should boast"; "For ye see your calling, brethren, how that not many wise men after the flesh, not many mighty, not many noble, are called: but God hath chosen the foolish things of the world to confound the wise; and God hath chosen the weak things of the world to confound the things which are mighty; and base things of the world, and things which are not, to bring to nought things that are: that no flesh should glory in his presence. But of him are ye in Christ Jesus, who of God is made unto us wisdom, and righteousness, and sanctification, and redemption: that, according as it is written, He that glorieth, let him glory in the Lord." Someone may say, "If that be so, we can just wait and let God have His way; for it makes no difference what I do. Surely that doctrine will teach men to presume." On the contrary, this doctrine invariably produces the opposite effect.

*How are we elected?* "Through sanctification of the Spirit." That is to say, the sovereign grace of God, operating through the mighty power of the Divine Spirit separates us unto Christ. What had Lazarus to do with his own return to life? Jesus Christ commanded, "Lazarus, come forth"— and he obeyed, as he could obey no other voice than the voice of the Son of God.

If we are really Christians, we are elect "through sanctification of the Spirit." We are not chosen in sin, nor ordained to eternal life without any provision being made for the removal of sin: "God, having raised up his Son Jesus, sent Him to bless you, in turning away every one of you from his iniquities."

Furthermore: *The manner of the separation is here very clearly set forth:* "Unto obedience and sprinkling of the blood of Jesus Christ." "This is His commandment, that ye should believe on the name of the Lord Jesus Christ." When the gospel was preached by Paul and Barnabas at Antioch in Pisidia, we read that "as many as were ordained to eternal life believed." Their election was manifested by their faith. The sanctification of the Spirit, that is, their separation unto God, issued in their believing the gospel and obeying God. Convicted of sin and righteousness and judgment, they believed; hence the blood of sprinkling was applied, and they were washed from their sins and made white in the blood of the Lamb.

That is how all men are saved. We may not enter into the secret counsels of the Eternal, but we know that certain are elect "through the foreknowledge of God." We can know who the elect are only as we have proof that they are sanctified by the Spirit unto obedience and sprinkling of the blood of Jesus Christ. One thing is certain: No one may be sure of his election until he is sure that he has repented of his sins, and obtained forgiveness through faith in Christ.

Someone perhaps will say, "But, sir, I do believe in Him. I have confessed my sins to Him, and received salvation at His hand." If that be so, you may thank God that you are among the elect; and the proof of your election is that you have been touched by the Spirit of God, and led to obey the divine command, and believe on the Lord Jesus Christ. In other words, your calling has been effected "through sanctification of the Spirit, unto obedience and sprinkling of the blood of Jesus Christ." Thus are we brought into filial relationship to God, becoming His children, "and if children, then heirs, heirs of God, and joint heirs with Jesus Christ." So much, briefly, for the doctrine itself.

Let me show you now, for a few moments, SOME OF THE PRACTICAL IMPLICATIONS OF THIS DOCTRINE. I have heard men speak to this effect: Undoubtedly the principle of election is taught in the Word, but why preach it? It is there for the comfort of God's believing people, but surely you do not expect such a doctrine to be effective in the conversion of sinners?

On the contrary, I believe *the doctrine of election is a soul-saving doctrine.* It is set forth in the Scripture not only to be believed, but to be preached.

I recall many years ago preaching during the Christmas season when away from home on this text, "Before that Philip called thee, when thou wast under the fig tree, I saw thee." In the sermon I explained in simple fashion that Philip supposed he was bringing Nathanael to Christ,—even as he supposed that he had himself found Christ, for he said, "We have found him, of whom Moses in the law, and the prophets, did write, Jesus of Nazareth, the son of Joseph." But as Philip and Nathanael approached, the Master said, "Behold an Israelite indeed, in whom is no guile." To this Nathanael replied, "Whence knowest thou me?" And He answered, "Before that Philip called thee, when thou wast under the fig tree, I saw thee." As though He had said, "Philip imagines that he has really brought you to me, but he was only the Shepherd's crook. I laid hold of him, and through him, I laid hold of you. You have not chosen me, but I have chosen you. You exercised your will in coming to me, but your will was exercised under the constraints of grace."

Well, I preached after that fashion, and for another Pastor. But when the service was over the Pastor rather shook his head and said, "I am not sure about the wisdom of preaching that doctrine." "Why not?" I asked, "Is it not in the Book?" "Oh yes, it is in the Book." I said, "Do you not think the Holy Ghost can take care of His own Word? If it is in the Book for us to read, why should it not be there for us to preach?" But he feared that it would lead men to presume.

The following Sunday I preached the same sermon, that is, the same in argument, from my own pulpit, and I remember it was the first Sunday in the year. There was a man in the congregation that Sunday evening with whom the Lord had been dealing for many months, although I was unaware of it at the time. He was rather a noted man in the town; he was, in fact, rather notorious for his profanity. His wife was a member of the church of which I was Pastor. When I assumed the pastorate of the church she came to me and said she was concerned about her husband, and that she would like me to pray for his conversion. But she said, "I have promised the Lord that if He will save my husband I will go to another church with him." I asked her why she had promised the Lord she would go to another church, to which she replied that she was sure her husband would never become a Baptist, and she was so anxious that he should be converted that she was willing to go to any church with him.

I said to her, "You are a Baptist from conviction, are you not? You believe the position you have taken to be supported by the teaching of Scripture?" To all of which she replied in the affirmative. And then I said, "And yet you promise the Lord that if He will do for you the greatest thing He can possibly do, you will show your gratitude by setting aside your own convictions of truth?" She again insisted that she had made this pledge because she was sure her husband would never come to a Baptist church; but I told her it was not half so great a miracle for the Lord to make a Baptist of him as it would be to make a Christian of him. I told her that she ought not to bargain with the Lord, but ask Him outright to save her husband, and to leave the future with Him.

I promised her that I would join her in unceasing prayer that her husband might be saved. His case was laid upon my own heart, and for two or three years I never prayed without praying for that man. For more than a year he never crossed the threshold of a Baptist church—but we prayed on. Then one Sunday evening he walked in with his wife, and sat up on the right side of the church. I learned later that he came of himself, without her invitation. He missed a few Sundays, and then came again; and in a little while he came again, at last becoming a regular Sunday evening hearer. He was not an easy man to approach,—the sort of man you instinctively feel must be left entirely to the Lord.

But after about a year he began to come to the morning service occasionally, and at length became as regular in his attendance at the morning service as at the evening.

I had a Bible class on Friday evenings, and after a while I learned that in the summertime he was accustomed to sit outside on the steps where he could hear through the open window. Of course, he would not come in, for that would be too great a surrender! One evening about December, sometime before Christmas, he appeared at the prayer meeting in his wife's absence. I went to the door and managed to shake hands with him. I said, "I am glad to see you here to-night, Mr. So-and-So," and half apologetically he said, "My wife is away, and the house had to be represented you know. Good-night"—and was gone!

Much I now tell you I learned afterwards, but I am relating it to you now as an illustration of how this principle of election is used of the Spirit of God to bring souls to Christ.

On the first Sunday in the year, to which I have referred, when I preached the sermon which I had preached the preceding Sunday when away from home, I felt led to say in the course of my exposition that when the Good Shepherd goes out after His sheep He always finds them, that it was impossible for the human will to thwart Him, that He does really go after His sheep, as is said in the parable, "until he find it." I said something to this effect: When they will not come without, He sometimes sends His dogs after them, but He has His own way of compelling their submission to His will. Then I continued: There are some of you who have come here week after week, and month after month, and I know very well what you have said in your hearts—and perhaps even aloud to some of your friends. You have gone out of that door angry, and have vowed that you would never go to hear that preacher again—but you have come again and again, and here you are this evening. Why do you come? Because you cannot help it. You have come repeatedly after vowing that you would not come, because the Good Shepherd constrains you to come.

I told them I knew what I preached was enough to empty any church in the world if the Holy Spirit did not compel people to listen to it, that the gospel is the most unpalatable message imaginable unless and until it is energized by the power of the Holy Ghost. The gospel humbles men in the dust; it leaves them no room for boasting whatsoever. It is contrary to everything that is in human nature, and only the grace of the Holy Ghost can make the Word of God palatable to the natural man. I told my hearers that I was not surprised that they should dislike my message, nor did I wonder that they went from the church angry.

Then I said something to this effect: You think you come here to listen to a preacher, and you go away having a mental quarrel with him, saying, "How dare any man talk to me like that?" Then I explained it was open to them to dissent from my opinions, and that they might with impunity entirely reject my counsel; but that if I were the ambassador of the King of kings, charged with the delivery of His message, and if the message I delivered was His word, then, in rejecting it, they were dealing with God Himself. I said, "You may do what you like with me, but I beg of you to beware how you strive with your Maker." I think I quoted that text: "Woe unto him that striveth with his Maker! Let the potsherd strive with the potsherds of the earth. Shall the clay say to him that fashioneth it, What makest thou? or thy work, He hath no hands?"

I learned afterwards that that particular man did that night what he had done many times before: When he went home from church Sunday nights he was accustomed to pace the floor and scold his wife for having taken him to church. He would say, "He hit me all over to-night, and I will never go to hear him again." He would warn his wife not to dare to ask him to go—but she did not need to: When Sunday came he went to church of his own accord.

On this particular night of which I speak he said much the same thing, but late that night he left his home and went to a barn across the road where he kept his horses, and went up into the hayloft, and there in the small hours of the morning, alone with God, he yielded himself to the sovereign Saviour. The following Sunday he rose in the after-meeting and gave his testimony. Turning round in his seat he addressed the young men present, warning them not to delay their surrender to Christ. He was an illiterate man, coarse in his speech, but I give you his own words. He said, "Boys, I wrastled with the Lord for nigh on to forty years, but the first Sunday of this year He was one too many for me, and He downed me!"

That was his conception of what it was to be saved: utterly subdued, completely conquered by sovereign grace.

And that is the gospel. Not always is the conflict so open and manifest as in this case, but the principle is always the same. Every soul that is really saved is saved because God in sovereign mercy has willed to save him. You see, therefore, dear friends, that this gospel, or *this principle of the gospel, provides a firm foundation for our faith to rest upon.* Do you find it easy to believe people? As you grow older, does it become easier to trust people? I confess I do not. I have been betrayed a thousand times. Sometimes in my haste I have said, "I will never trust anybody again." In a moment of weakness I have appropriated the Psalmist's saying, exclaiming, not in my haste, but at my leisure, "All men are liars." Have you ever said that? I do not mean that all people are deliberately untruthful, and that no one is worthy of trust—far from that. But I do say that human flesh has its limitations, and even those who would be true sometimes find it impossible to fulfil their promises. The more experience of life I have, at all events, the more deeply do I feel the need of Someone Who can be trusted, of some one Person in this universe of change and uncertainty upon Whose word I can absolutely depend.

And there is such a person—but *there is only One!* There is not a second. But there is One, and He can never break His word. There is no power in the universe that can thwart His will; nor can anyone even retard the fulfilment of His promise. I give thanks to God that He has been pleased to unveil Himself to me in Jesus Christ as being absolutely sovereign in all realms. My soul reposes in Him. I trust Him absolutely. No matter who else may break his word, my gracious God will never fail in the fulfilment of His promise,—

> Firm as His throne, His promise stands,
>   And He can well secure
> What I've committed to His hands,
>   Till that decisive hour.

Others may fail in the execution of their programme, but He can never fail. He is God; He is over all God blessed for ever.

But lest you should think there is even the suggestion of cynicism in what I have said, let me make clear to you that there is one person whom I find it more difficult to trust than anybody else, and that is myself. Oh so often I have promised myself what I would do, and what I would try. I have planned to do so much that I later discovered to be impossible. As I look back upon my Christian course, I see so much of vacillation and irresolution in the record that I have to confess I should be afraid to say, "I am on my way to heaven, and I am determined to arrive." I *know* I am on my way to heaven. I know I *shall* arrive. But my confidence is in the will of Another, not in my own. And when I see so clearly that He has willed it from all eternity, that He chose me, and that by His sovereign and effectual grace He called me because He had ordained me to everlasting life, I can say, Though I cannot trust myself, or anybody else, I can trust God, and I can say with confidence that I know I am saved, and I am on my way to glory.

I want none of your Arminianism. I do not want you to put me on an elevator and tell me that there is a steel rope from the top to the bottom, but that it is connected to the cage by a little bit of hemp. I want it to be steel all the way through. If you could show me that my salvation is conditioned upon any human effort, upon any degree of human merit, howsoever infinitesimal it may be, then you would have destroyed my hope of ever reaching heaven. But when I learn that my glorious Lord is the Alpha and the Omega, the Beginning and the Ending, and that it is all of God, and all of grace, I can say, Hallelujah, I am saved with an everlasting salvation.

I have no time to elaborate this doctrine, to show *its application to the progress of grace in the soul,* to the soul's growth in grace and in the knowledge of Christ, except merely to point out that this "God of peace Who brought again from the dead that great Shepherd of the sheep, through the blood of the everlasting covenant, our Lord Jesus," will also make us perfect to do His will, "working in us that which is well pleasing in his sight, through Jesus Christ." Our hope for the future, as for the past and the present, is wholly in God. How can we put off the "old man," and put on the "new"? How can we obtain the victory over the world, the flesh, and the devil? How dare we hope that we shall ever be able to stand without fault before the throne of God? I know of only one ground of hope, and it is this:

> He wills that I should holy be,—
> Who can withstand His will?
> The counsel of His grace in me
> He surely will fulfil.

It may require more power in my case than in yours. There may be more of the old man to subdue in some of us than in others; but it makes no difference in the end however much there may be. Our circumstances may be as varied as our temperaments, but whatever our situation, however difficult our circumstances may be, it is written, "Greater is he that is in you than he that is in the world." It is the indwelling presence of the sovereign God and Saviour that gives us hope.

I would point out to you also that this doctrine should be *of great encouragement to us in the work of the Lord,* for, as in respect to the initial stages of the Christian life, this great doctrine of election makes it possible for us to believe and to keep on believing, so it makes the preaching of the gospel a worthy and useful occupation. I cannot persuade people to come to Christ—can you? I cannot tell you how often people have said to me, "Can you not do something for my husband?" Or in another case, perhaps, "Can you do something for my boy?" And sometimes it may be I am asked to do something for a daughter. But how impotent we are to deal with the hearts of men, to change their dispositions, to turn them from darkness to light, and from sin to holiness! It is a task that is entirely beyond human power.

What, therefore, is the use of my coming here to-night? What is the use of my preaching next Sunday? Of what profit can it be for you teachers to come before your classes Sunday and teach them the Word of God? Do you not know that all the people whom you are trying to teach are by nature wholly set against everything that you try to do for them? If you preach and teach the gospel your teaching opposes everything that is in them. We might therefore just as well give up unless we can be assured that God is with us, and that He will do what we have found impossible.

I have turned for comfort often to that word in Acts which records the appearance of the Lord to Paul when he was in Corinth, saying, "Be not afraid, but speak, and hold not thy peace: for I am with thee, and no man shall set on thee to hurt thee: for I have much people in this city." Paul did not know it,—at least he did not know who they were, but the Lord knew; and therefore He bade him go on with his testimony, saying, "I have much people in this city."

You see, therefore, that we have a foundation for our faith, as Christian workers, also, if God be for us, working with us. "Therefore, my beloved brethren, be ye steadfast, unmoveable always abounding in the work of the Lord, forasmuch as ye know that your labour is not in vain in the Lord."

*11*

# Clarence Edward Noble Macartney

*1879-1957*

Born in Northwood, Ohio, where his father pastored the Covenanter Church, Clarence Macartney received his education at the University of Wisconsin, Princeton University, and Princeton Theological Seminary. Ordained to the Presbyterian ministry in 1905, he served the First Presbyterian Church of Paterson, New Jersey (1905–1914), the Arch Street Church in Philadelphia (1914–1927), and First Presbyterian Church of Pittsburgh (1927–1953). He was moderator of the Presbyterian Church U.S.A. (1924–1925).

While Macartney was ministering at Arch Street in Philadelphia, Harry Emerson Fosdick preached his sermon "Shall the Fundamentalists Win?" and the fundamentalist-modernist controversy heated up. Macartney took his stand for the orthodox Christian faith and was careful to contact Fosdick to be certain he was quoting him accurately. "He was very decent and dignified in his attitude," Fosdick wrote in *The Living of These Days*. "While his theological position was in my judgment incredible, he was personally fair-minded and courteous" (p. 146). Macartney's response to Fosdick's published sermon was to preach two sermons under the title "Shall Unbelief Win?" and review the basics of the orthodox Christian faith as they related to Fosdick's views of fundamentalist theology.

126

A gifted pulpiteer, Macartney was at his best when preaching biographical sermons, and many of his sermon series have been published. He preached without notes before him and often without a pulpit between him and his congregation. He wrote more than fifty books in various fields of study, including American history, biography, and biblical preaching. Macartney never married. The autobiography of Clarence Macartney was titled *The Making of a Minister*, published by Channel Press in 1961.

# While He Is Near

Seek ye the LORD while he may be found, call ye upon him
while he is near.

Isaiah 55:6

One of the old Saxon kings set out with an army to put down a
rebellion in a distant province of his kingdom. When the insur-
rection had been quelled and the army of the rebels defeated,
the king placed a candle over the archway of his castle where he
had his headquarters and, lighting the candle, announced
through a herald to all those who had been in rebellion against
him that all who surrendered and took the oath of loyalty while
the candle was burning would be spared. The king offered them
his clemency and mercy, but the offer was limited to the life of
that candle.

Every great offer of life and of time has its candle limitations.
This is true of the offer of fortune and prosperity, or knowledge,
or health, or affection. There is a limited period of time in which
to make use of their offer and their opportunity. This is true most
of all of the greatest offer ever made to man, the offer of eternal
life through Jesus Christ, God's Son.

The fifty-fifth chapter of Isaiah is one of the great invitation
chapters of the Bible. It rings with that favorite word of God,
"Ho, every one that thirsteth, come ye to the waters." This is a
word which resounds in the Bible from the book of Genesis to
the book of Revelation. When Noah had finished the ark, God
said to him, "Come . . . into the ark." In the great parable of the
supper Jesus represents God as saying to men, "Come, for all
things are now ready." Christ himself in unforgettable music said,

"Come unto me, all ye that labor and are heavy laden." This word "come" sounds through all the history and narrative and prophecy and warning and appeal and judgment and apocalypse of the Bible. It is the word that is written over the gates of heaven in letters of light to greet our pilgrim feet. And with this word, the divine revelation comes to a conclusion when John hears the voice of the angel using almost the very language of Isaiah, and saying, "The Spirit and the bride say, Come. . . . And let him that is athirst come. And whosoever will, let him take the water of life freely."

### Seek Ye the Lord

To seek the Lord is life's great, but greatly neglected, business. Men give their time and energy and strength and enthusiasm to other things and other quests, things which in the end fail and betray and disappoint the soul. The divine love here wonders at the way men seek something else rather than God. Inviting the soul to come to the waters and drink of the water of life, divine love says, "Wherefore, do ye spend money for that which is not bread and your labor which satisfieth not?"

But God never disappoints. The bread that he offers is real bread and the water that he offers is the water of life. Cardinal Wolsey in his dying hour exclaimed,

> Had I but served my God with half the zeal
> I served my king, he would not in mine age
> Have left me naked to mine enemies.

But where and when did you ever hear of a man who in the time of his defeat or overthrow or death regretted the time and search he had given to find God, or who said, "If I had only served myself as I have served my God, I would not now be left naked to my foes"? God made the soul, and the soul was made for God. And the soul will never be satisfied—with the true and deep and abiding satisfaction—with anything but God. The great end of life is to know God and to be known of him, and God can be found. The Bible rings with a thousand promises that if we seek God we shall find him, and Christian history is bright with the illuminated letters of believers who testified that they tasted and found that God was good.

### How to Seek the Lord

The way to seek God is charted in the Bible and in the history of believing souls. The roads that lead to God are clearly and unmistakably marked and "he that runs may read."

The Bible is one place where we seek God. It was given for that purpose. It is a lamp unto our feet and a light unto our path. How many men have found in the pages of the Bible the path that leads away from sin and brings the soul to God! The Bible speaks to the soul of man, for it was made for the soul, and the entrance of God's word giveth light. Jesus said, "Search the scriptures; for in them ye think ye have eternal life: and they are they which testify of me." The Bible is a light which lights the way to God.

The Waldensian preachers sometimes traveled about as merchants and dealt in jewels and precious stones as a way of obtaining access to the families of the nobility. When they had disposed of their rings and trinkets and were asked if they had nothing more to sell, they answered, "Yes, we have jewels still more precious than any you have seen. We will be glad to show you these also if you will promise not to betray us to the clergy. We have here a precious stone so brilliant that by its light a man may see God. And another which radiates such a fire that it enkindles the love of God in the heart of its possessor." Then, unwrapping their bundle, they brought out a Bible. It is indeed the most precious of all precious stones, for by its light a man sees God and can find God. That is the reason—and the only reason—for reading the Bible. That is why it is profitable and necessary every day to read the sacred page.

We can find God by prayer. God stands by his promise that they who seek him in prayer will find him. "Call upon me. . . . I will deliver thee." Promise after promise flashes on page after page of the Bible that if we seek God we shall find him, and that if we ask it shall be given unto us. Not that we get everything for which we ask, for that would often not be good for us, but that if we seek God in prayer we shall find his will for us and rejoice in it. How earnestly the prophets and the apostles, Abraham, Moses, Elijah, Samuel, Joshua, and David in his fall, sought God and found him. How earnestly Christ sought God in prayer, in the desert place before it was day, on the mountaintop, in the Garden of Gethsemane, and in the last hour on the cross. If God is not real to you, how earnestly have you sought him in prayer?

God is to be sought by repentance. To seek him in the Bible, to seek him in prayer, will not avail unless we seek him also with repentance. "Seek ye the Lord while he may be found, call upon him while he is near." Then comes this word about repentance—"Let the wicked forsake his way, and the unrighteous man his thoughts: and let him return unto the Lord, and he will have mercy upon him; and to our God, for he will abundantly pardon."

There is no sincere seeking after God without repentance, for repentance is the evidence that the soul wants God more than the things of this world. For thirty years, perhaps, Jacob had failed to keep his vow to go to Bethel and worship, the vow that he had made when in his dream he saw the ladder reaching unto heaven and the angels of God ascending and descending. Now, with his family sunk in idolatry, Jacob had settled down in the lush pastures of Shechem, more interested apparently in his flocks and herds than in seeking God or keeping the vow that he had made so many years before. Then the voice of God spoke to Jacob, "Go up to Bethel, and dwell there." And Jacob arose and went to Bethel. But before he made that journey he destroyed and buried the idols which his family had accumulated. That was the proof that he was in earnest when he went to seek God at Bethel, and when he came to Bethel in repentance God appeared unto him again and blessed him. There is no doubt that one reason for the little knowledge of God that some people have and the little enjoyment of God which they enjoy is that they do not truly seek him with repentance, that their religious profession and their Christian associations do not mean a change, an abandonment, a relinquishment, in their lives.

### When to Seek the Lord

"Seek ye the Lord while he may be found." This gracious and tender invitation has an earnest and solemn note in it. God is to be sought after and found, not next week, nor next year, but today, while he is near, and while he may be found.

But is God not always near? Is he not closer than breathing? Is he not, as Paul said on Mars' Hill, "not far from every one of us"? In his providence and government God is always near to us. But there are times when God is near to us in grace, in our opportunity to reach out after God, to find him and know him as our Saviour. There is a sense in which God cannot always be found, when he is not always near. Because this life is the time for seeking him, and because our hearts change, there are times when we can and will seek after God, and there are times when we have no interest in God.

God is near to the soul in time of sickness. Sickness teaches us our weakness, our littleness, our dependence upon God. After he had preached for many years, Thomas Chalmers, the great Scottish preacher, had an illness that lifted him into a higher sphere and he soared aloft. God has private doors by which he enters men's lives, and one of those doors is sickness. How quickly the sky and the winds of life can change! Yesterday all was bright and fair and prosperous; today you are brought low. All your strength is spent and you learn how weak man is and how dependent upon God. In the time of sickness we make a new appraisal of life. How poor are some of the things that we have sought after, how rich the things we have neglected! Then we realize our shortcomings and our failures, the things we would like to change if we get well again, the things we will not do again that we have been doing, the things which we have left undone and which now we will do. God then is near. Call on him!

God is near in the time of sorrow. Sorrow is one of God's greatest ministers. Life without sorrow would be like earth without rain or dew. As in the beautiful figure of Isaiah, the rain cometh down from heaven and the snow, and causeth the earth to bring forth and bud, that it may give seed to the sower and bread to the eater, so is the rain of sorrow to the soil of life if we make use of it. What a preacher sorrow is! What chords it strikes! Then, for a time at least, the heart is softened, affections are purified, defiling passions spread their dark wings and depart, hatreds expire, and the soul moves Godward.

In my office as a minister it is my privilege to meet many souls in a time of sorrow, and I have often thought, if only now the soul would take this flood tide and sail on it! If only now, while it has the light, it would walk toward God, for now he can be found, now he is near! But so often the precious moment is lost, the rain of heaven is wasted, and the soul goes back to its old ways and its old life.

God is near in conscience. Conscience is God's faithful oracle in the heart of man. As long as conscience can be troubled, there is the hope of spiritual health. And how often, and in how many ways, conscience speaks to our souls. When, after the Fall, the man and the woman heard the voice of God walking in the garden, they were afraid, and hid themselves among the trees. What was it that made them afraid when God was near in the garden? It was conscience. When the prophet Nathan, with his matchless parable of the ewe lamb of the poor man slaughtered to feed the rich man's guest, awakened the conscience of David, he knew that God was near and sought him and his mercy in penitence and in prayer. When Herod heard of the preaching of Jesus and dismissed all other accounts and theories as to Jesus, and said, "It is John, whom I beheaded: he is risen from the dead," it was conscience that was speaking within him.

There are men in the Bible who are like ships which emerge for a moment out of the mist into the sunlight and then again disappear into the mist and fog. I mean men like Herod, when he heard John preach; and Pilate, when Jesus stood before him; and Felix and King Agrippa, when Paul preached to them—men who had a special moment of divine grace, a truce of God, as it were, when their conscience was aroused, when they might have chosen Christ and eternal life, but turned away and disappeared into the darkness. They did not seek God while he could be found or call upon him while he was near. I speak now as God's minister to that conscience, to that soul within you. You can hear, and you do hear, the voice of God. God offers you his grace, his pardon, his amazing love. What will you do with it? By so many ways, by so many providences—pain, sorrow, failure, joy, trouble, and tribulation—God draws nigh to your soul. "In an acceptable time have I heard thee."

But God is not always near. In the first place, because the disposition of the heart and the life changes. There is many a man, a stranger to Christ today, who can look back, if he is willing, to some hour or some experience in his life when he knew that God was near and that he was near to God, and he has never been that near again. I once received into the church at a communion service a man over eighty years of age. He came to church for a time and then dropped out and went back to his old life. The explanation undoubtedly was this: He told me that when he was a youth in a boys' school in New England, the school was swept by a revival, and many of the boys were converted and took Christ for time and eternity. The voice of God spoke to him too and urged him to take Christ as his Saviour, but he deliberately set himself against yielding and refused the call of God's Holy Spirit. God was near to him then, and never that near again. That was his hour. God said then, "Today! Now!" but he said, "Tomorrow!" And tomorrow never came.

This is the only life in which God draws nigh to us as our Saviour, and the only life in which we can choose him as a Saviour. Men have asked the question: If a soul refuses the call of God in this life, and remains impenitent even unto death, is it not possible that in the life after death he should have another offer of salvation, and there, under new environment and new circumstances, and with a new vision of Christ, should repent and believe and be eternally saved? All that we can answer is that there is no indication or intimation of that in the Scriptures. If that were so, then it would leave without meaning all the urgings and pleadings of Christ and the apostles and the Holy Spirit to choose God in this life. It would leave without meaning that large number of the parables of Jesus which deal with men in their relations to God and time and eternity, and leave man at death in his fixed and finished destiny.

Even if the gospel were preached to a man in the life to come, what possible forces or influences could work on him there and persuade him to choose God as his Saviour, if in this life he heard the same gospel and refused to do so? What could be clearer, as an answer to that question, than those words of Jesus at the end of his great parable, when he said, "If they hear not Moses and the prophets, neither will they be persuaded, though one rose from the dead." Realizing that his own unhappy destiny was fixed and unchangeable, the rich man besought Abraham to send someone from the world of the dead to preach to his five brothers so that they might repent in time and escape the fate that had befallen him. Abraham reminded him that they had Moses and the prophets to listen to all their life, but he answered, "Nay, father Abraham, but if one went unto them from the dead, they will repent." It was as if he had said: "I had Moses and the prophets, but I paid no attention to them; but if someone had come from the dead and preached to me, I would have repented." But Abraham answered, and, of course, it is Christ who is speaking: "If they hear not Moses and the prophets, neither will they be persuaded, though one rose from the dead." In other words, there are no conceivable influences and forces working in the future life which could persuade a man to believe in Christ if he will not believe on him in this life.

"Seek ye the LORD while he may be found, call upon him while he is near." The only life in which to seek God is this life, and in this life there are times of grace and special opportunity when God in his providence speaks to our soul, and we know and feel that he is near, and that we can and ought to choose him. Those special opportunities, those special moments, those special hours, have their end, and time itself has its end, when, as Christ said, "And the door was shut." But now the door is open. Now the precious light of divine grace shines upon your path. While ye have the light, walk in it. "Ho, everyone that thirsteth, come ye to the waters." "The Spirit and the bride say, Come. . . . And let him that is athirst come. And whosoever will, let him take the water of life freely." "Seek ye the LORD while he may be found, call upon him while he is near."

# Frank William Boreham

*1871–1959*

The author of more than sixty books of sermons and essays, Frank William Boreham was once introduced at a pastors' conference as "the man whose books are in all our libraries and whose illustrations are in all our sermons." He was the last student personally selected by Charles Spurgeon to attend his Pastors College.

Boreham graduated in 1894 and was immediately commissioned to go to New Zealand to pastor the Mosgiel Baptist Church. He continued there until 1906 when he moved to the Hobart Tabernacle in Hobart, Tasmania; and in 1916 he moved to Melbourne.

An omnivorous reader, especially of biography and autobiography, Boreham determined to read a book a week. He digested what he read and used it in the pulpit or in the essays that made his name famous.

On May 11, 1911, while ministering in Hobart, Boreham launched the biweekly sermon series on "the texts that made history," beginning with "Martin Luther's Text" (Romans 1:17). The series continued for 125 Sunday evenings and is embodied in five valuable volumes that have been reprinted by Kregel.

Boreham and his wife returned to England in 1928 where he began a preaching tour that drew thousands to hear him, not only in England but also in Canada and the United States. The

Borehams returned to Australia where he served as visiting pastor in several churches, preached widely, and continued to write.

Boreham's autobiography is called *My Pilgrimage* (reprint edition, Judson Press, 1950), and the official biography is *The Story of F. W. Boreham* by T. Howard Crago (Marshall, Morgan and Scott, 1961).

# Hudson Taylor's Text

John 19:30

*I*

The day on which James Hudson Taylor—then a boy in his teens—found himself confronted by that tremendous text was, as he himself testified in old age, "a day that he could never forget." It is a day that China can never forget; a day that the world can never forget. It was a holiday; everybody was away from home; and the boy found time hanging heavily upon his hands. In an aimless way he wandered, during the afternoon, into his father's library, and poked about among the shelves. "I tried," he says, "to find some book with which to while away the leaden hours. Nothing attracting me, I turned over a basket of pamphlets and selected from among them a tract that looked interesting. I knew that it would have a story at the commencement and moral at the close; but I promised myself that I would enjoy the story and leave the rest. It would be easy to put away the tract as soon as it should seem prosy." He scampers off to the stableloft, throws himself on the hay, and plunges into the book. He is captivated by the narrative, and finds it impossible to drop the book when the story comes to an end. He reads on and on. He is rewarded by one great golden word whose significance he has never before discovered: *"The Finished Work of Christ!"* The theme entrances him; and at last he only rises from his bed in the soft hay that he may kneel on the hard floor of the loft and surrender his young life to the Saviour who had surrendered everything for him. If, he asked himself, as he lay upon the hay, if the whole work was finished, and the whole debt paid upon the Cross, what is there left for me to do? "And then," he tells us, "there dawned upon me the joyous conviction that there was nothing in the world to be done but to fall upon my knees, accept the Saviour and praise Him for evermore."

*"It is finished!"*

*"When Jesus, therefore, had received the vinegar he said, 'It is finished!' and He bowed His head and gave up the ghost."*

*"Then there dawned upon me the joyous conviction that, since the whole work was finished and the whole debt paid upon the Cross, there was nothing for me to do but to fall upon my knees, accept the Saviour and praise Him for evermore!"*

## II

*"It is finished!"*

It is really one word: the greatest word ever uttered; we must examine it for a moment as a lapidary examines under a powerful glass a rare and costly gem.

It was a *farmer's* word. When, into his herd, there was born an animal so beautiful and shapely that it seemed absolutely destitute of faults and defects, the farmer gazed upon the creature with proud, delighted eyes. *"Tetelestai!"* he said, *"tetelestai!"*

It was an *artist's* word. When the painter or the sculptor had put the last finishing touches to the vivid landscape or the marble bust, he would stand back a few feet to admire his masterpiece, and, seeing in it nothing that called for correction or improvement, would murmur fondly, *"Tetelestai! tetelestai!"*

It was a *priestly* word. When some devout worshiper, overflowing with gratitude for mercies shown him, brought to the temple a lamb without spot or blemish, the pride of the whole flock, the priest, more accustomed to seeing the blind and defective animals led to the altar, would look admiringly upon the pretty creature. *"Tetelestai!"* he would say, *"tetelestai!"*

And when, in the fullness of time, the Lamb of God offered Himself on the altar of the ages, He rejoiced with a joy so triumphant that it bore down all His anguish before it. The sacrifice was stainless, perfect, finished! *"He cried with a loud voice Tetelestai! and gave up the ghost."*

This divine self-satisfaction appears only twice, once in each Testament. When He completed the work of Creation, He looked upon it and said that it was very good; when He completed the work of Redemption He cried with a loud voice *Tetelestai!* It means exactly the same thing.

*III*

The joy of finishing and of finishing well! How passionately good men have coveted for themselves that ecstasy! I think of those pathetic entries in Livingstone's journal. "Oh, to finish my work!" he writes again and again. He is haunted by the vision of the unseen waters, the fountains of the Nile. Will he live to discover them? "Oh, to finish!" he cries; "if only I could finish my work!" I think of Henry Buckle, the author of the *History of Civilization*. He is overtaken by fever at Nazareth and dies at Damascus. In his delirium he raves continually about his book, his still unfinished book. "Oh, to finish my book!" And with the words "My book! my book!" upon his burning lips, his spirit slips away. I think of Henry Martyn sitting amidst the delicious and fragrant shades of a Persian garden, weeping at having to leave the work that he seemed to have only just begun. I think of Doré taking a sad farewell of his unfinished *Vale of Tears;* of Dickens tearing himself from the manuscript that he knew would never be completed; of Macaulay looking with wistful and longing eyes at the *History* and *The Armada* that must for ever stand as "fragments"; and of a host besides. Life is often represented by a broken column in the churchyard. Men long, but long in vain, for the priceless privilege of finishing their work.

*IV*

The joy of finishing and of finishing well! There is no joy on earth comparable to this. Who is there that has not read a dozen times the immortal postscript that Gibbon added to his *Decline and Fall?* He describes the tumult of emotion with which, after twenty years of closest application, he wrote the last line of the last chapter of the last volume of his masterpiece. It was a glorious summer's night at Lausanne. "After laying down my pen," he says, "I took several turns in a covered walk of acacias which commands a prospect of the country, the lake and the mountains. The air was temperate, the sky was serene, the silver orb of the moon was reflected from the waters, and all nature was silent." It was the greatest moment of his life. We recall, too, the similar experience of Sir Archibald Alison. "As I approached the closing sentence of my *History of the Empire,*" he says, "I went up to Mrs. Alison to call her down to witness the conclusion, and she saw the last words of the work written, and signed her name on the margin. It would be affectation to conceal the deep emotion that I felt at this event." Or think of the last hours of Venerable Bede. Living away back in the early dawn of our English story—twelve centuries ago—the old man had set himself to translate the Gospel of John into our native speech. Cuthbert, one of his young disciples, has bequeathed to us the touching record.

As the work approached completion, he says, death drew on apace. The aged scholar was racked with pain; sleep forsook him; he could scarcely breathe. The young man who wrote at his dictation implored him to desist. But he would not rest. They came at length to the final chapter; could he possibly live till it was done?

"And now, dear master," exclaimed the young scribe tremblingly, "only one sentence remains!" He read the words and the sinking man feebly recited the English equivalents.

"It is finished, dear master!" cried the youth excitedly.

*"Ay, it is finished!"* echoed the dying saint; "lift me up, place me at that window of my cell at which I have so often prayed to God. Now glory be to the Father and to the Son and to the Holy Ghost!" And, with these triumphant words, the beautiful spirit passed to its rest and its reward.

## V

In his own narrative of his conversion, Hudson Taylor quotes James Proctor's well-known hymn—the hymn that, in one of his essays, Froude criticizes so severely:

> Nothing either great or small,
> Nothing, sinner, no;
> Jesus did it, did it all,
> Long, long ago.

> *"It is Finished!"* yes, indeed,
> Finished every jot;
> Sinner, this is all you need;
> Tell me, is it not?

> Cast your deadly doing down,
> Down at Jesus' feet;
> Stand in Him, in Him alone,
> Gloriously complete.

Froude maintains that these verses are immoral. It is only by "doing," he argues, that the work of the world can ever get done. And if you describe "doing" as "deadly" you set a premium upon indolence and lessen the probabilities of attainment. The best answer to Froude's plausible contention is the *Life of Hudson Taylor*. Hudson Taylor became convinced, as a boy, that "the whole work was finished and the whole debt paid." "There is nothing for me to do," he says, "but to fall down on my knees and accept the Saviour." The chapter in his biography that tells of this spiritual crisis is entitled "The Finished Work of Christ," and it is headed by the quotation:

Upon a life I did not live,
Upon a death I did not die,
Another's life, Another's death
I stake my whole eternity.

And, as I have said, the very words that Froude so bitterly condemns are quoted by Hudson Taylor as a reflection of his own experience. And the result? The result is that Hudson Taylor became one of the most prodigious toilers of all time. So far from his trust in "The Finished Work of Christ" inclining him to indolence, he felt that he must toil most terribly to make so perfect a Saviour known to the whole wide world. There lies on my desk a Birthday Book which I very highly value. It was given me at the docks by Mr. Thomas Spurgeon as I was leaving England. If you open it at the twenty-first of May you will find these words: *"'Simply to Thy Cross I cling' is but half of the Gospel. No one is really clinging to the Cross who is not at the same time faithfully following Christ and doing whatsoever He commands";* and against those words of Dr. J. R. Miller's in my Birthday Book, you may see the autograph of *J. Hudson Taylor.* He was our guest at the Mosgiel Manse when he set his signature to those striking and significant sentences.

## VI

*"We Build Like Giants; We Finish Like Jewelers!"*—so the old Egyptians wrote over the portals of their palaces and temples. I like to think that the most gigantic task ever attempted on this planet—the work of the world's redemption—was finished with a precision and a nicety that no jeweler could rival.

*"It is finished!"* He cried from the Cross.

*"Tetelestai! Tetelestai!"*

When He looked upon His work in Creation and saw that it was good, He placed it beyond the power of man to improve upon it.

To gild refined gold, to paint the lily,
To throw a perfume on the violet,
To smooth the ice, or add another hue
Unto the rainbow, or with taper-light
To seek the beauteous eye of heaven to garnish,
Is wasteful and ridiculous excess.

And, similarly, when He looked upon His work in Redemption and cried triumphantly *"Tetelestai,"* He placed it beyond the power of any man to add to it.

There are times when any addition is a subtraction. Some years ago, White House at Washington—the residence of the American Presidents—

was in the hands of the painters and decorators. Two large entrance doors had been painted to represent black walnut. The contractor ordered his men to scrape and clean them in readiness for repainting, and they set to work. But when their knives penetrated to the solid timber, they discovered to their astonishment that it was heavy mahogany of a most exquisite natural grain! The work of that earlier decorator, so far from adding to the beauty of the timber, had only served to conceal its essential and inherent glory. It is easy enough to add to the wonders of Creation or of Redemption; but you can never add without subtracting. *"It is finished!"*

## VII

Many years ago, Ebenezer Wooton, an earnest but eccentric evangelist, was conducting a series of summer evening services on the village green at Lidford Brook. The last meeting had been held; the crowd was melting slowly away; and the evangelist was engaged in taking down the marquee. All at once a young fellow approached him and asked, casually rather than earnestly, "Mr. Wooton, what must *I* do to be saved?" The preacher took the measure of his man.

"Too late!" he said, in a matter of fact kind of way, glancing up from a somewhat obstinate tentpeg with which he was struggling. "Too late, my friend, too late!" The young fellow was startled.

"Oh, don't say that, Mr. Wooton!" he pleaded, a new note coming into his voice. "Surely it isn't too late just because the meetings are over?"

"Yes, my friend," exclaimed the evangelist, dropping the cord in his hand, straightening himself up, and looking right into the face of his questioner, "It's too late! You want to know what you must *do* to be saved, and I tell you that you're hundreds of years too late! The work of salvation is done, completed, *finished!* It was finished on the Cross; Jesus said so with the last breath that He drew! What more do you want?"

And, then and there, it dawned upon the now earnest inquirer on the village green as, at about the same time, it dawned upon young Hudson Taylor in the hay-loft, that *"since the whole work was finished and the whole debt paid upon the Cross, there was nothing for him to do but to fall upon his knees and accept the Saviour."* And there, under the elms, the sentinel stars witnessing the great transaction, he kneeled in glad thanksgiving and rested his soul for time and for eternity on "the Finished Work of Christ."

## VIII

"The Finished Work of Christ!"
"Tetelestai! Tetelestai!"
"It is finished!"

It is not a sigh of relief at having reached the end of things. It is the unutterable joy of the artist who, putting the last touches to the picture that has engrossed him for so long, sees in it the realization of all his dreams and can nowhere find room for improvement. Only once in the world's history did a finishing touch bring a work to absolute perfection; and on that day of days a single flaw would have shattered the hope of the ages.

*13*

# Donald Grey Barnhouse

*1895-1960*

You had no doubt who the preacher was when from your radio speaker you heard, "This is *The Bible Study Hour* from Philadelphia, Pennsylvania." It was Donald Grey Barnhouse, distinguished pastor of Tenth Presbyterian Church (1927–1960), author, conference speaker, editor of *Revelation* magazine, which later became *Eternity,* and one of the American church's greatest exponents of Reformed theology blended with premillennial dispensationalism. His speaking was precise and his approach somewhat dogmatic and he usually opened his prayers with "Through the Lord Jesus Christ we come unto Thee, our Father and our God, and in the Holy Spirit. . . ."

Barnhouse was educated at the Bible Institute of Los Angeles (1913–1915), Princeton Theological Seminary (1915–1917), and Eastern Baptist Theological Seminary (1926–1927). After serving in the army in World War I, he ministered in Europe as a missionary and a pastor from 1919 to 1925.

For years through *The Bible Study Hour,* Barnhouse taught "the whole Bible using the Epistle to the Romans as the point of departure," an approach he had used when he began his ministry at Tenth Presbyterian Church. His ten-volume commentary on Romans, published by Eerdmans, grew out of this intensive series. Barnhouse was a master of illustrative material and boasted that he could make an illustration out of anything. He traveled widely in Bible teaching ministry, spoke often at British Keswick, and conducted large Bible classes in key cities in the United States.

Barnhouse published a number of books on biblical themes, including *The Invisible War; Teaching the Word of Truth; His Own Received Him Not, BUT—; Guaranteed Deposits;* and *God's Methods for Holy Living.*

# Justification without a Cause

Being justified freely by his grace through the redemption that
is in Christ Jesus.

Romans 3:24

Though all sinned and are falling short of the glory of God, the
Bible tells us that the Lord Jesus Christ brought us back to glory.
The glory which man lost in Adam, and which he could never
regain by his own efforts, the Lord Jesus Christ secured and
brought to us by His redemptive death. "For it became him, for
whom are all things, and by whom are all things, in bringing
many sons into glory, to make the author of their salvation perfect through sufferings" (Heb. 2:10, margin).

How were we brought back to the glory which had been lost
to us forever so far as any worth in ourselves was concerned? Our
text in the third of Romans now sets it forth: "Being justified
freely by his grace through the redemption that is in Christ Jesus"
(Rom. 3:24).

When man first sinned, God had no way of testing him other
than His own perfect glory. Man, of course, had come short of that
glory, and there was nothing to do but declare him dead in trespasses and sins and to evict him from the presence of God. But in
the same way that God declared man to be a sinner, falling short
of His glory, so God declares a man righteous, justifying him freely
by His grace through the redemption that is in Christ Jesus.

## Definitions

We have now come to the point in our study where we must
set forth the true meaning of the term *justify,* and the cognate

146

words *justification, just,* and *justifier.* I turn to the dictionary and am not at all satisfied with the definition that is given there. Even the Oxford English Dictionary falls short of the Biblical meaning when it defines the verb "justify" in the following terms: "To absolve, acquit, exculpate; especially in theology, to declare free from the penalty of sin on the ground of Christ's righteousness, or to make inherently righteous by the infusion of grace." There is an approach to the truth but there is far more involved in the idea. Perhaps we can come to a truer meaning if we proceed, as a doctor would in making a diagnosis, by a process of elimination. Let us find some of the things that the term does not mean, and then we will be able to establish better what is the true meaning.

First of all, the verb *justify* is not a mere synonym for forgiveness. It includes forgiveness but it also includes so much more that to speak of justification in terms of forgiveness only is to lose the true sense of the word. Take, for example, a convict who has committed a great crime. The man against whom the crime was committed might freely forgive the criminal for the wrong that had been done, but that would not change his status before the law. He would still be a criminal, guilty in every way. Forgiveness does not take away guilt. Nor does the word mean nothing more than pardon. The law itself might pardon the criminal, but thenceforward he is nothing more than a pardoned criminal. But justification is far more than this.

When we consider God's justifying the ungodly, it is necessary that we think clearly in order not to fall into similar errors. We must not look upon justification as a making up of the deficit that is owed by man. For example, if we should say, arbitrarily, that each man owed to God one hundred per cent, and that one man had performed fifty per cent and another thirty and another twenty, we must never think of God making up the lack and giving the first man fifty, the second man seventy and the third man eighty in order to total, in each case, the one hundred per cent that was demanded by God. God rejects with a curse all that man has done and gives him a new and different one hundred per cent in each case.

### No Time Element

Nor must we think of justification in terms of the life span of the individual. There have been those who wrongly thought that God applies forgiveness to an individual from the time of his birth up to the time of his salvation. If, for example, a young man is twenty when he trusts in Christ, there are those who believe that his sin from birth to the age of twenty is removed. If such were the case, it would constitute one of the strongest arguments for delaying salvation. The man who was able "to call his shots well" could postpone accepting Christ till the latest possible moment in his life, and thus have the grace of God for the longest period of his sinful existence. There have been some foolish enough to claim that such a principle is true.

The Bible teaches, of course, that, whatever justification is, it happens to a man instantaneously, and that it covers his whole being in the totality of his existence. When a man is justified, he is accepted in his person and being in all of his life, past, present, and future.

## Cleansing

Perhaps I can make the matter clearer by a simple story. When I was still in my teens in California, I was invited to speak on a certain occasion at a county Christian Endeavor convention some distance from my home. The home where I was to be entertained was in a new subdivision; and, though the sidewalk had been laid, the street was not yet paved. As I walked toward the house, I noticed in front a large puddle of water that covered a good portion of the street. It had evidently been there for days for there were indications that small boys had been playing around its edges, perhaps wading in it, and there was the wreck of a small wooden boat lying near it.

My hostess had a small boy, four or five years of age, dressed in clean clothes, who was pleading with his mother to allow him to go outside to play. She finally was persuaded by him and gave him permission to go out on the front steps only, with strict warning that he was not to go down the front walk to the gate or street. As I sat by the window reading, I noticed the conduct of the boy. First he went to the bottom step and began to play. After a while he left the step and went two or three paces down the walk. Then he came back to the step and played for a few minutes, leaving again to go down the walk five or ten steps. He then returned once more to play on the steps. A moment later, he went all the way down to the gate and climbed up on its lower bar. He then returned to the steps to play for a brief period. Once more he went down to the gate, and this time he opened it and swung on it. He then returned to the steps and seemed to give up the idea of any further excursion. He played so long on the steps that I became engrossed in my reading and did not look out the window to watch his movements. Suddenly there was an outcry from the boy. He had fallen from the sidewalk into the mud puddle. Covered with mud and water, he came crying toward the gate. His mother, who had heard him as soon as I, met him at the gate. She took him by the hand and led him firmly around toward the back of the house. He was whimpering: "Don't whip me; don't whip me, mama." As they passed the window, I heard his mother say: "Stop your crying. I forgive you." When his mother told him that he was forgiven, his crying stopped. Forgiveness for him meant but one thing:

remission of penalty. He would not receive the thrashing he deserved. But forgiveness meant much more to the mother. She stripped the dirty clothes from him, and I heard unmistakable sounds of a boy being scrubbed. She put fresh clothes on him, and in a few minutes brought him into the room where I was reading, sat him firmly down on a chair and said, "Now you sit there and talk to Mr. Barnhouse."

The application is simple. We are all sinners. By virtue of the grace of Christ, God first pronounces that we are forgiven. To us that may mean remission of penalty: We shall not go to the lake of fire which we deserve by virtue of our sin. But to God, because His nature is grace, it means much more. The blood of Jesus Christ cleanses us so that we stand before Him in Christ dressed in Christ's righteousness. But even that is not all.

### Declared Righteous

We have seen that man is not merely a forgiven criminal still suffering for his crime; and we have seen that man is not merely a pardoned criminal, forgiven of the guilt and of the penalty. There is more. Our text declares that the sinner is justified: that is, he is forgiven, pardoned, and declared to be essentially righteous. This is far more than being declared innocent. God does not proclaim that the sinner is innocent. It would have been wonderful if fallen men had been restored to the position of Adam before the fall, yet how precarious would have been that state for the first parents were not able to maintain it. But when we are justified we are lifted much higher than Adam. We are made higher than the angels through Christ who was made lower than the angels (Heb. 2:7). We are made higher than the seraphs and the cherubs. We are made higher than Lucifer was before he became Satan. We are counted as one in Christ, and are given the position of sons with the Father, and are destined to share the government of the universe with the Creator. Righteousness now belongs to the justified one even as it belongs to God, for we have been made partakers of the divine nature (2 Peter 1:4), and are a new creation (2 Cor. 5:17). This does not mean that we are sinless, but it does mean that we have been declared righteous.

This means that the sinner can look away from himself and look to the cross of the Lord Jesus Christ. We are not for a moment teaching that a man can believe and then do as he pleases, for though we believe in eternal security, we do not believe in eternal presumption. But we *are* insisting that there is only one meaning to justification in the sight of the living God and in the light of His revealed Word. Therefore, let no man consider his *feelings,* but let him *trust* in the Word of God about the cross of the Lord Jesus Christ.

## Freely

All of this change takes place, as the text says, "freely," and "by his grace." The word translated *freely* carries with it a rich connotation. It is found nine times in the New Testament and is revealed to man "without price, without return, without cause." It is the word that is twice used in the well known verse, "Freely ye have received, freely give" (Matt. 10:8). It is the word that is twice used at the end of the Bible to tell all men that they may take of the water of life freely (Rev. 21:6; 22:17).

But the richest meaning is to be found in a verse that speaks of the manner in which men hated Christ when He was here on earth. In the upper room when the Lord Jesus talked about the hatred which the world would bear to the believer, because the world already bore the same hatred to Him, He concludes the passage with the word: "This cometh to pass, that the word might be fulfilled which was written in their law, They hated me without a cause" (John 15:25). The translators have used three English words— *without a cause*—to translate the one Greek word. What was the manner of the hatred of men toward Christ? The answer is: "without a cause." That is the meaning of our word here. "Freely ye have received, freely give," could be translated, "Ye have received without any remuneration; give without any remuneration." Our text would then read: "Being justified without a cause in you."

When we understand this, we can see the true basis of our salvation. There was absolutely nothing within man that could recommend him to God. God did not sit in Heaven and look down upon this earth until He had found something in some men that recommended them to Him. He gave salvation to men who deserved Hell. There will not be one person in Heaven who deserved Heaven except the Lord Jesus Christ. He is the only one who merited Heaven. But an innumerable company who merited Hell are going to be in Heaven simply because the grace of God decided that they should be there.

## Not a Reward

We must even move away from the heresy that thinks that salvation is a reward for faith. It is false to conceive of God as looking over the population of earth with a sort of frustrated longing, saying, "O, where in humanity is another man in whom I can find a bit of faith which I can reward with salvation?" Such is not the Biblical picture of God. Rather do we see God proceeding in the majesty of His eternal Being, on the plane of deity, and counting as righteous those who believe in Christ because it pleases Him to declare them righteous. There is no difference between the method wherein He declares them to be sinners and the method wherein He declares them righteous.

One evening I was speaking in Washington, D.C., and at the close of the meeting a group of about a dozen men crowded around me to ask questions. One of them was fighting all that I had been teaching. He insisted that justification could not be *entirely* God's work. It stood to reason, he said, that God would not justify a man without finding in him something on which to base the justification. Patiently, I took him through many of the verses which show that there is nothing in man upon which God bases His choice. He argued that he had been preaching to some men in a particular school, that some of them had accepted Christ, and that surely when the decision had been reached it was because of something that was in them. I asked him to tell me what it would be, and he looked at me triumphantly and said, "Their faith!" And then he started to quote Ephesians 2:8–9, "For by grace are ye saved through faith . . ." Suddenly his voice trailed off to silence, and I could see the working of his mind as he began to comprehend what was the very next clause in the verse. I would not let him stop but insisted that he go on. "And where did the faith come from?" I pressed him. And he was man enough to finish the quotation: "And that not of yourselves: it is the gift of God: not of works, lest any man should boast."

### All a Gift

He left that and started on a different track. He presented another verse that had to do with seeking. I pointed out to him that an earlier verse in the third chapter of Romans states that there is "none that seeketh after God," that these invitations to seek were given to those who were already believers, and not to the Gentiles round about. After about five starts, each of which was effectively blocked by plain statements from the Word of God, he said, "But . . . but . . . that would mean that God does it all!" There was almost wonderment in his voice, and I let the Word of God sink in and do its work. Then, suddenly, there burst upon him the full realization that we are justified freely, or, as the Greek could have it, justified without a cause.

That is the glorious truth which our hearts must feed upon. Our justification does not have its roots in us: If it were otherwise we would always be in constant doubt as to whether we had properly fulfilled the requirements. But when we know that we are justified without a cause in ourselves, then we know that it is all based upon the loving nature of God's being, and we can rest quietly, assured that the life that He gives is because of the love that He is.

> Awake, my soul, in joyful lays,
> And sing my great Redeemer's praise;
> He justly claims a song from me,
> His loving kindness, oh, how free.
>
> He saw me ruined in the fall,
> And loved me, notwithstanding all.
> He saved me from my lost estate,
> His loving kindness, oh, how great.

Justified by His grace, without a cause in us. How shall we define such grace? In my ministry I have found it easier to illustrate grace than it is to define it, and there comes to my mind a story that I used in my earliest ministry. It had slipped my mind for many years but comes back today, strong and fresh. When I was in my teens I was invited to speak for a week in a little church in Southern California. There was such blessing that I was invited to continue for a second week, but I was in a quandary for I had no more sermons. I went in to Los Angeles to get some books; and, while I was browsing at the shelves of a store, I ran across a little book (which I did not buy) whose name I do not remember and which I have never seen since. I remember one story out of it which I frequently used in those days, and which comes back to me only today.

## A Better Pitcher

In the days of Moody, there was a minister named Harry Morehouse who often helped Moody in his campaigns. One morning he was walking along the street in a poor part of one of our great cities and witnessed a minor tragedy. A small boy, who could not have been more than five or six years of age, came out of a store with a pitcher of milk in his hands. The little fellow was making his way carefully along the street when he slipped and fell, the pitcher breaking, and the milk running all over the sidewalk. He let out a wail, and Harry Morehouse rushed to see if he were hurt. There was no physical damage but he would not be consoled, crying out over and over, "My mama'll whip me! My mama'll whip me."

Mr. Morehouse said to him, "Maybe the pitcher is not broken in too many pieces; let us see if we can put it together again." The boy stopped crying at once, as he had no doubt seen bits of crockery glued together to remake a broken plate or cup. He watched as Mr. Morehouse placed the base of the pitcher on the sidewalk and started building up the pieces. There were one or two failures and the pieces fell apart. At each failure the boy started crying again, but was silenced by the big preacher who was helping him so much. Finally, the entire pitcher was reconstructed from the pieces, and it stood there in perfect shape on the sidewalk. The little fellow was given the handle, and he poked it toward the place where it belonged, and, of course, knocked the whole thing apart once more. This time there was no stopping his tears, and it was then that Mr. Morehouse gathered the boy in his arms and walked down the street with him to a nearby crockery store. He entered with the lad and bought a new pitcher. Then he went back to the milk store, had the pitcher washed and filled with milk. Carrying the boy on one arm and the pitcher of milk in the other hand, he followed the boy's instructions until they arrived at his home. Very gently he deposited the lad on his front steps, carefully put the pitcher in his hands and then said to him, "Now will your mama whip you?" A smile broke on the boy's streaked face, and he answered, "Aw, no sir! 'Cause it's a lot better pitcher 'n we had before."

## God's Grace

The story may be very simple, but it represents faintly what the Lord Jesus Christ did for me and for you. Whether you will accept the fact or not, you had dropped the pitcher of your life and its milk was spilled beyond regathering. You may have spent much time in trying to patch the pieces together again, but God assures you that you are broken beyond repair. It was when we were thus, broken and hopeless, in the despair of our lost soul and our crashed hopes that the Lord Jesus intervened to save us. He may have watched our efforts at patching for a while, until we could come to the place where we believed beyond question that it is impossible for us to repair our lives in a way that would ever satisfy the holiness of the Heavenly Father. It was then that He carried us in His arms and purchased for us an entirely new nature, a new life, which He imparted to us on the basis of His loving kindness and tender mercies. It was not because there was good in us, but because there was grace in Him. It was not because there was righteousness in our hearts, but because there was grace in His heart.

No one had to plead with Him to save us; He did not come because of any promptings of His earthly mother, for example; but He came from Heaven because He, the Lord Jesus Christ, was full of all grace, and that grace was abounding to us through the redemption which He provided in dying for us. It was not our works that saved us but His grace. It was not our character that recommended us to Him, but His grace. If He had not been all grace, we would have forever lain in the misery of our broken hopes. But His very name is love. He is gracious. And that is why I know in this hour that I have new life. He justified me freely, without any cause in me, and all by His grace. And thus I am saved by grace.

*14*

# Charles Edward Fuller

*1887-1968*

*B*orn in southern California to devout Christian parents, Charles Edward Fuller graduated cum laude from Pomona College in 1910 and went to work in the family orange groves. The next year he married, and when bad weather wiped out the crop in 1913, he and his wife moved to Placentia where he became manager of a packing house.

In July 1916 Fuller heard Paul Rader preach at the Church of the Open Door in Los Angeles and was greatly moved by the message. He drove to a secluded spot, knelt on the floor in the backseat of the car, and yielded himself to Jesus Christ. He had been a professed Christian for many years and was active in a local church, but this step brought him new life and spiritual motivation. In later years Charles Fuller looked on that experience as his true conversion to Christ.

Following his commitment to Christ, Fuller studied for three years at the Bible Institute of Los Angeles and was greatly influenced by the dean, R. A. Torrey. Fuller started a very successful Bible class in Placentia, which later became Calvary Baptist Church. He was ordained May 4, 1925. On January 5, 1930, the church began to broadcast the evening service, and Fuller discovered that he was made for radio preaching. He pastored the church until 1932 and the next year organized the Gospel Broadcasting Association, the umbrella organization for his radio ministry, which included a Thursday evening *Radio Bible Class,*

*The Sunday School Hour,* and a Sunday evening broadcast called *Heart to Heart Hour.* Later the name was changed to *The Radio Revival Hour* and finally *The Old-Fashioned Revival Hour.*

Eventually the radio program became a coast-to-coast Sunday afternoon live broadcast from the municipal auditorium in Long Beach, California. The auditorium seated some thirty-five hundred people and an estimated twenty million people listened each week by radio. One of the features of the program was Mrs. Fuller reading letters from listeners, usually introduced by her husband, who said, "And now, here's Mrs. Fuller with the letters. Go ahead, Honey." In 1958 the program left the auditorium and became a taped half-hour broadcast. Fuller resigned from active ministry in 1967 and died on March 18, 1968. The program continued into the early 1980s, and there was even a short-lived television broadcast.

Charles Fuller had a personal burden to help train effective preachers and he founded Fuller Theological Seminary in honor of his father, Henry Fuller.

The official biography is *Give the Winds a Mighty Voice: The Story of Charles E. Fuller* by Daniel P. Fuller (Word, 1972).

# Seven Marvels of God's Mercy

Please take your Bibles and turn to Isaiah the first chapter, verse 18, where you find seven marvels of God's mercy and His divine compassionate love. "Come now, and let us reason together, saith the LORD: though your sins be as scarlet, they shall be as white as snow; though they be red like crimson, they shall be as wool."

It was to Isaiah, one of God's choicest prophets, that God committed the task of constantly warning and exhorting Judah to return from their backsliding ways, to return to Jehovah God. God was ever willing to extend pardon and mercy and compassionate love to all who would return; but to those who refused to return to Jehovah, God said He would execute judgment. And so Isaiah warns the disobedient, the stubborn, the stiff-necked—those who hear but continue to reject and to spurn God's forgiveness of sins through faith in Jesus Christ.

Isaiah's prophecy has sixty-six chapters, and they may be divided into three great sections. Each of these sections is marked at the beginning with an earnest call and at its close by a solemn warning.

Section 1 covers chapters 1 to 48 and opens with the earnest call: "Come now, and let us reason together, saith the LORD: though your sins be as scarlet, they shall be as white as snow, and though they be red like crimson, they shall be as wool." The solemn warning is in chapter 48 and verse 22: "There is no peace, saith the LORD, unto the wicked." That's the first section.

The second section is from chapters 49 to 57. The earnest call is chapter 49, verse 1: "Listen, O isles, unto me; and hear ye people afar; the LORD hath called me and he hath made my mouth like a sharp sword, and made me a polished shaft in his quiver, to restore the preserved of Israel, to give light to the gentiles, that thou mayest be my salvation unto the end of the earth." The solemn warning at the close of section two is in chapter 57, verse 21, "There is no peace, saith my LORD, to the wicked."

The third section of Isaiah goes from chapter 58 to the end of the book. The earnest call is in Isaiah 58:13 and 14. "Cry aloud, spare not, lift up thy voice like a trumpet." That is, "Sound the call, show my people their transgressions" (v. 1). "If thou turn away thy foot from the sabbath, from doing thy pleasure on my holy day; and call the sabbath a delight [lovers of pleasure more than lovers of God, not doing your own ways]. . . . Then shalt thou delight thyself in the LORD; and I will cause thee to ride upon the high places of the earth, and feed thee with the heritage of Jacob." One of the evidences of the breaking of God's commandments is occupation with pleasures and athletic contests and stores being open on the beloved holy day that should be set apart for worship of Jehovah God.

The solemn warning is in 66:15: "Behold the LORD will come with fire, and with his chariots like a whirlwind, to render his anger with fury, and his rebuke with flames of fire." *These* things are written for our admonition and instruction and hence, the last warning. We look ahead to the Second Coming of Christ, His coming according to 2 Thessalonians 1:8–9, "For he is coming in flaming fire to take vengeance on them that know not God and that obey not the gospel." Wake up! He's suddenly going to intervene Himself in the affairs of men, and then you'll have all the space travel if you're in Christ Jesus! For then you'll "be caught . . . up to meet the Lord in the air; and so shall we ever be with the Lord" (1 Thess. 4:17). I'm going to have the best space trip that the world's ever seen, and it will not be man-made. According to Jude 14, "Behold, the Lord cometh with ten thousands of his saints." For what purpose? To execute judgment upon all the ungodly. Read Revelation 19:11–16. It tells us that Jesus will come and tread "the winepress of the fierceness and wrath of Almighty God." Judgment is ahead for this old world, and only those that are in Christ Jesus will be worthy to escape those things that are about to come upon the earth.

Now to section one. May we meditate upon the earnest call of that section found in chapter 1, verse 18. I quote it again, "Come now, and let us reason together, saith the LORD: though your sins be as scarlet, they shall be as white as snow; though they be red like crimson, they shall be as wool." Here, beloved, in this verse we find one of God's precious diamonds of mercy, pardon and compassionate love. This diamond of mercy has seven facets, seven sides all reflecting God's *Shekinah* glory.

Have you ever noticed that it is the custom in the jewelry shops to display diamonds on a dark cloth background? And by so doing, the contrast is made more plain between the light and the darkness. It's more marked. The diamonds shine with more brilliance against the dark purple or black background. Now that's exactly what God has done in the first chapter of Isaiah. Over against the background, dark and damnable as it is, this diamond with its seven facets of God's mercy shines above the brightness of the noonday sun.

In Isaiah chapter 1, verses 2–17, we find a very dark background, spiritually speaking. In verses 2–9, God unveils man's thoughtlessness. "Why," He says, "the ox knows his owner, and the ass his master's crib: but [man] does not know [his Creator]"—by nature, children of disobedience, children of wrath, alienated and cut off from the life that's in Christ Jesus. Man—created originally in God's image, but through sin fallen and afar off—does not know as much as the dumb beasts. It's a pretty dark background. Man—natural man, laden with iniquity, evil doers, corrupters—have forsaken the Lord, all going astray, each man to his own way, dead in trespasses and sins, going backwards.

Consider verse 6 of the first chapter. "From the soul of the foot even unto the head there is no soundness in it." Man—there's none righteous, only wounds and bruises and putrefying sores because of sins. "They have not been closed, neither bound up, neither mollified with ointment." And that's God's picture of you outside of Christ Jesus. In verses 10–17, God unveils man's formalism of worship, warning those who have a form of godliness, but no power. But over against this dark background, God's seven-faced diamond of mercy shines out with brilliancy.

The first facet is *that God should forgive at all.* God hates sin, but He loves the sinner, and by one man's disobedience back in the Garden of Eden, sin entered the world, and through sin, death—both physical and spiritual death. The day that Adam sinned, he died spiritually and later died physically. By nature every man is separated spiritually from God, and it's appointed unto men once to die physically, and after that the judgment. God might have dealt with sinful man only according to law and justice, but God is not willing that any should perish, and the good news is that God forgives. "In whom we have redemption . . . even the forgiveness of sins." I care not what your state may be—a Pharisee, righteous in your own eyes, or a sinner down in skid row in the gutter—God will forgive you of your sin.

The second facet of this marvelous diamond is, not only that God forgives at all, but *that God should be willing to forgive all.* Yes, God is willing to save to the uttermost all that come unto Him through the Lord Jesus, for Christ is the Lamb of God who takes away the sins of the world. He bore our sins in His own body on the tree. He's willing to take *all* your sins and put them behind His back and bury them in the deepest sea, never to remember them against you anymore forever—if you're willing to come as a humble, poor, hell-bound sinner and say, "God be merciful to me, a sinner."

The third facet on God's diamond of mercy is *that He is willing to reason with sinners.* "Come . . . let us reason," that is, "let us put the matter right and settle the matter once for all." "Put an end to all reasoning" is literally what it means. Settle your soul's destiny once for all, for "he that heareth My word and believeth on Him that sent me, hath everlasting life and shall not come into condemnation, but is passed from death unto life." Come, today, on the last broadcast of *The Old-Fashioned Revival Hour* from the municipal auditorium and settle your eternal destiny once for all through faith in Jesus Christ.

The fourth facet is *that God should offer to reason with us after all He has done for us.* Did you ever stop to think that after God gave His only begotten Son that whosoever believes in Him should not perish but have everlasting life, that He's willing to sit down and reason with you? Why should He? He's provided His Son, the way is open, the table is ready, all things are prepared; why should He sit down and reason with you? Simply because He loves you and He's not willing that any should perish, but that all should come to repentance. Truly, where sin abounds, grace much more abounds. Oh, the longsuffering and the patience of God! Some of you have heard the Gospel for years and you're still in your sins, with your heart hardened. God have mercy on you! I have often said that if you go on rejecting the Gospel the day will come when you'll become past feeling. But if there's the slightest desire, a pull towards things eternal, come now and trust Christ.

The fifth facet is *that God not only forgives but transforms the sinner.* "Though your sins be as scarlet"—deeply, deeply ingrained, deeply dyed, outstanding, innumerable, so that all can see them—"they shall be as white as snow." The cleansing blood of Jesus Christ, God's Son, does the work, cleansing you from all unrighteousness. Now note this, please. The cleansing blood of Jesus does not wash scarlet sins white. He does not wash scarlet sins white, but He washes scarlet *sinners* white as snow. And He puts your sins away, never to bring them to remembrance. Romans 8:1 says, "There is therefore now no condemnation to them which are in Christ Jesus."

The sixth facet is that God should forgive, transform and make us new creations *on such simple terms:* "Come now, and let us reason together." Reconciliation has been made; come and approach Him with boldness. Come now—the way is open and His ear is ever open to the cry of the believing, confessing sinner. God says, "Him that cometh to Me, I will in no wise cast out."

160

*God's longsuffering* is the seventh facet—bearing patiently with man's many refusals. I plead with you at the close of this beloved hour. God's table is loaded with spiritual things—forgiveness, righteousness from Christ Jesus. Blessings are ready, so come and eat and drink. God says, "Ho, everyone that thirsteth, come ye to the waters, and he that hath no money; come ye, buy, and eat; yea, come, buy wine and milk without money and without price."

Now it's up to you—it's up to you.

Let's bow our heads for prayer.

Out in the great radio audience, God is speaking to you, the Jehovah God of eternity. He says, "Now come, son, let us reason together. Come now, I'm willing to receive you if you make the first move." And like the prodigal son of old, the father saw him coming afar off. He ran, fell on his neck and had compassion and kissed him. And the moment that you make a move towards God, God runs to meet you. He's not willing that any should perish. And out in the great radio audience, I say today, Come now. God is willing to pardon you, willing to receive you, willing to wash you from your sins and make you white as snow.

While our heads are bowed and Christians are praying here in this wonderful audience at Long Beach today, in the quiet of the hour while we're praying, how many will put up their hands and say, "Brother Fuller, I need Christ as my personal Savior. I want to accept Him today, and I'm coming now." Will you put your hand up, and say by that, "Please remember me in prayer; I want to accept Him." Anyone here on the lower floor? God bless you two right there. Anyone else? Anyone else? Quickly! God bless you, another one there in front. God bless you back there, young lad in the back. Anyone else? Quickly! Put your hands up on the lower floor, up in the balconies to my left, anyone? Yes, God bless you, I'll have to move around. Up in the balconies to the rear. Put them up high. Yes, in the balconies to the right. Anyone up there, put your hands up and say "Pray for me," that you want to accept Christ as your personal Savior. Anyone else on the lower floor? God bless you, young man; I see your hand. Anyone else, just before we close?

Heavenly Father, give these that have raised their hands the courage to come to the front when the opportunity arrives. Out over the radio audience, may thousands send in their names that we might pray for them, that they have accepted Christ as their personal Savior. For we ask it in His name and for His sake. Amen.

I want you to stand. We're going to sing "God Be with You Till We Meet Again." Everybody stand, please, and the chorus choir's going to sing. Don't anyone leave now, you'll miss the climax of the meeting. And those of you who have raised your hands for prayer, while we're singing "God Be with You Till We Meet Again," would you come right over. Please give us the front seats here for just a moment. Thank you so much. And those of you who raised your hands for prayer, out of the balcony, anywhere in the auditorium, come right down to the front. The personal workers will help you while we're singing "God Be with You Till We Meet Again."

[The chorus choir and the congregation begin to sing.]

Come on. God bless you, young lad. Whether you raised your hand or not, come on down to the front here. You folks, come on right now. Step out, come on down. God bless you!

[Dr. Fuller continued the invitation and then closed the service.]

This is Charles E. Fuller bidding you good-bye and God's richest blessing upon you.

# Harry Emerson Fosdick

*1878-1969*

Harry Emerson Fosdick considered himself a "theological liberal but a temperamental conservative" and even preached sermons criticizing the modernists for failing to appreciate the true meaning of religious tradition.

He was born in Buffalo, New York, and received his education at Colgate University, Columbia University, and Union Theological Seminary. Ordained a Baptist minister in 1903, he pastored First Baptist Church of Montclair, New Jersey, from 1904 to 1915, when he became professor of practical theology at Union Seminary, a position he held until 1946.

In 1919 Fosdick became an assistant minister ("stated pulpit supply") at First Presbyterian Church in New York City, and it was there on May 21, 1922, that he delivered his famous sermon "Shall the Fundamentalists Win?" which was later printed and distributed widely. Fosdick claimed that the sermon was "a plea for tolerance" but he admitted in his autobiography, "If ever a sermon failed to achieve its object, mine did" (p. 145). The storm broke, conservative Presbyterians opposed the presence of a liberal preacher in one of their pulpits, and Fosdick resigned from the church in 1925.

He was then called to New York's Park Avenue Baptist Church, and one of the members, John D. Rockefeller Jr., offered to build him a new edifice where he could freely carry on his ministry. The Riverside Church was dedicated February 8, 1931, and Fosdick remained its senior minister until he retired in 1946.

His sermons were carried over the *National Vespers* radio broadcast and published in numerous books that were widely read. He sought to integrate modern knowledge with ancient religious principles and to bring Christians together without the "barriers" erected by denominational creeds and theological debates.

Fosdick's autobiography, *The Living of These Days* (Harper, 1956), should be read in conjunction with the official biography, *Harry Emerson Fosdick: Preacher, Pastor, Prophet*, by Robert Moats Miller (Oxford, 1985). For Fosdick's approach to preaching, see *Preaching as Counseling* by Edmund Holt Linn (Judson Press, 1966). *Riverside Sermons* (Harper, 1958) contains forty representative sermons selected by Charles L. Wallis.

# The Essential Elements
# in a Vital Christian Experience

The worse the world is without, the deeper we all need to go within. The profound meanings of inward, personal, Christian experience become not less but more important in a turbulent and dismaying era. What, then are *the essential elements* in a vital religious life, so basic that from Quaker to Roman Catholic all Christians at their best have shared them? Are they not *a great need, a great salvation, a great gratitude,* and *a great compulsion?*

Often the doom of Christianity has been announced. Many a time it has sinned against light and fallen on evil days. It has been used as a mere counter in a political game, as Napoleon used it and as more than one dictator would like to use it now. Often it has faced new world views and refused new knowledge. Time and again it has identified itself with some contemporary social *status quo* and has seemed to collapse with the downfall of the system it was tied to. How often the cry has risen which Voltaire voiced in the eighteenth century: "Ere the beginning of the nineteenth century Christianity will have disappeared from the earth"! But it has not disappeared. Its expressions change but at the heart of it are creative factors that everlastingly keep their hold: a great need, a great salvation, a great gratitude, and a great compulsion.

First, then, *a great need.* No one achieves a vital, personal, Christian experience without a profound sense of need. While many think of need as a sign of weakness, the fact is that there is no truer test of the status of any creature in the scale of existence than the size, amplitude, and quality of his needs. See this strange creature, man, that the materialists tell us is but an accidental bundle of atoms drifting toward oblivion. That estimate of man seems to some of us incredible if only because of what it takes to meet this creature's needs. If he wanted only food for his body, like some animals, then an animal he would be. But he has curiosity that must explore the farthest stars and build great telescopes to get at the stars he cannot see. That is an incredible thing for a mere bundle of atoms to need to do. The badge of man's dignity, the sign of his greatness, is this outreach of want without whose satisfaction he cannot be content. He needs music and books and art—not telephones and airplanes only, though that is mysterious enough, but ideals for himself and his society, a clear conscience, great purposes to live for, and high faiths to live by, if at his best he is to be content. Such need is incredible in a mere bundle of atoms. *Need, first of all, is not a sign of weakness but the mark of a creature's status in the scale of existence.* Consider, then, the fact that age after age millions of folk have sought a personal experience of Christ because they needed him.

To different people *this need comes in different ways.* With many it appears as a *sense of inadequacy* in meeting the demands of life. For the demands of life can be terrific. A father lately had to say farewell for the last time to his sixteen-year-old son. There on the hospital bed lay the boy, ill of an insidious disease but with no idea that he was going to die. And one evening the father, as though it were a matter of course, not at all revealing what he knew, had to say "Good night, son," and hear the boy say "Good night, Dad," knowing all the time that that was the final good-by and that before morning the boy would die. What demands life makes on us! Who can meet them? Not simply when they come suddenly but when they come slowly in the long drag of the years, putting burdens on us difficult to sustain, who can face life's demands, whether in youth or age, without a need of spiritual reinforcement to meet the strain?

To others this experience comes mainly through *moral failure*. For sin is a Trojan horse. We welcome it through a breach in our walls as the ancient city did, expectant of happiness, but it has inside it many hostile forces we never suspected, that in the night come creeping out! *Habit,* for example, so that we start free to sin and then wake up to discover that we are not free to stop. *Guilt,* for example, so that we begin with high anticipation of pleasure only to find that our sin passes from anticipation through committal into memory, and, changing its visage, becomes guilt and settles down to haunt us like a ghost. Explicit punishment, for example, for there is something terrific in this universe that finds out a man's mistakes and even at long last lays a heavy hand upon them. Perhaps, worst of all, we sin thinking only of ourselves and our pleasures and then discover that we have involved others and that the consequences of our evil blast the hopes and happiness of those for whom we really care. So, age after age, people facing moral failure and its tragic aftermath have sought a personal experience of Christ, his forgiveness and re-establishment, because they needed him.

To others this experience comes not so much from life's demands or even from moral failure, as from a positive vision of *life's possibilities*. When I was a boy I do not recall that I needed great music. I had little chance to hear any. Once, as a lad, I was taken to a symphony but I did not like it. Then one day some really great music broke through. That was a strange experience; to use Wordsworth's words, it disturbed "me with the joy of elevated thoughts." I awoke to a new need, something that ever afterward I must have to be content—a solace, comfort, incentive, and inspiration. That is a strange experience, to break into a new realm of need, where something you have not known before becomes necessary to you, and that experience is most often reduplicated through the awakening influence of great personalities. Remember Alcibiades saying to Socrates: "There is one experience I have in the presence of this man alone, such as nobody would expect in me; and that is, to be made to feel ashamed; he alone can make me feel it. For he brings home to me that I cannot disown the duty of doing what he bids me, but that as soon as I turn from his company I fall a victim to the favours of the crowd." Above all others, Christ has so disturbed people. They could not live beside him and still be what they were. They awoke to a new sense of need from a new vision of possibility.

Whatever way it comes to us, this is the first element in a vital Christian experience. If someone says he feels no such need, that is a pity. Some feel no need of music, or of books, or of the beauty of God's out-of-doors, and that fact is a revelation of their status in the scale of existence. What kind of person do you think he is who does not need interior resources of spiritual power to face life's strains, conquer its temptations, and fulfill its possibilities?

The second element in a vital Christian experience is a *great salvation*. To be sure, that word troubles me. Words can fall into bad company and be dragged down by their associates. When St. Paul's Cathedral in London was finished, the architect displayed it to the king on a state occasion and the king called it amusing, awful, and artificial. The architect was overjoyed at the royal compliment for in those days "amusing" meant "amazing," "awful" meant "awe-inspiring," and "artificial" meant "artistic." So words change their meaning, and "salvation" has often walked in undesirable intellectual company and gotten incredible connotations. I beg of you today to use the word, since there is no other to be used, in its finest and best sense.

If a man has ever been lost in the woods at night or on the sea in a fog in a small boat without a compass, and then help has come, he ought to know what it feels like to be saved. If a man has ever been unemployed and the long succession of days that were hard and nights that were terrible have worn him down, and then employment has come again, he ought to know what it means to be saved. If our family life was ever in peril and we had almost given up hope, and then a better spirit came and the rift in the lute was mended and what we cared more for than anything else in the world became lovely again, we ought to know what it means to be saved. And in the same realistic sense, if we have ever known a desperate need for help to stand life's strains, overcome its temptations, and fulfill its possibilities, and then victory has come through the revelation of power that Christ has brought, the word "salvation" ought to have a vivid place in our vocabulary. At any rate, across the ages millions of people have found a great need thus met by a great salvation.

This experience comes to most of us in two general ways. To many it *is opportunity for a second chance*. They have failed, messed up their lives, and have only the remnants left of their first opportunity. Then they face that amazing, unbelievable offer of a second chance. A friend of mine attended cooking school sometime since and the title of one of the announced lectures has fascinated my imagination ever since—"Putting the Lure into the Leftovers." That lesson is needed far outside a cooking school. Who has not needed *that*? The Prodigal in the far country with only the remnants of his first opportunity left needed something that would put the lure into those leftovers, and, all the ages since, men like Augustine—afterwards St. Augustine—who ran away from home and lived with his mistress, and even after he had felt Christ's attraction cried: "The worse that I knew so well had more power over me than the better that I knew not," have needed something or someone who could put the lure into the leftovers. Who of us here has not thus failed, made a mess of some first chance, stood with only the remnants left, and then faced that incredible miracle of forgiveness that reestablishes the old relationships as though we had not broken them, and offers a second chance?

Along with this first factor in a saving experience goes *strength to make something of the second chance*. For any kind of failure, moral failure in particular, is a Svengali to the soul. It hypnotizes us, and, casting upon us its horrid spell, towers over us, saying, You cannot; you have failed; you are whipped. Who has not experienced that? And who has not cried out for someone who could defeat that incantation, break that enchantment, and lift him up to answer back, as Paul answered even in a Roman prison, I can—"In Him who strengthens me, I am able for anything."

Sometimes I think we preachers, overawed by the formal dignity of the pulpit, talk too anonymously and impersonally. Here I am today, an older man talking to you about the secret of spiritual power in general, when all the time what I am really seeing in my imagination's eye is that young man I was years ago, shot all to pieces, done in and shattered in a nervous breakdown, foolishly undertaking too much work and doing it unwisely, all my hopes in ashes and life towering over me, saying, You are finished; you cannot; you are done for. People ask me why in young manhood I wrote *The Meaning of Prayer.* That came out of young manhood's struggle. I desperately needed a second chance and reinforcement to carry on with it. I was sunk unless I could find at least a little of what Paul had in mind when he said, I can—"In Him who strengthens me, I am able for anything."

That is salvation—forgiveness, a second chance, reinforcement, power, the voice of a friend out of the fog where all direction has been lost, saying, I am here, and, You can! Across the ages Christ has meant that to men—a great need met by a great salvation.

The third element in a personal experience of Christ is a *great gratitude.* One cannot understand the New Testament or the driving power of the Christian church at its best without taking the measure of the fact that a profound need met by a profound salvation has issued in a profound gratitude.

Mark this strange fact that the church is the only organization in the world that advertises itself as a company of sinners. That fact is worth walking around. In the second century Celsus the pagan jeered at the Christians because of this. To the heathen world it seemed a ridiculous, incredible thing that a great company of people should advertise themselves as sinners and to their fellowship welcome sinners. And still it is a unique phenomenon. Where else will you find people standing up to say that they have done those things they ought not to have done and have left undone those things they ought to have done and there is no health in them? And even when we do not use those words, how difficult it is to find a scripture or a human without the accent of penitence!

> When the worldling, sick at heart,
>   Lifts his soul above;
> When the prodigal looks back
>   To his Father's love;
> When the proud man, from his pride,
>   Stoops to seek thy face;
> When the burdened brings his guilt
>   To thy throne of grace.

Here is a unique phenomenon, the founding of a world-wide fellowship explicitly made up of sinners. One cannot understand what that means until one sees that a great need, met by a great salvation, has issued in a great gratitude.

That, of course, is the reason why the Lord's Supper, to a Christian who understands it, is the climax of Christian worship. The early Christians called it the Eucharist. What does Eucharist mean? It is the Greek word for "thank you." Just as in France we say *Merci,* or in Italy, *Gratia,* so in modern Greece we say *Eucharisto,* that is, Eucharist, thank you. The Lord's Supper is the church of Christ, knowing that it is made up of sinners, having faced a profound need, met with a profound salvation, going up before the cross of Christ, the symbol of the price paid for our help, to express a great gratitude.

The ethical implications of such gratitude are immense. Gratitude, someone has said, is the mother of all virtues. That is a defensible proposition. Here is a man who has no spark of gratitude anywhere concealed about his person. He thinks life has been egregiously unjust to him. He is resentful and rebellious about life. You will get no great living out of him. Or here is another man who thinks life consists in getting what you have earned. It is *quid pro quo,* so much for so much, and he suspects he is breaking about even; he is getting what he earns and is earning what he gets. You will find no superior living in such a man. But here is a man who feels that no matter what he does he never can pay back the debt he owes. To be sure, there is injustice in his experience and *quid pro quo* too, but when life is taken as a whole, he feels that he has received what he never could deserve or earn. In all ages the finest living has come out of folk like that.

This is not simply a matter of religion. Consider, for example, the millions of us born in democratic nations, who have strolled into the privileges of democracy and nonchalantly have settled down there without a grateful thought. We have even been dominated by resentfulness over the failures of democracy or by nonchalance toward its liberties. But who can take the measure of these present days and not rise to another attitude? Freedom is precious in the world today. It was won for us, before we were born, by our fathers, who with thought, labor, and sacrifice built a democratic nation where the rights of individual souls and of minorities would be respected. We should be grateful. Our lives, our fortunes, our sacred honor are owed to democracy. There is something to be said for the idea that gratitude is the mother of all virtues. Certainly, there is no such thing as a vital Christian experience without it. Need of Christ, salvation in Christ, gratitude toward Christ—those three phrases are, as it were, the stethoscope where we can hear the very heartbeat of the gospel.

The fourth element in a creative experience of Christ is a *great compulsion.* For it stands to reason that if a man has known a deep want, met by a great redemption issuing in a profound thankfulness, then something has gotten hold of him. He is not his own. He has been taken possession of. He is under a powerful inner compulsion.

Now compulsion is a part of every man's life. One way or another, life coerces all of us and no one of us can escape the word "must." But how vast the difference between those mere creatures of circumstance, pushed and pulled by outward chance and fortune, on one side, and, on the other side, the elect spirits of the race whose compulsion is from within! The great musicians, the Beethovens, Tschaikowskys, Brahms, must write music. Why must they? No one makes them. But they know the need that only music can supply; they have had an experience of music bringing to them its saving satisfaction; they have a gratitude toward music that no words can express; and so they are under a compulsion strong as steel and ineluctable as destiny. They must give their lives to music. The elect spirits of the race know this compulsion from within.

So Paul said: "I must also see Rome." Why must he? No one made him undertake that risky adventure that ended with his beheading on the Appian Way. I must see Africa, said Livingstone. Why must he? No one coerced him from his Scottish home to die in his tent in Africa with his face fallen into the open pages of the Bible, a sacrifice to his high endeavor to paint the dark continent white. Here is the secret of man's greatness and his liberty, to have compulsion not from without but from within. And in quieter lives among our friends or in our families, who of us has not known such characters, who could have said: "O Love that wilt not let me go"?

No need of the modern world is so deep as the need for this kind of character. We could muddle along without much more scientific invention. We could get by with no more skyscrapers and gadgets. But we cannot get by without more Christian character if by that we mean what we have been talking about. Theologies change; creeds alter; the world views of one generation are incredible to the next; the mental patterns that Paul, Augustine, Calvin used we cannot exactly copy. But when we range up into this experience of profound need met in Christ by a great salvation, that issues in a deep gratitude so that we are inwardly taken possession of by a high compulsion, we not only overpass the differences between our contemporary sects but the differences between the centuries. Paul would understand *that*, and St. Augustine and Luther and Phillips Brooks. In that experience is the real communion of the saints. When one pleads for that one is pleading for the basic structural material without which no decent society can be built. When one pleads for that one is pleading for a quality of character without which man at his best cannot be satisfied. If you lack it, seek it. If you have a little of it, deepen it—a great need, a great salvation, a great gratitude, a great compulsion.

*16*

# Robert Greene Lee

*1886-1978*

His parents were sharecroppers who nurtured their son in the Word of God. Converted in a revival meeting in 1898, Robert Greene Lee felt a call to preach, was educated at Furman University, graduating in 1913, and had further studies at Tulane. During several student pastorates, he developed his oratorical style of preaching.

After pastoring Baptist churches in South Carolina and Louisiana, in 1927 Lee accepted the call to Belleview Baptist Church in Memphis, Tennessee, where he served for thirty-two years. During that long pastorate, he baptized more than seven thousand people and received more than twenty-four thousand into church membership. Three times he was elected president of the Southern Baptist Convention. He published more than thirty volumes of sermons and he preached his most famous sermon "Pay Day—Some Day" over a thousand times.

Lee was a gifted wordsmith and knew how to use repetition, alliteration, and verbal imagery to get and hold the attention of his hearers and then lead them to decision. Rather than exegete and explain a passage, Lee laid hold of a major theme in the text and developed it with great creativity. Some of his sermons are woven around a repeated theme, like a concerto or a symphony, with each variation bringing out a new truth. Lee was one of the last of the traditional Southern pulpit orators. When he was at his best, he kept congregations spellbound. On more than one occasion he confessed that he had "laid a foundation for a skyscraper but built a chicken coop on it."

*Robert G. Lee* by John Hus (Zondervan, 1963) and *The Preaching of Robert G. Lee* by Paul Gericke (Christ for the World Publishers, 1967) are early studies of this great pulpiteer.

# Pay Day—Some Day

Arise, go down to meet Ahab king of Israel, which is in Samaria: behold, he is in the vineyard of Naboth, whither he is gone down to possess it. And thou shalt speak unto him, saying, Thus saith the LORD, Hast thou killed, and also taken possession? And thou shalt speak unto him, saying, Thus saith the LORD, In the place where dogs licked the blood of Naboth shall dogs lick thy blood, even thine.

And of Jezebel also spake the LORD, saying, The dogs shall eat Jezebel by the wall of Jezreel.

1 Kings 21:18–19, 23

I introduce to you Naboth. Naboth was a devout Israelite who lived in the foothill village of Jezreel. Naboth was a good man. He abhorred that which is evil and clave to that which is good. In spite of the persecution of the prophets he did not shrink from making it known that he was a worshiper of Jehovah. He was an example of one who had not bowed the knee nor given a kiss to Baal.

Naboth would not change his heavenly principles for loose experiences. He would not dilute the stringency of his personal righteousness for questionable compromises. Now Naboth had a vineyard surrounding his house. This little vineyard, fragrant with blossoms in the days of the budding branch and freighted with fruit in the days of the vintage, was a cherished ancestral possession. This vineyard was near the summer palace of Ahab—situated about twenty miles from Samaria—a palace unique in its splendor as the first palace inlaid with ivory.

173

174

I introduce to you Ahab—the vile, egotistical, covetous toad who squat-ted upon the throne of Israel—the worst of Israel's evil kings. King Ahab had command of a nation's wealth and a nation's army, but he had no com-mand of his lusts and appetites. Ahab wore rich robes, but he had a sin-ning and wicked and troubled heart beneath them. Ahab ate the finest food the world could supply—and this food was served to him in dishes splen-did by servants obedient to his every beck and nod—but he had a starved soul. Ahab lived in palaces sumptuous within and without, yet he tormented himself for one bit of land more.

Ahab was a king, with a throne and a crown and a scepter, yet he lived all of his life under the thumb of a wicked woman—a tool in her hands. Ahab has pilloried himself in the contempt of all right-thinking, right-living, God-fearing men as a mean and selfish rascal who was the curse of his country. The Bible introduces him to us in words more appropriate than these when it says: "But there was none like unto Ahab, which did sell himself to work wickedness in the sight of the LORD, whom Jezebel his wife stirred up. And he did very abominably in following idols, accord-ing to all things as did the Amorites, whom the LORD cast out before the children of Israel" (1 Kings 21:25–26).

"And Ahab made a grove; and Ahab did more to provoke the LORD God of Israel to anger than all the kings of Israel that were before him" (1 Kings 16:33).

I introduce to you Jezebel, daughter of Ethbaal, King of Tyre (1 Kings 16:31), and wife of Ahab, the King of Israel—a king's daughter and a king's wife, the evil genius at once of her dynasty and of her country. Infinitely more daring and reckless was she in her wickedness than was her wicked husband. Masterful, indomitable, implacable, the instigator and supporter of religious persecution, called "the authentic author of priestly inquisi-tions," a devout worshiper of Baal, she hated anybody and everybody who spoke against or refused to worship her false and helpless god. As blunt in her wickedness and as brazen in her lewdness was she as Cleopatra, fair sor-ceress of the Nile. She had all the subtle and successful scheming of Lady Macbeth, all the adulterous desire and treachery of Potiphar's wife (Gen. 39:7–20), all the boldness of Mary Queen of Scots, all the cruelty and whimsical imperiousness of Katherine of Russia, all the devilish infamy of a Madame Pompadour, and, doubtless, all the fascination of personality of a Josephine of France.

Most of that which is bad in all evil women found expression through this painted viper of Israel. She had that rich endowment of nature which a good woman ought always to dedicate to the service of her day and generation. But—alas!—this idolatrous daughter of an idolatrous king of an idolatrous people engaging with her maidens in worship unto Ashtoreth—the personification of the most forbidding obscenity, uncleanness, and sensuality—became the evil genius who wrought wreck, brought blight, and devised death. She was the beautiful and malicious adder coiled upon the throne of the nation.

I introduce to you Elijah the Tishbite, the prophet of God at a time when by tens of thousands the people had forsaken God's covenants, thrown down God's altars, slain God's prophets with the sword (1 Kings 19:10). The young prophet, knowing much of the glorious past of the now apostate nation, must have been filled with horror when he learned of the rank heathenism, fierce cruelties, and reeking licentiousness of Ahab's idolatrous capital—at a time when Jezebel "set herself, with Ahab's tacit consent, to extirpate the religion of Jehovah from the land of Israel." Holy anger burned within him like an unquenchable Vesuvius or the flames of Martinique.

Elijah! Heir to the infinite riches of God he! Elijah! Attended by the hosts of heaven he! Little human companionship he had! But he was not lonely—because God was with him, and he was sometimes attended by the hosts of heaven. He wore a rough sheepskin cloak, but there was a peaceful, confident heart beneath it. He ate bird's food and widow's fare, but was a physical and spiritual athlete. He had no lease of office or authority, yet everyone obeyed him. He grieved only when God's cause seemed tottering. He passed from earth without dying—into celestial glory. Everywhere where courage is admired and manhood honored and service appreciated he is honored as one of earth's heroes and one of heaven's saints. He was "a seer, and saw clearly; a hero, and dared valiantly; a great heart, and felt deeply."

And now with these four persons introduced we want to turn to God's Word and see the tragedy of pay day some day! We will see the corn they put into the hopper and then behold the grist that came out the spout.

The first scene in this tragedy of "pay day—some day" is—

## I. The Real Estate Request

"And it came to pass after these things, that Naboth the Jezreelite had a vineyard, which was in Jezreel, hard by the palace of Ahab king of Samaria. And Ahab spoke unto Naboth, saying, Give me thy vineyard, that I may have it for a garden of herbs, because it is near unto my house: and I will give thee for it a better vineyard than it; or, if it seem good to thee, I will give thee the worth of it in money" (1 Kings 21:1–2).

Thus far Ahab was quite within his rights. No intention had he of cheating Naboth out of his vineyard or of killing him to get it. Honestly did he offer to give him its worth in money. Honestly did he offer him a better vineyard for it.

176

Ahab had not, however, counted upon the reluctance of all Jews to part with their inheritance of land. By peculiar tenure every Israelite held his land, and to all land-holding transactions there was another party, even God, "who made the heavens and the earth." Throughout Judah and Israel, Jehovah was the real owner of the soil; and every tribe received its territory and every family its inheritance by lot from Him, with the added condition that the land should not be sold forever. "The land shall not be sold for ever: for the land is mine; for ye are strangers and sojourners with me" (Lev. 25:23). "So shall not the inheritance of the children of Israel remove from tribe to tribe: for every one of the children of Israel shall keep himself to the inheritance of the tribe of his fathers. . . . But every one of the tribes of the children of Israel shall keep himself to his own inheritance" (Num. 36:7, 9).

Thus we see that the permanent sale of the paternal inheritance was forbidden by law. Ahab forgot—if he had ever really known it—that for Naboth to sell for money or to swap for a better vineyard his little vineyard would seem to that good man like a denial of his allegiance to the true religion to sell it when jubilee restoration was neglected in such idolatrous times.

Fearing God most and man least, and obeying the One whom he feared the most and loved the most, he said: "The LORD forbid it me, that I should give the inheritance of my fathers unto thee" (1 Kings 21:3).

True to the religious teachings of his father with real-hearted loyalty to the covenant God of Israel, he believed he held the land in fee simple from God. His father and grandfather, and doubtless grandfather's father, had owned the land before him. All the memories of childhood were tangled in its grapevines. His father's hand, folded now in the dust of death, had used the pruning blade among the branches, and because of this every branch and vine were dear. His mother's hands, now doubtless wrapped in a duststained shroud, had gathered purple clusters from those bunch-laden boughs, and for this reason he loved every spot in his vineyard and every branch on his vines. The ties of sentiment, of religion, and of family pride bound and endeared him to the place. So his refusal to sell was quick, firm, final, and courteous.

So with "the courage of a bird that dares the wild sea," he took his stand against the king's proposal.

And that brings us to the second scene in this tragedy. It is—

## II. The Pouting Potentate

Naboth's quick, firm, courteous, final refusal took all the spokes from the wheels of Ahab's desire and changed it into a foiled and foaming whirlpool of sullen sulks.

"And Ahab came into his house heavy and displeased because of the word which Naboth the Jezreelite had spoken to him: for he had said, I will not give thee the inheritance of my fathers. And he laid him down upon his bed, and turned away his face, and would eat no bread" (1 Kings 21:4).

What a ridiculous picture! A king acting like a spoiled and sullen child—impotent in disappointment and ugly in petty rage! A king, whose victories over the Syrians have rung through many lands—a conqueror, a slave to himself—whining like a sick hound! A king, rejecting all converse with others, pouting like a spoiled and petulant child that has been denied one trinket in the midst of one thousand playthings! A king, in a chamber "ceiled with cedar, and painted with vermilion" (Jer. 22:14), prostituting genius to theatrical trumpery.

What an ancient picture we have of great powers dedicated to mean, ugly, petty things. Think of it! In the middle of the day, the commander-in-chief of an army seized by Sergeant Sensitive. General Ahab made prisoner by Private Pouts! The leader of an army laid low by Corporal Mopishness! A monarch moaning and blubbering and growlingly refusing to eat because a man, a good man, because of the commandments of God and because of religious principles, would not sell or swap a little vineyard which was his by inheritance from his forefathers.

What an ancient picture of great powers and talents prostituted to base and purposeless ends and withheld from the service of God! What an ancient spectacle! And how modern and up-to-date, in this respect, was Ahab, king of Israel. What a likeness to him in conduct today are many talented men and women. I know men and women—you know men and women—with diamond and ruby abilities who are worth no more to God through the churches than a punctured Japanese nickel in a Chinese bazaar!

So many there are who, like Ahab, withhold their talents from God—using them in the service of the Devil. People there are, not a few, who have pipe-organ abilities and make no more music for the cause of Christ than a wheezy saxophone in an idiot's hands. People there are, many of them, who have incandescent-light powers who make no more light for God than a smoky barn lantern, with smoke-blackened globe, on a stormy night. People there are—I know them and you know them—with locomotive powers doing pushcart work for God. People there are—and how sad 'tis true—who have steam-shovel abilities who are doing teaspoon work for God. Yes!

Now look at this overfed bull bellowing for a little spot of grass outside his own vast pasture lands—and, if you are withholding talents and powers from the service of God, receive the rebuke of the tragic and ludicrous picture.

And now, consider the third scene in this tragedy of "pay day—some day." It is—

## III. The Wicked Wife

When Ahab would "eat no bread," the servants went and told Jezebel. What she said to them, we do not know. Something of what she said to Ahab we do know. Puzzled and provoked at the news that her husband would not eat—that he had gone to bed when it was not bedtime—Jezebel went to investigate. She found him in bed with his face turned to the wall, his lips swollen with mulish moping, his eyes burning with cheap anger-fire, his heart stubborn in wicked rebellion. He was groaning mournfully and peevishly petulant—having, up to the moment when she stood by his bedside, refused to eat or cheer up in the least.

At first, in a voice of solicitousness, she sought the reason of his choler. In "sweet" and anxious concern she said: "Why is thy spirit so sad, that thou eatest no bread?" (1 Kings 21:5). And then, as the manner of women is unto this day, she doubtless put her hand on his forehead to see if he had temperature. He had temperature all right. Like the tongue of the wicked, he was set on fire of hell. Then he told her, every word full of petulance and mopish peevishness as he spoke: "Because I spake unto Naboth the Jezreelite, and said unto him, Give me thy vineyard for money; or else, if it please thee, I will give thee another vineyard for it: and he answered, I will not give thee my vineyard" (1 Kings 21:6).

With her tongue, sharp like a razor, she prods Ahab as an ox driver prods with sharp goad the ox which does not want to press his neck into the yoke, or as one whips with a rawhide a stubborn mule. With profuse and harsh laughter this old gray and gaudy guinea of Satan derided this king of hers for a cowardly buffoon and sordid jester.

What hornet-like sting in her sarcasm! What wolf-mouth fierceness in her every reproach! What tiger-fang cruelty in her expressed displeasure! What fury in the shrieking of her rebuke! What bitter bitterness in the teasing taunts she hurled at him for his scrupulous timidity! Her bosom with anger was heaving! Her eyes were flashing with rage under the surge of hot anger that swept over her.

"Are you not the king of this country?" she chides bitingly, her tongue sharp like a butcher's blade. "Can you not command and have it done?" she scolds as a common village hag who has more noise than wisdom in her words. "Can you not seize and keep?" she cries with reproach. "I thought you told me you were king in these parts! And here you are crying like a baby and willing to eat not anything because you do not have courage to take a bit of land. You! Ha! Ha! Ha! Ha! You the king of Israel, and allow yourself to be disobeyed and defied by a common clodhopper from the country. You are more courteous and considerate of him than you are of your queen! Shame on you! But you leave it to me! I will get the vineyard for you, and all that I require is that you ask no questions. Leave it to me, Ahab!"

"And Jezebel his wife said unto him, Dost thou now govern the kingdom of Israel? arise, and eat bread, and let thine heart be merry: I will give thee the vineyard of Naboth the Jezreelite!" (1 Kings 21:7).

Ahab knew Jezebel well enough to know assuredly that she would do her best, or her devil's worst, to do what she said she would do. So slowly, as a turtle crawls out of the cold mud when the hot sunshine hits it, he came out of his sulks, somewhat as a snake arouses and uncoils from winter sleep. He doubtless asked her, with a show of reluctant eagerness, how she was going to get Naboth's vineyard. She, if she acted as human nature naturally expresses itself, tickled him under the chin with her lily white and bejeweled fingers, or kissed him peckingly on the cheeks with her lips screwed in a tight knot, and said something akin to these words: "That's my secret just now; just leave it to me!"

She was the polluted reservoir from which the streams of his own iniquity found mighty increase. She was the poisonous pocket from which his cruel fangs fed. She was the sulphurous pit wherein the fires of his own iniquity found fuel for intenser burning. She was the Devil's grindstone which furnished sharpening for his weapons of wickedness.

I suppose Ahab considered himself the master of his wife. But it was her mastery over him that stirred him up to more and mightier wickedness than his own heart was capable of conceiving, than his own mind was capable of planning, than his own will was capable of executing.

What a tragedy when any woman thinks more of paint than purity, of vulgarity than virtue, of pearls than principles, of adornment than righteous adoration, of hose and hats than holiness, of dress than duty, of mirrors than manners! What a tragedy when any woman sacrifices decency on the altar of degradation—visualizing the slimy, the tawdry, the tinseled!

Know ye not yet, ye women, that the degeneracy of womanhood helps the decay of manhood? Know ye not that when woman is lame morally man limps morally?—that when woman slips morally man slumps morally?—when woman fags in spiritual ideals man sags in spiritual ideals? Study history as much as you please and read the Bible as often as you will, and you will see that the moral and spiritual life of no nation, no community, no city, no village, no countryside, no home, no school, no church ever rises any higher or flows any stronger than the spiritual life of the women.

Who was it who caused Samson to have his eyes punched out and to be a prisoner of the Philistines, after he had been judge in Israel for twenty years? Delilah—a woman! Who was it caused David to stake his crown for a caress? Bathsheba—a woman. Who was it danced Herod into hell? Herodias—a woman! Who was it who was like a heavy chain around the neck of

Governor Felix for life or death, for time and eternity? Drusilla—a woman! Who was it, by lying and diabolical stratagem, sent the spotless Joseph to jail because he refused her dirty, improper proposal? Potiphar's wife.

So also it was a woman, a passionate and ambitious idolatress, even Jezebel, who mastered Ahab. Take the stirring crimes of any age, and at the bottom more or less consciously concerned, the world, almost invariably, finds a woman. Only God Almighty knows the full story of the foul plots hatched by women. This was true, as we shall presently see, with the two under discussion now. But let me say, incidentally, if women have mastered men for evil, they have also mastered them for good—and we gladly make declaration that some of the fairest and most fragrant flowers that grow in the garden of God and some of the sweetest and most luscious fruit that ripens in God's spiritual orchards are there because of woman's faith, woman's love, woman's prayer, woman's virtue, woman's tears, woman's devotion to Christ.

But we must not depart further from the objective of this message to discuss that. Let us come to the next terrible scene in this tragedy of sin. The next scene is—

## IV. A Message Meaning Murder

Jezebel wrote letters to the elders of Jezreel. And in these letters she made definite and subtle declaration that some terrible sin had been committed in their city for which it was needful that a fast should be proclaimed in order to avert the wrath of heaven.

"So she wrote letters in Ahab's name, and sealed them with his seal, and sent the letters unto the elders and to the nobles that were in his city, dwelling with Naboth. And she wrote in the letters, saying, Proclaim a fast, and set Naboth on high among the people: and set two men, sons of Belial, before him, to bear witness against him, saying, Thou didst blaspheme God and the king. And then carry him out, and stone him, that he may die" (1 Kings 21:8–10).

This letter, with cynical disregard of decency, was a hideous mockery in the name of religion. Once get the recusant citizen accused of blasphemy, and, by a divine law, the property of the blasphemer and rebel went to the crown. "Justice! How many traitors to sacred truth have dragged the innocent to destruction!"

Surely black ink never wrote a fouler plot or death scheme on white paper since writing was known among men. Every syllable of every word of every line of every sentence was full of hate toward him who had done only good continually. Every letter of every syllable was but the thread which, united with other threads, made the hangman's noose for him who had not changed his righteous principles for the whim of a king. The whole letter was a diabolical death-warrant.

Moreover, Jezebel's deeds showed that when she went down to market, as it were, she would have in her basket a nice vineyard for her husband when she returned. She said to herself: "This man Naboth has refused my honorable lord on religious grounds, and by all the gods of Baal, I will get him yet on these very same grounds." She understood perfectly the passion of a devout Jew for a public fast; and she knew that nothing would keep the Jews away. Every Jew and every member of his household would be there.

"Proclaim a fast." Fasting has ever been a sign of humiliation before God, of humbling one's self in the dust before the "high and lofty One that inhabiteth eternity." The idea in calling for a fast was clearly to declare that the community was under the anger of God on account of a grave crime committed by one of its members, which crime is to be exposed and punished. Then, too, the fast involved a cessation of work, a holiday, so that the citizens would have time to attend the public gathering.

"Set Naboth on high!" "On high" meant before the bar of justice, not in the seat of honor. "On high" meant that Naboth was put where every eye could watch him closely and keenly observe his bearing under the accusation. "And set women, base fellows, before him."

And let them "bear witness against him!" In other words, put him out of the way by judicial murder, not by private assassination. "And then carry him out, and stone him, that he may die!" A criminal was not to be executed within a city, as that would defile it! Thus Christ was crucified outside the walls of Jerusalem! We see that Jezebel took it for granted that Naboth would be condemned.

And so one day, while Naboth worked in his vineyard, the letters came down to Jezreel. And one evening, while Naboth talked at the cottage door with his sons or neighbors, the message meaning murder was known to the elders of the city. And that night, while he slept with the wife of his bosom, the hounds of death let loose from the kennels of hell by the jewel-adorned fingers of a king's daughter and a king's wife were close on his heels. The message meaning murder was known to many but not to him, until they came and told him that a fast had been proclaimed—proclaimed because God had been offended at some crime and that His wrath must be appeased and the threatening anger turned away, and he himself, all unconscious of any offense toward God or the king, set in the place of the accused, even "on high among the people," to be tried as a conspicuous criminal.

Consider now—

## V. The Fatal Fast

And what concern they must have created in the household of Naboth, when they knew that Naboth was to be "set on high," even in the "seat of the accused," even before the bar of "justice," because of a ferocious message calling religion in to attest a lie. And what excitement there was in the city when, with fawning readiness to carry out her vile commands, the elders and nobles "fastened the minds" of the people upon the fast—proclaimed as if some great calamity were overhanging the city for their sins like a black cloud portending a storm, and proclaimed as if something must be done at once to avert the doom. Curious throngs hurried to the fast to see him who had been accused of the crime which made necessary the appeasing of the threatening wrath of an angered God.

And they did! "And there came in two men, children of Belial, and sat before him" (1 Kings 21:13). Satan's hawks ready to bring death to God's harmless sparrow! Satan's eagles ready to bury their cruel talons in God's innocent dove. Satan's bloody wolves ready to kill God's lamb! Satan's boars ready with keen tusks to rip God's stag to shreds! Reckless and depraved professional perjurers they were! "And the men of Belial witnessed against him, even against Naboth, in the presence of the people, saying, Naboth did blaspheme God and the king" (1 Kings 21:13).

Then strong hands jerked Naboth out of the seat of the accused. Doubtless muttering curses the while, they dragged him out from among the throngs of people, while children screamed and cried, while women shrieked in terror, while men moved in confusion and murmured in consternation. They dragged him roughly to a place outside the walls of the city and with stones they beat his body to the ground. Naboth fell to the ground as lily by hailstones beaten to earth, as stately cedar uprooted by furious storm. His head by stones is crushed, as eggs crushed by heel of giant. His legs are splintered! His arms are broken! His ribs are crushed. Bones stick out from the mass of human flesh as fingers of ivory from pots of red paint. Brains, emptied from his skull, are scattered about. Blood spatters like crimson rain. Naboth's eyes roll in sockets of blood. His tongue between broken jaws becomes still. His mauled body becomes—at last—still. His last gasp is a sigh. Naboth is dead— dead for cursing God and the king as many were led to believe!

And we learn from 2 Kings 9:26, that by the savage law of those days his innocent sons were involved in this overthrow. They, too, that they might not claim the inheritance, were slain. And Naboth's property, left without heirs, reverted to the crown.

No doubt Naboth's righteous austerity had made him extremely unpopular in many ways in "progressive Jezreel." And since Jezebel carried out her purpose in a perfectly legal and orderly way and in a "wonderfully" democratic manner, we see a fine picture of autocracy working by democratic methods. And when these "loyally patriotic citizens" of Jezreel had left the bodies of Naboth and his sons to be devoured by the wild dogs which prowled after nightfall in and around the city, they sent and told Queen Jezebel that her bloody orders had been bloodily and completely obeyed! "Then they sent to Jezebel, saying, Naboth is stoned, and is dead" (1 Kings 21:14).

I do not know where Jezebel was when she received the news of Naboth's death. Maybe she was out on the lawn watching the fountains splash. Maybe she was in the sun parlor, or somewhere listening to the musicians thrum on their instruments. But, if I judge this painted human viper by her nature, I say she received the tragic news with devilish delight, with jubilant merriment.

What was it to her that yonder, over twenty miles away, sat a little woman who the night before had her husband but who now washes her crushed and ghastly face with her tears? What did it matter to her that in Jezreel only yesterday her sons ran to her at her call but today are mangled in death? What did it matter to her that outside the city walls the dogs licked the blood of a godly husband? What mattered it to her that Jehovah God had been defied, His commandments broken, His altars splattered with pagan mud, His holy Name profaned? What mattered it to her that the worship of God had been dishonored?

What did she care if a wife, tragically widowed by murder, walked life's way in loneliness? What did she care that there was lamentation and grief and great mourning, Rachel weeping for her children because they were not? What did she care if justice had been outraged just so she had gotten the little plot of land close by their place within which was evil girt with diadem? Nothing! Did pang grip her heart because innocent blood had been shed? Just as well ask if the ravenous lion mourns over the lamb it devours.

Trippingly, as a gay dancer, she hurried in to where Ahab sat. With profuse caresses and words glib with joy she told him the "good" news. She had about her the triumphant manner of one who has accomplished successfully what others had not dared attempt. Her "tryout" in getting the vineyard was a decided "triumph." She had "pulled the stunt." She had been "brave" and "wise"—and because of this her husband now could arise and hie him down to the vineyard and call it his own.

"And it came to pass, when Jezebel heard that Naboth was stoned, and was dead, that Jezebel said to Ahab, Arise, take possession of the vineyard of Naboth the Jezreelite, which he refused to give thee for money: for Naboth is not alive, but dead" (1 Kings 21:15).

And it was the plot hatched in her own mind and it was her hand, her lily-white hand, her queen's hand, that wrote the letters that made this tragic statement true.

And the next scene in this tragedy of "pay day—some day" is—

## VI. The Visit to the Vineyard

How Jezebel must have paraded with pride before Ahab when she went with tidings that the vineyard which he wanted to buy was now his for nothing! How keen must have been the sarcasm of her attitude when she made it known by word and manner that she had succeeded where he failed—and at less cost! How gloatingly victorious were the remarks which she made which kept him warmly reminded that she had kept her "sacred" promise! What a lovely fabric, stained and dyed red with Naboth's blood, she spread before him for his "comfort" from the loom of her evil machinations!

"And it came to pass, when Ahab heard that Naboth was dead, that Ahab rose up to go down to the vineyard of Naboth the Jezreelite, to take possession of it" (1 Kings 21:16). Ahab rose up to go down—from Samaria to Jezreel. He gave orders to his royal wardrobe keeper to get out his king's clothes, because he had a little "business" trip to make to look over some property that had come to him by the shrewdness of his wife in the real estate market!

Jehu and Bidkar, the royal charioteers, make ready the great horses such as kings had in those days. Jehu was the speed-breaking driver of his day, known as the one who drove furiously. The gilded chariot is drawn forth. The fiery horses are harnessed and to the king's chariot hitched. The outriders, in gorgeous garments dressed, saddle their horses and made ready to accompany the king in something of military state. Then, amid the clatter of prancing hoofs and the loud breathing of the chariot horses—eager-eyed, alert, strong muscled, bellows-lunged, stouthearted, and agile of feet—Jehu drives the horses to the chariot hitched up to the palace steps.

Out from the palace doors, Jezebel walking, almost strutting, proudly and gaily at his side, comes Ahab. Down the steps he goes while Jezebel, perhaps, waves a bejeweled hand to him or speaks a "sweet" good-bye. Bidkar opens the chariot door. Ahab steps in. Then, with the crack of his whip or a sharp command by word of mouth, Jehu sends the great horses on their way—away from the palace steps, away from the palace grounds, away through the gates, away, accompanied by the outriders, away down the road to Jezreel!

*Where is God?* Where is God? Is He blind that He cannot see? Is He deaf that He cannot hear? Is He dumb that He cannot speak? Is He paralyzed that He cannot move? *Where is God?* Well, wait a minute, and we shall see.

Over there in the palace Jezebel said to Ahab, her husband: "Arise! Get thee down and take possession of the vineyard of Naboth." And over yonder in the wilderness way, out yonder where the tall cedars waved like green plumes against a silver shield, against the moon blossoming in its fulness like a great jonquil in the garden of the patient stars, out yonder where the only music of the night was the weird call of whippoorwill and the cough of coyote and the howl of wolf, out yonder God had an eagle-eyed, hairy, stouthearted prophet, a great physical and spiritual athlete, Elijah. "And the word of the LORD came to Elijah." And God said to Ellijah: "Arise, go down."

Over here, in the palace, Jezebel said to Ahab: "Arise, get thee down!" And out there, near Carmel, God said to Elijah: "Arise!" I am so glad that I live in a universe where, when the Devil has his Ahab to whom he can say, "Arise," God has His Elijah to whom He can say, "Arise!"

"And the word of the LORD came to Elijah the Tishbite, saying, Arise, go down to meet Ahab king of Israel, which is in Samaria: behold, he is in the vineyard of Naboth, whither he is gone down to possess it. And thou shalt speak unto him, saying, Thus saith the LORD, Hast thou killed, and also taken possession? And thou shalt speak unto him, saying, Thus saith the LORD, In the place where the dogs licked the blood of Naboth shall dogs lick thy blood, even thine" (1 Kings 21:17–19).

As Ahab goes down to Jezreel, the voice of Jehu, as he restrains the fiery horses, or the lash of his whip as he urges them on, attracts the attention of the grazing cattle on adjacent pasture land. The sound of clanking hoofs of cantering horses resounds in every glen by the roadway. The gilded chariot catches the light of the sun and reflects it brightly, but he who rides therein is unmindful of the bloodstains on the ground where Naboth died.

And that brings us to the other scene in this tragedy of "pay day—some day." It is—

## VII. The Alarming Appearance

The journey of twenty-odd miles from Samaria to Jezreel is over. Jehu brings the horses to a stop outside the gate to the vineyard. The horses stretch their necks trying to get slack on the reins. They have stood well the furious pace at which they have been driven. Around the rim of their harness is the foam of their sweat. On their flanks are, perhaps, the marks of Jehu's whip. They breathe as though their great lungs were a tireless bellows. The outriders line up in something of military formation. The hands of ready servants open the gate to the vineyard. Bidkar opens the chariot door. And Ahab steps out into Naboth's vineyard. There, no doubt, he sees, in the soft soil, Naboth's footprints. Close by doubtless, the smaller footprints of his wife he sees.

Naboth is dead, and the coveted vineyard is now Ahab's through the "gentle scheming" of the queen of his house. Perhaps Ahab, as he walks into the vineyard, sees Naboth's pruning hook among the vines. Or he notices the fine trellis work which Naboth's hands had fastened together for the growing vines. Perhaps, in a corner of the vineyard, is a seat where Naboth and his sons rested after the day's toil, or a well where sparkling waters refreshed the thirsty or furnished water for the vines in time of drouth.

And while Ahab strolls among the vines that Naboth tended, what is it that appears? Snarling wild beasts? No. Black clouds full of threatening storm? No, not that. Flaming lightning which dazzles him? No. War chariots of his ancient enemies rumbling along the road? No. An oncoming flood sweeping things before it? No; not a flood. A tornado goring the earth? No. A huge serpent threatening to encircle him and crush his bones in its deadly coils? No; not a serpent. What then? What alarmed Ahab so? Let us follow him and see.

As he converses with himself, suddenly a shadow falls across his path. Quick as a flash Ahab whirls on his heels, and there before him stands Elijah, prophet of the living God. Elijah's cheeks are swarthy; his eye is keen and piercing; like coals of fire, his eyes burn with righteous indignation in their sockets; his bosom heaves; his head is held high. His only weapon is a staff; his only robe a sheepskin, and a leather girdle about his loins.

Like an apparition from the other world, like Banquo's ghost at Macbeth's feast, with suddenness terrifying, stands before Ahab. Ahab had not seen Elijah for five years. Ahab thought Elijah had been cowed and silenced by Jezebel, but now the prophet confronts him with his death-warrant from the Lord God Almighty.

To Ahab there is an eternity of agony in the few moments they stand thus, face to face, eye to eye, soul to soul! His voice is hoarse, like the cry of a hunted animal. He trembles like a hunted stag before the mouths of fierce hounds. Suddenly his face goes white. His lips quiver. He had gone to take possession of a vineyard, coveted for a garden of herbs; and there he is face to face with righteousness, face to face with honor, face to face with judgment. The vineyard, with the sun shining upon it now, is as black as if it were part of the midnight which has gathered in judgment.

"And Ahab said to Elijah, Hast thou found me, O mine enemy?" (1 Kings 21:20). And Elijah, without a tremor in his voice, his eyes burning their way into Ahab's guilty soul, answered: "I have found thee: because thou hast sold thyself to work evil in the sight of the LORD." Then, with every word a thunderbolt, and every sentence a withering denunciation, Elijah continued: "God told me to ask you this: Hast thou killed, and also taken possession? . . . Thus saith the LORD, In the place where dogs licked the blood of Naboth shall dogs lick thy blood, even thine. . . . Behold, I will bring evil upon thee, and will take away thy posterity. . . . And will make thine house like the house of Jeroboam the son of Nebat, and like the house of Baasha the son of Ahijah, for the provocation wherewith thou hast provoked me to anger, and made Israel to sin!"

And then, plying other words mercilessly like a terrible scourge to the cringing Ahab, Elijah said: "And of Jezebel also spake the LORD, saying, The dogs shall eat Jezebel by the wall of Jezreel. Him that dieth of Ahab in the city the dogs shall eat; and him that dieth in the field shall the fowls of the air eat."

And, with these words, making Ahab to cower as one cowers and recoils from a hissing adder, filling Ahab's vineyard to be haunted with ghosts and the clusters thereof to be full of blood, Elijah went his way—as was his custom so suddenly to appear and so quickly to disappear. Ahab had sold himself for nought, as did Achan for a burial robe, and a useless ingot, as did Judas for thirty pieces of silver which so burned his palms and so burned his conscience and so burned his soul until he found relief in the noose at the rope's end.

And when Ahab got back in the chariot to go back to Jezebel—the vile toad who squatted upon the throne to be again with the beautiful adder coiled upon the throne—the hoofs of the horses pounding the road pounded into his guilty soul Elijah's words: "Some day—the dogs will lick thy blood! Some day the dogs will eat Jezebel—by the ramparts of Jezreel." God had spoken! Would it come to pass?

And that brings us to the last scene in this tragedy of "pay day—some day." It is—

### VIII. Pay Day—Some Day

Does pay day come? As to Ahab and Jezebel, pay day comes as certainly as night follows day, because sin carries in itself the seed of its own fatal penalty. Dr. Meyer says: "According to God's constitution of the world, the wrongdoer will be abundantly punished." The fathers sow the wind and the children reap the whirlwind. One generation labors to scatter tares, and the next generation reaps tares and retribution immeasurable.

To the individual who goes not the direction God points, a terrible pay day comes. To the nation which forgets God, pay day will come in the awful realization of the truth that the "nations that forget God shall be turned into hell." When nations trample on the principles of the Almighty, the result is that the world is beaten with many stripes. We have seen nations slide into Gehenna—and the smoke of their torment has gone up before our eyes day and night.

The certainty of pay day—some day for all who regard not God or man is set forth in the words of an unknown poet:

> You'll pay. The knowledge of your acts will weigh
> Heavier on your mind each day.
> The more you climb, the more you gain,
> The more you'll feel the nagging strain.
> Success will cower at the threat
> of retribution. Fear will fret
> Your peace and bleed you for the debt;
> Conscience collects from every crook
> More than the worth of what he took.
> You only thought you got away
> But in the night you'll pay and pay.

All these statements are but verification of Bible truth:

"Whoso diggeth a pit shall fall therein: and he that rolleth a stone, it will return upon him" (Prov. 26:27).

"Therefore shall they eat of the fruit of their own way, and be filled with their own devices. For the turning away of the simple shall slay them, and the prosperity of fools shall destroy them" (Prov. 1:31–32).

"Even as I have seen, they that plow iniquity, and sow wickedness, reap the same" (Job 4:8).

"The gods are just—and of our vices made instruments to scourge us."

When I was pastor of the First Baptist Church of New Orleans, all that I preached and taught was sent out over the radio. In my "fan mail" I received letters from a young man who called himself "Chief of the Kangaroo Court." Many nasty, critical things he said. Sometimes he wrote a nice line—and a nice line was in all the vulgar things he wrote like a gardenia in a garbage can.

One day I received a telephone call from a nurse in the Charity Hospital of New Orleans. It was about this fellow who so often dipped his pen in slop, who seldom thrust his pen into nectar. She said: "Pastor, there is a young man down here whose name we do not know, who will not tell us his name. All he will tell us is that he is chief of the Kangaroo Court. He is going to die. He says that you are the only preacher he has ever heard—and he has never seen you. He wants to see you. Will you come down?" "Yes," I replied. And I quit what I was doing and hurried down to the hospital.

The young nurse met me at the entrance to the charity ward and took me in. Inside were several beds against the wall on one side and against the wall on the other side. And in a place by itself was another bed. To this bed, on which lay a young man about eighteen or nineteen years old, slender, hollow-eyed, nervous, the nurse led me. "This is the chief of the Kangaroo Court," she said simply.

I looked upon the young man, "Hello," I said kindly.

"Howdy do?" he answered, in a voice that was half a snarl.

"What can I do for you?" I asked, trying to make him see my willingness to help him.

"Not a thing! Nothin' 'tall," he said grouchily, "unless you throw my body to the buzzards when I am dead—if the buzzards will have it!"

A rather painful silence, in which I looked kindly at him and he wildly at me, ensued.

Then he spoke again. "I sent for you, sir, because I want you to tell these young fellows here something for me. I sent for you because I know you go up and down the land and talk to many young people. And I want you to tell 'em and tell 'em every chance you get, that the Devil pays only in counterfeit money."

This was in desperate earnestness, in his eyes and in his voice. I held his hand as he died. I saw his eyes glaze. I heard the last gurgle in his throat. I saw his chest heave like a bellows and then become quiet.

When he died, the little nurse called me to her, excitedly. "Come here!" she called.

"What do you want, child?" I asked.

"I want to wash your hands! It's dangerous to *touch* him."

Pay day had come!

But what about Ahab? Did pay day come for him? Yes. Consider how. Three years went by. Ahab is still king. And I dare say that during those three years Jezebel had reminded him that they were eating herbs out of Naboth's vineyard. I can hear her say something like this as they sat at the king's table: "Ahab, help yourself to these herbs. I thought Elijah said the dogs were going to lick your blood. I guess his dogs lost their noses and lost the trail."

But I think that during those three years, Ahab never heard a dog bark that he did not jump.

One day Jehoshaphat, king of Judah, visited Ahab. The Bible tells us what took place—what was said, what was done.

"And the king of Israel said unto his servants, Know ye that Ramoth in Gilead is ours, and we be still, and take it not out of the hand of the king of Syria? And he said unto Jehoshaphat, Wilt thou go with me to battle to Ramoth-gilead? And Jehoshaphat said to the king of Israel, I am as thou art, my people as thy people, my horses as thy horses" (1 Kings 22:3–4).

"So the king of Israel and Jehoshaphat the king of Judah went up to Ramoth-gilead" (1 Kings 22:29).

Ahab, after Jehoshaphat had promised to go with him, in his heart was afraid, and had sad forebodings, dreadful premonitions, horrible fears. Remembering the withering words of Elijah three years before, he disguised himself—put armor on his body and covered this armor with ordinary citizen's clothes.

"And the king of Israel said unto Jehoshaphat, I will disguise myself, and enter into the battle; but put thou on thy robes. And the king of Israel disguised himself, and went into the battle" (1 Kings 22:30).

The Syrian general had given orders to slay only the king of Israel—Ahab.

"But the king of Syria commanded his thirty and two captains that had rule over his chariots, saying, Fight neither with small nor great, save only with the king of Israel" (1 Kings 22:31).

Jehoshaphat was not injured, although he wore his royal clothes.

"And it came to pass, when the captains of the chariots saw Jehoshaphat, that they said, Surely it is the king of Israel. And they turned aside to fight against him: and Jehoshaphat cried out. And it came to pass, when the captains of the chariots perceived that it was not the king of Israel, that they turned back from pursuing him" (1 Kings 22:32–33).

While war steeds neighed and war chariots rumbled and shields clashed on shields and arrows whizzed and spears were thrown and swords were wielded, a death-carrying arrow, shot by an aimless and nameless archer, found the crack in Ahab's armor.

"And a certain man drew a bow at a venture, and smote the king of Israel between the joints of the harness: wherefore he said unto the driver of his chariot, Turn thee thine hand, and carry me out of the host; for I am wounded. And the battle increased that day: and the king was stayed up in his chariot against the Syrians, and died at even: and the blood ran out of the wound into the midst of the chariot. . . . And one washed the chariot in the pool of Samaria; and the dogs licked up his blood; and they washed his armour; *according unto the word of the LORD which He spake*" (1 Kings 22:34–35, 38).

But what about Jezebel? Did her pay day come? Yes—after twenty years. After Ahab's death, after the dogs licked the blood, she virtually ruled the kingdom. But I think that she went into the temple of Baal on occasions and prayed her god Baal to protect her from Elijah's hounds.

Elijah had been taken home to heaven without the touch of the deathdew upon his brow. Elisha had succeeded him.

"And Elisha the prophet called one of the children of the prophets, and said unto him, Gird up thy loins, and take this box of oil in thine hand, and go to Ramoth-gilead: and when thou comest thither, look out there Jehu the son of Jehoshaphat the son of Nimshi, and go in, and make him arise up from among his brethren, and carry him to an inner chamber; then take the box of oil, and pour it on his head, and say, Thus saith the LORD, I have anointed thee king over Israel. Then open the door, and flee, and tarry not. So the young man, even the young man the prophet, went to Ramoth-gilead. And when he came, behold, the captains of the host were sitting; and he said, I have an errand to thee, O captain. And Jehu said, Unto which of all us? And he said, To thee, O captain. And he arose, and went into the house; and he poured the oil on his head, and said unto him, Thus saith the LORD God of Israel, I have anointed thee king over the people of the LORD, even over Israel. And thou shalt smite the house of Ahab thy master, that I may avenge the blood of my servants the prophets, and the blood of all the servants of the LORD, at the hand of Jezebel. . . . And I will make the house of Ahab like the house of Jeroboam the son of Nebat, and like the house of Baasha the son of Ahijah: And the dogs shall eat Jezebel in the portion of Jezreel, and there shall be none to bury her. And he opened the door, and fled" (2 Kings 9:1–7, 9–10).

"Then Jehu came forth to the servants of his lord: and one said unto him, Is all well? wherefore came this mad fellow to thee? And he said unto them, Ye know the man, and his communication. And they said, It is false; tell us now. And he said, Thus and thus spake he to me, saying, Thus saith the LORD, I have anointed thee king over Israel. Then they hasted, and took every man his garment, and put it under him on the top of the stairs, and blew with trumpets, saying, Jehu is king" (2 Kings 9:11–13).

Mounting his chariot, commanding and taking with him a company of his most reliable soldiers, furiously did he drive nearly sixty miles to Jezreel.

"And when Jehu was come to Jezreel, Jezebel heard of it." Pause! Who is Jehu? He is the one who, twenty years before the events of this chapter from which we quote, rode down with Ahab to take Naboth's vineyard, the one who throughout those twenty years never forgot those withering words of terrible denunciation which Elijah spoke. And who is Jezebel? Oh! The very same one who wrote the letters and had Naboth put to death. And what is Jezreel? The place where Naboth had his vineyard and where Naboth died, his life pounded out by stones in the hands of ruffians. "And when Jehu was come to Jezreel, Jezebel heard of it; and she painted her face, and tired her head, and looked out at a window. And as Jehu entered in at the gate, she said, Had Zimri peace, who slew his master?"

Pause again just here. "Had Zimri peace, who slew his master?" No; "there is no peace, saith my God, to the wicked." And he lifted up his face to the window, and said, "Who is on my side? who? And there looked out to him two or three eunuchs. And he said, Throw her down" (2 Kings 9:30–33).

These men put their strong men's fingers into her soft feminine flesh and picked her up, tired head and all, painted face and all, bejeweled fingers and all, silken skirts and all—and threw her down. Her body hit the street and burst open. Some of her blood splattered on the legs of Jehu's horses, dishonoring them. Some of her blood splattered on the walls of the city, disgracing them.

And Jehu drove his horses and chariot over her. There she lies, twisting in death agony in the street. Her body is crushed by the chariot wheels. On her white bosom are the black crescent-shapes of horses' hoofs. She is hissing like an adder in the fire.

"And when he was come in, he did eat and drink, and said, Go, see now this cursed woman, and bury her: for she is a king's daughter. And they went to bury her: but they found no more of her than the skull, and the feet, and the palms of her hands" (2 Kings 9:34, 35).

God Almighty saw to it that the hungry dogs despised the brains that conceived the plot that took Naboth's life. God Almighty saw to it that the mangy lean dogs of the back alleys despised the hands that wrote the plot that took Naboth's life. God Almighty saw to it that the lousy dogs which ate carrion despised the feet that walked in Baal's courts and then in Naboth's vineyard.

These soldiers of Jehu went back to Jehu and said: "We went to bury her, O king," but the dogs had eaten her.

And Jehu replied: "This is the word of the LORD, which he spake by his servant Elijah the Tishbite, saying, In the portion of Jezreel shall dogs eat the flesh of Jezebel."

"And the carcass of Jezebel shall be as dung upon the face of the field in the portion of Jezreel; so that they shall not say, This is Jezebel" (2 Kings 9:37).

Thus perished a female demon, the most infamous queen that ever wore a royal diadem.

Pay day—some day! God said it—and it was done! Yes, and from this we learn the power and certainty of God in carrying out His own retributive providence, that men might know that His justice slumbereth not. Even though the mill of God grinds slowly, it grinds to powder; "and though His judgments have leaden heels, they have iron hands."

And when I see Ahab fall in his chariot and when I see the dogs eating Jezebel by the walls of Jezreel, I say, as the Scripture saith: "O that thou hadst hearkened to my commandments; then had thy peace been as a river, and thy righteousness as the waves of the sea!" And as I remember that the gains of ungodliness are weighted with the curse of God, I ask you: "Wherefore do ye spend money for that which is not bread? and your labour for that which satisfieth not?"

And the only way I know for any man or woman on earth to escape the sinner's pay day on earth and the sinner's hell beyond—making sure of the Christian's pay day on earth and the Christian's heaven beyond the Christian's pay day—is through Christ Jesus, who took the sinner's place upon the cross, becoming for all sinners all that God must judge, that sinners through faith in Christ Jesus might become all that God cannot judge.

# Fulton John Sheen

*1895-1979*

During his years of active ministry, Bishop Fulton J. Sheen was probably the best-known Roman Catholic prelate in the United States. Ordained in 1919, from 1926 to 1950 he taught philosophy and theology at Catholic University, Washington, D.C. In 1950 he became national director for The Society for the Propagation of the Faith and brought several notable Americans into the Roman Catholic Church. However, it was as a radio and television personality that he reached his greatest audience and achieved his popularity.

From 1930 to 1952 Bishop Sheen spoke weekly over the *Catholic Hour* radio program, but it was his television program *Life Is Worth Living* (1951–1957) that made a religious celebrity out of him. It is estimated that thirty million viewers tuned in Bishop Sheen every week, an audience surpassed only by comedian Milton Berle. The remarkable thing is that Bishop Sheen gave his electrifying (and often humorous) sermons without the aid of script, cue cards, or teleprompter. He used a blackboard to clarify and illustrate his points, always drawing an angel in the corner of the board to remind us that he was speaking about holy things; and at the close of each television season, he thanked his "writers"—Matthew, Mark, Luke, and John.

Sheen wrote two syndicated newspaper columns, one of them for the Roman Catholic press, and he was the author of more than fifty books, some of which appeared on the best-seller list.

He resigned all of his church offices in 1969 to devote himself to writing and occasional preaching assignments.

Bishop Sheen's autobiography, *Treasure in Clay*, was published posthumously by Doubleday/Image in 1982, and Ignatius Press brought out a new edition in 1993. McGraw-Hill published his television talks in five series from 1954 to 1957 under the title *Life Is Worth Living*. A selection of his best sermons and articles is found in *From the Angel's Blackboard*, edited by Patricia A. Kossmann (Triumph Books, 1995).

# Life Is Worth Living?

Is life worth living, or is it dull and monotonous? Life *is* monotonous if it is meaningless; it is *not* monotonous if it has a purpose. The prospect of seeing the same program on television for a number of weeks is this problem in minor form. Will not repetition of the same format, the same personality, the same chalk, the same blackboard, and the same angel create monotony? Repetition does generally beget boredom. However, two beautiful compensations have been given a television audience to avoid such boredom: one is a dial, the other is a wrist. Put both together and all the forces of science and advertising vanish into nothingness.

Life is monotonous if it has no goal or purpose. When we do not know why we are here or where we are going, then life is full of frustrations and unhappiness. When there is no goal or over-all purpose, people generally concentrate on motion. Instead of working toward an ideal, they keep changing the ideal and calling it "progress." They do not know where they are going, but they are certainly "on their way." Life is then like a radio in the early days. Remember? No one seemed to be interested in getting a particular program. He was interested only in picking up distant places, sitting up all night, turning the dial. The next morning he would say with glee, "You know, at three o'clock last night I got Washington, then Mobile, and I even heard Peoria."

Those who have no ultimate destiny for life really can never say they are making progress; if there is no fixed point, they can never say whether they are getting to their goal or not. Life under these circumstances is boring. A sculptor after hacking and cutting away at a block of marble all day was asked, "What are you making?"

He said, "I really don't know. I haven't seen the plans."

People live ten, twenty, thirty, fifty years without a plan. No wonder they find their existence humdrum and tiresome. If they were farmers, they would probably plant wheat one week, root it up and plant barley the next; then dig up the barley and plant watermelon; then dig up the watermelon another week and plant oats. Fall comes around and they have no harvest; if they repeated that process for years, they could go crazy. It is the meaninglessness of life that makes it wearisome.

Some change their philosophy of life with every book they read: One book sells them on Freud, the next on Marx; materialists one year, idealists the next; cynics for another period, and liberals for still another. They have their quivers full of arrows, but no fixed target. As no game makes the hunter tired of the sport, so the want of destiny makes the mind bored with life.

Boredom can lead to revolution. A boy is given a BB gun. If the father gives him a target, for example, a bull's-eye in the side of a barn or an old tin can, the boy is happy to shoot at it, and use his gun as it ought to be used. As soon as the target is rejected or ignored or not given, generally he goes in for shooting anything, particularly school windows. The revolutionary spirit in the world today is born of such purposeless and meaningless existence.

A university kept dogs for experimental purposes in two separate cages. In one cage were dogs without fleas; in the other were dogs with fleas who were waiting to be dipped and "defleaed." The professors noted that the dogs with fleas were more tranquil than the dogs without fleas, because they had something to keep them busy. The others howled and barked and in general created many problems of canine delinquency. The scientists concluded that physiological economy is directed to work and the expenditure of energy. The restlessness of the flealess dogs was a kind of regulatory mechanism for keeping the organism fit. In the higher realms, man's powers are directed to the expenditure of energy for an over-all purpose; if he lacks it, his giddiness and restlessness and consequent boredom are the price he has to pay. The most bored people in life are not the underprivileged but the overprivileged. The moral is not to have "fleas" or annoyances and troubles; but the moral is to have something to *do* and *live for*, not for today and tomorrow, but *always*.

When life has no intentional destiny; when it has no bivouac, no harbor, no ideal, it is full of mediocrity and tedium. It then becomes completely exteriorized with consequent loss of much power and peace.

As Stephen Vincent Benét put it:

198

Life is not lost by dying; Life is lost
Minute by minute, day by dragging day,
In all the thousand small uncaring ways.

Where there are no inner resources, but only staleness and flatness, such people say life has frustrated them: *No! They have frustrated life.* They excuse themselves saying they are bored because they are not loved: No! They are bored because they do not love; because they have denied love.

(Incidentally, just as soon as I began to quote that poem the camera moved toward me like an enemy tank. The one moment one must concentrate is when poetry is recited. Why cameramen want close-ups in poetical moments is not for me to divine. I must just remember to be prepared in subsequent programs. That Cyclops' eye, Camera No. 2, can be the most distracting thing in television.)

Thus far we have considered one alternative: Life does not seem worth living if it has no goal or purpose. On the other hand, life is thrilling if it has a destiny.

What we call the ultimate purpose of life is one beyond all immediate or proximate goals, such as a man wanting to become a farmer, or a woman wanting to become a nurse. The purpose that survives when these lesser goals have been achieved, is the ultimate goal. No one can have two final purposes in life any more than he can walk to the right and left at the same time. The final purpose is, therefore, unique—the grand powerhouse whence flows the current for all the particular tasks of living.

The best way to discover it is to study the nature of man. We are to some extent like the rest of creation. For example, we have existence, or being, like stones, oxygen, and sand. But man also has life, which makes him like flowers and trees, which vegetate and grow and reproduce. Man also has senses like the animal, by which he enters into contact with the great external environment, from stars to the food which lies at his finger tips. But man has something unique; he is not just the sum of all of these. What man has peculiar unto himself is the fact that man is a *thinking* and a *willing* being. First of all, he can think thoughts that surpass the knowledge of the senses, *e.g.*, causes, the beautiful, or the relatedness between things. But he also has freedom. He can choose, decide, and determine his targets both near and far.

This superior intellect and will of man wants many things, such as to make money, to be the head of a labor union (though the two are not mutually exclusive), to marry the boss's daughter, etc. But what he basically wants in common with all other humans, is happiness. This happiness obviously does not revolve around external things, such as a big income without income tax, for such things are *external* to him. He wants to be happy on the *inside*.

Man wants three things: life, knowledge, and love.

The *life* he wants is not a life for two more minutes, but the fullness of life without wrinkles, worry, or old age. The *truth* he wants is not only the knowledge of geography to the exclusion of literature or the truths of science to the exclusion of philosophy; he wants to know all things. Man is incurably curious.

Finally, he wants *love*. He needs it because he is incomplete within himself. He wants a love without jealousy, without hate, and above all, a love without satiety—a love with a constant ecstasy in which there is neither loneliness nor boredom.

Man does not find that enduring life, that all-embracing knowledge, that joyful love here below. Here he finds life is mingled with death; truth with error; love with hate.

He knows he would not be craving for such happiness, if it did not exist. He would not have eyes if there were no light or things to see. If there is the fraction, there ought to be the whole. His search then becomes like looking for the source of light in this theater. It is not under this blackboard, for here light is mingled with darkness; it is not under the camera, for there light is mingled with shadow. If we are to discover the source of light in this theater, we have to go out to this bright light shining above us. In like manner, if we are to find the source of the life, truth, and love that is in the world, we have to go to a Life that is not mingled with its shadow, death; to a Truth that is not mingled with its shadow, error; to a Love that is not mingled with its shadow, hate. We must go out to Pure Life, Pure Truth, Pure Love, and that is the definition of God. He is the ultimate goal of life; from Him we came, and in Him alone do we find our peace.

Many think, when we say that man's ultimate happiness is union with God, that God is to be conceived as something extrinsic to man, as a kind of a pious "extra," or that He is related to us as a reward for a good life, or as a medal is related to study. A gold medal at the end of the school year is not intrinsically related to study. Many do excellent work in school and get no medals. God and the happiness of Heaven are not related to us that way. Rather God and Heaven are related to one another as blooming to a rose, or as a peach to a peach tree, or as an acorn to an oak, namely, as our intrinsic perfection without which we are incomplete, and with which we are happy.

Over my head is a microphone. You cannot see it on your television. That microphone is at the end of a long iron pole and is actually only about eight inches above my head. I always admire the restraint of the boom man. He must be tempted a thousand times a night to hit a poor performer over the head with it. All he would have to do would be to let it drop. As he could hit an actor on the "bean," he could hit a Bishop on the "beanie." If the microphone were endowed with consciousness and we asked it, "When are you happy?" the microphone would say, "When I pick up sound."

"Are you happy when you hit a Bishop on the 'beanie'?"

"Only as an amusing distraction."

When are we most happy? When we do that for which we are made, as the microphone is happy when it does that for which it was made. Then there is a thrill and a romance to life.

It may be objected that there are people who are full of life who hate repetition; therefore, working toward the ideal goal is boring. No! Look at those who are full of life; they love repetition. Put a child on your knees and bounce it up and down two or three times; the child will say, "Do it again."

If you tell a child a funny story—I can remember my grandmother telling me the story of an Indian who came to kill a farmer who was splitting logs. The farmer induced the Indian to put his fingers in the split log for a second, which he did and was held prisoner. I never found out what happened to either the farmer or the Indian, but I said to her at least a thousand times, "Tell me again." The child never says, "That's an old story; I heard Uncle Ed tell it last week." He says, "Tell me again." You blow smoke through your nose or you blow it through your ears, as I once thought an uncle could do, and the child will say, "Do it again."

When Divine Life came to this earth, he re-echoed the lesson of the Thrill of Monotony. St. Peter asked how many times we should forgive. Peter thought seven times was enough. Our Lord said, "seventy times seven." There were three sweet monotonies in His Life—thirty years obeying, three years teaching, three hours redeeming. He passed on to us the thrill of being born again, which was made a condition for entering into the Kingdom of Heaven.

Because God is full of life, I imagine each morning Almighty God says to the sun, "Do it again"; and every evening to the moon and the stars, "Do it again"; and every springtime to the daisies, "Do it again"; and every time a child is born into the world asking for a curtain call, that the heart of God might once more ring out in the heart of the babe.

Life is full of romance and thrill when it has one over-all purpose, namely, to be one with a Life that is Personal enough to be a Father; one with a Truth that is Personal enough to be the Wisdom from whence come all Art and Science; and one that is Personal enough to be a Love that is a "Passionless Passion, a wild Tranquility."

Life is Worth Living when we live each day to become closer to God. When you have said your prayers, offered your actions in union with God, continue to enjoy the "Thrill of Monotony," and *Do it again!*

# David Martyn Lloyd-Jones

*1899–1981*

D. Martyn Lloyd-Jones left certain success as a medical doctor to follow Christ's call into ministry and as a result gained eternal rewards as a faithful servant of the Word. Lloyd-Jones was born in Cardiff, South Wales, and reared in the Calvinistic Methodist tradition of Whitefield. He began his medical training in London at the age of sixteen and passed every examination with brilliance. When he was only twenty-one, he was working in Harley Street with Lord Horder, the royal physician. He was so young, he had to wait until 1923 to receive his M.D. degree.

Lloyd-Jones's future was secure, but his heart was restless, and in 1926 he surrendered to preach the gospel. He served the Bethlehem Church in Sandfields, Aberavon, from 1927 to 1938 when he was called to be associate minister with G. Campbell Morgan at Westminster Chapel, London. When Morgan retired in 1943, Lloyd-Jones became the senior minister and remained at Westminster Chapel until his retirement in 1968.

It wasn't long before London and the entire United Kingdom realized that a prophet and a man of God had been raised up to help guide his people through the difficult postwar years. A thoroughgoing Calvinist, Lloyd-Jones made certain that every sermon or address was based on careful exegesis and that it proclaimed solid theology. He never really lost the approach of the physician, for many of his messages began with the diagnosis of the problem (sin), exposed the false remedies, and then announced the one and only remedy—faith in the Lord Jesus Christ.

In October 1955 he began his monumental series on Romans at the Friday-night Westminster Bible School and continued verse by verse until his retirement, ending in Romans 14. Also beginning in 1955 he expounded the Epistle to the Ephesians in 230 Sunday-morning messages.

Lloyd-Jones explained his convictions about preaching in his book *Preaching and Preachers* (Hodder & Stoughton, 1971). He defined preaching as "logic on fire" and "eloquent reason" and insisted that every sermon apply God's truth to both "the current situation" and to the personal needs of the people. The purpose of preaching was to "give men and women a sense of God and His presence." Along with his many volumes on Romans and Ephesians, he published sermon commentaries on the Sermon on the Mount, Habakkuk, and Psalm 73, as well as topical studies on matters relating to conversion, Christian unity, and healing. Lloyd-Jones's grandson Christopher Catherwood is overseeing the publication of additional sermon series and memoirs.

The official biography is by Iain H. Murray, *D. Martyn Lloyd-Jones: The First Forty Years*, and *D. Martyn Lloyd-Jones: The Fight of Faith* (Banner of Truth, 1982 and 1990). For a study of the preaching of D. Martyn Lloyd-Jones, see *The Sacred Anointing* by Tony Sargent (Hodder and Stoughton, 1994; American edition, Crossway, 1994).

# The Christian Message
# to the World

But God . . .
Ephesians 2:4

We now come to look at two wonderful words—"But God." These words obviously suggest a connection with something that has gone before. The word "but" is a conjunction, and yet it suggests always a contrast; and here we have the connection and the contrast. Look at them in their context, "And you hath he quickened, who were dead in trespasses and sins; wherein in time past ye walked according to the course of this world, according to the prince of the power of the air, the spirit that now worketh in the children of disobedience: among whom also we all had our conversation in times past, in the lusts of our flesh, fulfilling the desires of the flesh and of the mind; and were by nature the children of wrath, even as others. But God . . ."

With these two words we come to the introduction to the Christian message, the peculiar, specific message which the Christian faith has to offer to us. These two words, in and of themselves, in a sense contain the whole of the gospel. The gospel tells of what God has done, God's intervention; it is something that comes entirely from outside us and displays to us that wondrous and amazing and astonishing work of God which the apostle goes on to describe and to define in the following verses.

We shall take these words now in a general manner only. I do so for several reasons. One is that the text itself compels one to do so, but there are also certain special reasons for doing so. A charge frequently brought against the Christian message, and especially the evangelical form of that message, is that it is remote from life, that it is irrelevant to the immediate circumstances in which men and women find themselves. In other words, there is an objection on the part of some to the expository method of preaching the gospel; it is that it never seems to come to grips with the realities of the situation in which men and women find themselves from day to day, and that it is irrelevant to the whole world situation in which we find ourselves. I desire to show, therefore, that that charge is entirely unfounded; and further, that the idea that the business of Christian preaching is just to make topical references to contemporary events is, indeed, in a sense, to depart from the Christian message altogether. I would go so far as to say that there is nothing which really does deal with the contemporary situation save the Scripture, when its doctrines are understood, believed and applied.

That is what I propose to do now. I want to show the relevance of the gospel on a day such as Remembrance Sunday when instinctively almost, and certainly as the result of what is happening in the world in which we live, our minds are compelled to face, and to think of, the general situation in addition to our own particular situations. And, claiming as I do that the gospel deals with the whole of man and with the whole of his life in this world, it is important that we should see what it has to say about, and to do with, the position in which we find ourselves. You notice that the thing I am emphasising is the all-importance of method. The many who do not think in a Christian and biblical manner believe that the business of the Christian Church on a day such as this is to announce, for instance, a subject such as "The Geneva Conference—Possibilities," and then go on to say what we think the statesmen should do. That, it seems to me, is entirely false and contrary to the biblical method. The biblical method, rather, is to display God's truth, and then to show the relevance of that to any given situation. You do not start with the situation, you end with the situation. The Bible invites us at the outset to stop looking on the horizontal level, as it were, to stop merely looking at the world and at men; it invites us at the very beginning to lift up our eyes and to look at God. In other words, the whole case presented in the Bible from beginning to end is that life and man and the world simply cannot be understood until we see everything in the light of the truth about God, and in that context. Therefore we must start with the truth of God and only then go on to the immediate situation.

Let us proceed to show how that is done, and how it is done in the very passage which we are considering. We have considered in detail these first three verses in this chapter, and we have been doing so in order that we might see what we ourselves are like by nature and what the world is like by nature. You cannot begin to solve the problems of mankind until you know the truth about man. How futile it is to attempt to do so apart from that. You must start with the character, the nature, the being of man. Instead of starting with international conferences and talk about contemporary events, we need to go much further back and ask, Well now, what sort of a creature is man? Obviously all our conclusions and all our proposals are going to be governed by the answer to that question. If man is really an essentially good creature who only needs a little more instruction and knowledge and information, obviously the treatment is going to be comparatively simple. But if what the apostle Paul says here about man as he is by nature, and without Christ, is true, then equally obviously, treatment along such lines is going to be entirely hopeless, and to attempt it is sheer waste of time.

We must start with this doctrine. *What is true of man in sin?* What characterises man as he is in sin without the grace of God? We have already looked into this matter. Man is dead spiritually; he is governed by the devil, who operates through the mighty spiritual forces under his command, which in turn produce and control the mind and the outlook of the world. That is the position of man. And the result is that man, dominated by that evil power, lives a life of trespasses and sins; indeed he has been born in such a way, as the result of his descent from Adam, that his very nature is fallen. He starts with a polluted nature. And finally he is under the wrath of God. That is the apostle's statement in the first three verses.

What then is the relevance of all that to the present situation; what has it to say to us as we face the whole world situation at this present time? It is clear that a number of things can be very easily deduced from this teaching.

The first is that here we are given *the only real and adequate explanation of why there are such occurrences as wars.* Why do we have them? Why is man guilty of this final madness? Why is it that men kill one another and have even gloried in war? Why? What is the explanation of it all? There is only one answer; it is because man is as the apostle describes him. It is not only the teaching of the apostle Paul. You remember how James puts it in the fourth chapter of his Epistle, "Whence come wars among you?"—and answers the question—"even of the lusts that war in your members." That is the cause of war. It is man in his fallen condition. Now the realisation of this truth and fact is absolutely vital for us as a starting point. This is true of nations, it is true of classes, it is true of individuals. There is surely nothing which is quite so illuminating and contradictory as the way in which people think along one line when they are thinking of nations and along a quite different line when they are thinking of individuals. There is little point in talking eloquently about the sanctity of international contracts while you are dealing with people who break their own marriage contracts and other personal contracts, for nations consist of individuals. The nation is not something abstract, and we are not entitled to expect conduct from a nation which we do not find in the individual. All these things have to be taken together.

This is a principle that operates throughout society from top to bottom, from the individual to the nation, to the continent, to the whole world itself. The explanation of the state of the world according to the Bible is that man is governed by these desires of the flesh and of the mind. He is not so much interested in whether a thing is right or not, he is interested in the fact that he wants it, that he likes it, that he must have it. Of course we stand back aghast when a nation behaves like that. When Hitler walks in and annexes Austria we are horrified. Yes, people are horrified who do the very same thing in their personal lives. They do it in the matter of other men's wives; they do it in the matter of another man's post or position or business. It is the same thing exactly. There then is the principle. It is this lust that governs mankind. "Walking according to the course of this world" says the apostle, "we all had our conversation in times past in the lusts of the flesh, fulfilling the desires of the flesh and of the mind." The first deduction, therefore, is that here and here alone do we have an adequate explanation and understanding of why things are as they are.

The second deduction follows quite logically. It is that *while man continues to be thus governed, the world will continue to be as it is.* This is surely obvious. If it is the state of man in sin that has been responsible for the history of the past, obviously, while man remains unchanged, the history of the future is going to be unchanged. Here we confront and come into collision with the optimism of the natural man who is always so sure and confident that somehow or another we in our generation can put things right. He feels that whereas all other generations who have gone before us have failed, we are in a different position, in a superior position. We are educated, and cultured; we know whereas they did not know; we have advanced so much, we must succeed; we are going to succeed. But if you believe this biblical doctrine of man in sin you must see at once that that is a fatal fallacy. If our troubles are due to the lusts that are in mankind in sin, and which control men, while they remain, there will be wars. We have specific teaching to that effect from our blessed Lord Himself, who said, "There will be wars and rumours of wars." He said, also, "As it was in the days of Noah, so shall it be also in the days of the Son of man"; "Likewise also as it was in the days of Lot"—in Sodom—"even thus shall it be" (Luke 17:26–30). That is our Lord's view of history.

If we grasp this teaching we shall be delivered at once from all the false enthusiasm and the false hopes of men who really believe that by bringing in some new organisation you can outlaw war and banish it for ever. The answer of the Bible is that you cannot do so while man remains unregenerate. Is this depressing? My reply is that, whether it is depressing or not is not our concern; we should be concerned to know the truth. The modern man claims to be a realist. He has objected to Christianity because, according to him, it does not face the facts. It is not realistic, he says; it is always "pie in the sky," and you go into your chapels and you shut yourselves off and do not face the facts of life. Yet when we give him the facts he objects on the grounds that they are depressing. It is the political and philosophical optimists who are not realists; it is the people who have never faced the facts about man in sin who are shutting their eyes and turning their backs upon reality. The Bible faces it all; it has a realistic view of life in this world, and it alone has it.

Now let us look at *the specific, direct teaching of the gospel.* What has the Christian message to say about this state and this condition, the explanation of which we have just been considering? The answer is that it says, "But God." That is its message. What does that mean? The most convenient way of analysing this matter is to put it first of all negatively and then positively. I regret that I have to start with a negative again. I must do so, because so many forget these negatives, and thus deliver messages which cannot possibly be regarded as Christian at all. And yet they will be delivered in the name of Christianity and of the Christian Church. I am profoundly convinced that what is keeping large numbers of people from Christ and from salvation, and from the Christian Church is this terrible confusion of which the Church herself has been, and is, so guilty. There are many outside the Church today because in the first world war the Christian Church so frequently became a kind of recruiting office. Men are offended—and in a sense they were right to be offended. There are certain things which should never be confused. Let us note some of them.

What is this Christian message? We start by saying that *it is not a great appeal for patriotism:* That is not the Christian message. The Christian message does not denounce patriotism, or say that there is anything wrong in it. The man is to be pitied who does not love his country and his nation. There is nothing in the Scriptures against that. It is God who has divided up the nations and defined their bounds and their habitations. It is God's will that there should be nations. But it is not God's will that there should be nationalism, an aggressive nationalism. There is nothing wrong in a man honouring his own country and delighting in it: but it is utterly un-Christian to say "My country right or wrong." That is always wrong, that is fatally wrong; that is a complete denial of the teaching of Scripture. Take this great apostle who wrote this very Epistle to the Ephesians. Here is a

man who was a Jew, and if ever a man was proud of the fact of his nation-
ality it was the apostle Paul—"A Hebrew of the Hebrews, of the tribe of
Benjamin. . . ." He was once a narrow nationalist who despised others. The
Gentiles were dogs, outside the pale. But the thing in which he glories in
this Epistle, you remember, is this, "in whom ye also trusted." The Gentiles have come in, have been made "fellow heirs" with the Jews, the middle wall of partition has been broken down. "There is no longer Jew nor
Gentile, barbarian, Scythian, bond nor free, male nor female; all are one
in Christ." That is the Christian position. "But God. . . ." Here is the way
to break down that nationalistic spirit that leads to war. To believe that we
are always right and everybody else wrong is as wrong in nations as it is in
individuals. It is always wrong. The Christian message is not just an appeal
to patriotism. And if Christianity is portrayed in that form it is a denial, a
travesty of the message, and it is misleading in the eyes and the ears of those
who listen to it.

But, secondly, *the Christian message is not just an appeal to courage, or
heroism,* or to the manifestation of a great spirit of self-sacrifice. Let us be
clear about this also. Christianity does not condemn courage, it does not
condemn self-sacrifice, or heroism. These qualities, these virtues are not
specifically Christian. They are pagan virtues, which were taught and incul-
cated, admired and praised, before the Lord Jesus Christ ever came into
this world. Courage was the supreme virtue according to the Greek pagan
philosophers; it was the very essence of Stoicism. And that was why they
regarded meekness, the meekness taught by the Christian faith, as weakness. There was no word for meekness in Greek pagan philosophy. Courage,
and strength, and power—those were the things they believed in. That is
why, you remember, Paul tells us that the preaching of the cross was "to
the Greeks foolishness." That someone who was crucified in weakness
should be the Saviour, and that that should be the way of salvation, to them
was nonsense and rubbish. They placed no value on meekness and on humil-
ity; courage and power and heroism were the great virtues. So it is very
important that we should realise that it is no part of the Christian message
to exhort people to courage and heroism and to self-sacrifice. There is
nothing specifically Christian in such ideas. Christianity does not condemn
them, but that is not the Christian message. And the point I am emphasising is this, that when that has been presented as the Christian message
it has confused people, and has led to the very division which the gospel
itself was meant to heal.

But let us go on to a third matter. There are many people who seem to
think that the Christian message is that we should just appeal to the world
to put into practice the Christian principles. *Now this is the pacifist position,
so-called.* They say, Now, you Christian people, you are always preaching

about personal salvation and about doctrines and so on; why do you not do something about wars? Well then, we say, what do you want us to do? They reply, What you have to do is to tell the people to practise the Sermon on the Mount. Why do you not tell them to turn the other cheek and to love one another, and so on, then there would be an end of war? You have the solution; just get people to put into operation the principles of the teaching of Christ. What is the answer to that? The answer is the teaching of the first three verses in this second chapter of Paul's Epistle to the Ephesians. You can preach the Sermon on the Mount to people who are "dead in trespasses and sins" until you have exhausted yourself and you will be none the wiser, neither will they. They cannot practise it. They do not want to. They are "enemies and aliens in their minds." They are governed by "lusts." They "fulfil the desires of the flesh and of the mind." They are governed and ruled by this. How can they practise the Sermon on the Mount?

There is only one hope for man in sin, says Paul—"but God." Men need to be regenerated; they must be given a new nature before they can even understand the Sermon on the Mount leave alone begin to put it into practice. So it is but a travesty of the Christian message to speak of it as if it were but an appeal to men to rise up and to follow Christ in their own strength, and to put into operation Christian principles of teaching. It is as much a travesty of the gospel as is the preaching of patriotism and imperialism. It is equally non-Christian. It is indeed dangerous heresy, the ancient Pelagian heresy, because it fails to realise that man, being what he is in sin, cannot possibly implement such teaching. To expect Christian conduct from people who are not yet Christians is dangerous heresy. You see how important our teaching is, and how essential it is that we should be clear about the true application of the Christian message to the modern world. That is why we do not spend our time in talking about international conferences and about politics and international relationships, or industrial disputes, or in preaching always on the question of pacifism and against physical warfare. To do so is simply to waste time—though it would probably attract publicity. What is needed is that we should start with this fundamental principle, the doctrine of man in sin, in his deadness, in his hopelessness, in his complete helplessness.

To sum up at this point, the negative principle is that the Christian faith, the Christian gospel, has no direct message for the world except to say that the world as it is, is under the wrath of God, that it is under condemnation, and that all who die in that state will go to perdition. The only message of the Christian faith to an unbelieving world, in the first instance, is simply about judgment, a call to repentance, and an assurance that if they do repent and turn to Christ they shall be delivered. The Church, therefore, the Christian faith, has no message to the world apart from that.

But the Bible also teaches very plainly and clearly that while that is the message of God to the unbelieving world, God, nevertheless, has done something about that unbelieving world. What He has done in the first instance is this. *He has put a control upon the power of sin and of evil.* He has done so in this way. As I have already reminded you He has divided up the peoples of the world into nations. Not only so, He has ordained that there should be states and governments. He had ordained "the powers that be." "The powers that be," says Paul, in Romans 13, "are ordained of God"; whether it be a king or an emperor or a president of a republic, "the powers that be are ordained of God." It is God who has ordained magistrates and given them the sword of power. Why? Simply to keep the manifestations of evil within bounds and under control. For if God had not done this, if the lusts that operate in us all by nature and by inheritance from Adam were allowed unlimited and uncontrolled manifestation, the world would be hell, and it would have hurtled itself to perdition long ago and would have destroyed itself. God has put a limit upon it. He has put a bound even upon evil, He has held it in, He has restricted it. Indeed the apostle Paul in a most extraordinary statement in the Epistle to the Romans (chapter 1, verses 18 ff.) proves the matter by saying that sometimes, for His own end and purposes, God withdraws that restraint partially. He says that God "had given them over to a reprobate mind." There are times and seasons when God seems to relax the restraint that He has put upon sin and evil in order that we may see it in all its horror. It may well be that we are living at such a time. But that is what the Bible tells us about what God does directly about man in sin; He controls the manifestations of his foul and evil and fallen nature. That is the *general* message.

But what is the *particular* message? This is the thing that the apostle is concerned to emphasise most of all in this immediate paragraph. *The message to individuals is that we can be delivered out of this present evil world,* that we can escape the condemnation that is coming for certain upon this world. That is the message the apostle preached. It is a message to individuals. It does not say that the world can be put right if we only implement Christian teaching; it is not an appeal to people to reform themselves and to do this or that. No, it is a message which says that as the result of what God has done in Christ Jesus, His Son, our Lord and Saviour, we who were in the very warp and woof of that sinful, condemned world can be delivered out of it— "Who gave himself for our sins," he says to the Galatians, "that he might deliver us from this present evil world." The world is doomed, the world is going to be destroyed and punished, the devil and all his forces are going to perdition, and all who belong to that realm will suffer the same punishment. But the messages of the gospel to men and women individually is that they need not be participators in that. You can be taken out of it—"out of the kingdom of darkness" brought out from the power of Satan, unto god. That is its message to individual men and women. The world will remain as it is, but you can be delivered out of it, you can be taken out of it.

Not only that; we can also be introduced into and become citizens of a kingdom which is not of this world. As we go through this chapter we shall find Paul elaborating his own words. The marvellous thing, he says, is that you Gentiles are in Christ, and because of His blood, have become fellow citizens with the saints; you have become citizens in the kingdom of God, the kingdom of Christ, the kingdom of light, the kingdom of heaven—a kingdom that is not of this world, a kingdom which cannot be shaken, a kingdom which cannot be moved. That is the kingdom into which we enter.

This is the most thrilling news a man can ever hear. Now we are all citizens of this country, our native land, and we are all involved in what happens to this country. If this country goes to war we shall be involved. We did not escape the bombs in the first war any more than anybody else simply because we were Christians. We are all involved in it, we are citizens of this world and we share in the fate of this world. But thank God, here is something different. While remaining citizens of this world we become citizens of another kingdom, this other kingdom that has been opened to us by Christ—a spiritual kingdom, a kingdom that is not of this world, eternal in the heavens with God. That is the teaching of this message. "But God . . ."

The doctrine works itself out in practice like this. If I believe this message, from now on I *am not going to pin my hopes, nor rest my affections finally, on anything in this world.* The natural man does so, of course; he pins his hopes on this world and its mind, its outlook, its statesmen, its mentality, its pleasures, its joys. He lives for it, and all his hopes are centred here, his affections are here. Not so the Christian. The Christian, having been given to see that this world is doomed, that it is under the wrath of God, has fled from "the wrath to come." He has believed the gospel, he has entered this other kingdom, and his hopes and affections are set there now, not here. The Christian is a man, who, to use a scriptural phrase, knows that he is but "a stranger and a pilgrim" in this world. He is a mere sojourner, he does not any longer live for this world: he has seen through it, he sees beyond it. He is but a journeyman, a traveller, and, as James puts it (chapter 4) he is a man who has realised that his life is "but a vapour," a breath. So he does not regard this world as permanent; he does not lay down his plans and say, I am going to do this or that. Not at all! But rather,

"If the Lord will . . ."; it is all under God, and he realises how contingent it is. He does not any longer pin his faith or set his affections on this world.

But still more marvellous! *He is never taken by surprise over anything that happens in this world.* That is why I said earlier, that there is nothing that I know of that is so relevant to worldly circumstances as this gospel. The Christian is a man who is never surprised by what happens in the world. He is prepared for everything, prepared for anything. He is not at all surprised when a war breaks out. The non-Christian, and especially the idealist, of course, is greatly surprised. He really did believe at the end of the first world war that the League of Nations was going to abolish war for ever. There were many who believed that the Locarno Pact of 1925 was finally going to do it, and they were very happy. They were confident that there would never be another war like that of 1914–18. And when it came in 1939 they did not know how to explain it. But the true Christian, knowing that man is a creature who is governed by lusts, and that lust always produces war, knew perfectly well that no Locarno Pact or anything else could outlaw or abolish war. He knew that war might come at any time, and when it came he was not surprised. As Psalm 112 puts it in the seventh verse: "He shall not be afraid of evil tidings; his heart is fixed, trusting in the LORD." Believing as we do this biblical doctrine of man in sin, we should never be surprised at what happens in the world. Are you surprised at all the murders, the thefts, the violence, the robbery, all the lying and the hatred, all the carnality, the sexuality? Does it surprise you as you look at your newspapers? It should not do so if you are a Christian. You should expect it. Man in sin of necessity behaves like that; he cannot help himself, he lives, he walks in trespasses and sins. He does it individually, he does it in groups; therefore there will be industrial strifes and misunderstandings and there will be wars. Oh, what pessimism! says someone. I say, No, what realism! Face it, be prepared for it, do not expect anything better from a world like this; it is a fallen, sinful, godless, evil world; and while man remains in sin, it will be like that. And it is as much like that today as it was in the days of Sodom and Gomorrah and in the time of the flood!

But, thank God, I have not finished. I go on to say that the Christian is a man who, realising that he is living in such a world, and who, having no illusions at all about it, yet knows that he is linked to a Power that enables him not only to bear whatever may come to him in such a world, but indeed *to be "more than conqueror" over it all.* He does not just passively bear it, he does not merely put up with it, he does not just "stick it" and exercise courage. No, that is stoicism, that is paganism. The Christian, being in Christ, the Christian knowing something of what the apostle calls "the exceeding greatness of God's power to us-ward that believe," is strengthened, is enabled to endure; his heart does not quail, he is not defeated, indeed he can rejoice in tribulations. Let the world do its worst to him, let hell be let loose, he is sustained. "This is the victory that overcometh the world, even our faith." So that if things really do become impossible, the Christian has resources, he still has comforts and consolations, he still has a strength of which all others are ignorant.

Finally, the Christian is absolutely certain and assured that whatever the world and men may do *he is safe in the hands of God.* "We can confidently say," say the Scriptures, "the Lord is my helper, and I will not fear what man shall do unto me." Indeed he knows this, that man in his malignity may insult him, may persecute him, may ravage him, may even destroy his body; but he also knows that nothing shall ever be able to "separate him from the love of God which is in Christ Jesus our Lord." He knows that whatever may happen in this world of time, he is a son of God, an heir of glory. Indeed he knows this, that a day is coming when even this present sinful world shall be entirely redeemed, and there "shall be new heavens and a new earth wherein dwelleth righteousness." The Christian can look forward to this, that he, some glorious day in the future, when his very body shall be renewed and glorified, when it shall no longer be weak, when it shall be no longer subject to sickness and old age and disease, when it will be a glorified body like that of the risen Christ—he knows that he in this glorified body shall even walk the face of this very earth, out of which evil and sin and vileness shall have been burned by the fire of God. He will dwell in a perfect world, of which the Lamb, the Son of God, is the Light and the Sun, the Brightness and the Glory, and he shall enjoy it for ever and ever. That is what the Christian message, the Christian faith has to say to this wretched, distracted, unhappy, confused, frustrated, modern world. It is all the outcome of these essential doctrines which can be learned only in this Book which is God's Word. There is the world!—"But God . . ."

# Oswald Jeffrey Smith

*1889–1986*

Oswald Smith was born in a farmhouse near Odessa, Ontario, where his father worked for the railroad. In January 1906 Smith heard R. A. Torrey preach at Massey Hall in Toronto and gave his heart to Christ. He served for a year among the Indians in British Columbia as an agent for the Bible Society and for a short time attended Manitoba College in Winnipeg. He spent two years at the Toronto Bible College (1910–1912) and three at McCormick Seminary in Chicago (1912–1915). In 1915 he was ordained at the Buena Presbyterian Church in Chicago and returned to Toronto to serve as associate pastor of the Dale Presbyterian Church. There he met Daisy Billings and they were married September 12, 1916. She was the perfect helpmeet for him.

In October Smith became pastor of Dale Presbyterian Church when the senior pastor left for the front to minister to the troops. However, Smith's emphasis on evangelism and missions aroused opposition in the church and he was asked to leave. He and Daisy and their son Glen went to British Columbia to minister as part of the Shantymen's Christian Association. In 1919 he felt a call from God to return to Toronto, and in October he began a ministry called The Gospel Auditorium. The next year his flock became part of the Parkdale Tabernacle, which was part of the Christian & Missionary Alliance, and Smith became superintendent of the C. & M.A. work in eastern Canada. It was then that he came under the strong influence of Paul Rader.

Smith pastored the Alliance Tabernacle in Los Angeles for a year and then returned to Toronto, burdened to start a work that would emphasize missions, the Spirit-filled life, and evangelism. On September 9, 1928, he began the ministry that later became The People's Church, and he remained as pastor until 1959 when his son Paul succeeded him. Oswald J. Smith traveled through the world to awaken the church to evangelism, revival, and missions.

Smith was not only a powerful preacher, but he was also a prolific writer (over thirty-five books) and composer. His first song was "Joy in Serving Jesus" (1931), and more than two hundred followed, including "God Understands," "After," "Pray On," "The Song of the Soul Set Free," "Then Jesus Came," and "With Thy Spirit Fill Me." *The Story of My Life* is his autobiography (Marshall, Morgan & Scott, 1962), and the official biography is *Fire in His Bones* by Lois Neely (Tyndale, 1982). The Smiths' daughter Hope Evangeline wrote a poignant biography of her mother simply called *Daisy* (Baker, 1978).

# The Man God Uses

Never will I forget that period in my life when I wanted, more than anything else, to be used of God. As I rode my mule through the beautiful ravines of the Kentucky hills, or paced back and forth in my little lonely cabin among the mountaineers, I cried out to God in the agony of my soul, "Lord, use me. Make me a soul-winner. Send me out as an evangelist. Let me see revival. Don't let me settle down in an ordinary pastorate and accomplish nothing. I have only one life to live and I want to invest it for thee. Let me live for others. Enable me to win lost men and women to the Lord Jesus Christ. Let thy blessing rest upon my ministry."

Then I would pray like this: "Lord, what are the qualifications for evangelistic work? How may I be used by thee? Are there conditions to be met? If so, reveal them to me. What must I do? Make known the prerequisites. Help me to meet the conditions whatever they may be so that I may not waste my life. I must not fail."

Then as I studied God's Word I found the qualifications, and I faced them, one by one, as God revealed them to me. There they were, clearly stated. These conditions I now want to pass on to you, for I believe that you, too, want to be used of God. You, too, realize that you have but one life to live and you do not want to waste it. You want it to count for souls. You want to know the qualifications for the work of evangelism and revival. Let me mention them one by one, just as God revealed them to me so long ago.

Until God gives us a vision of the utter bankruptcy of the human race, we will not get far with our evangelistic work. We must know that the race is bankrupt. We must realize that men are dead in trespasses and in sins, that there is no good thing in any man. We must know something of the utter depravity of the human heart.

## 1. A Vision of the Total Bankruptcy of the Human Race

As long as we think there is a spark of divine life in the heart of man, we will not accomplish much in our evangelistic work; for we will then conclude that all we have to do is to fan that spark into a flame and all will be well.

That, you see, rules out the new birth entirely. There is then no need of conversion, for if man already has life, he does not have to receive life. He has merely turned his back on his Father God and has wandered away. The work of the evangelist, then, is to persuade him to right about face, to turn back to God.

Such an idea implies that we are all children of God, which according to the Bible is untrue. Until we have been born again, we are children of Satan and we do not belong to the family of God at all. Only the new birth can make us children of God. No, my friend, there is no spark of divine life in any man; therefore there is nothing to fan into a flame. Men are dead, lost, undone, utterly depraved, with no hope of life apart from a new birth.

That is why I say that we must realize something of the utter bankruptcy of the human race. We must know that man who is dead must be quickened into life, that he is utterly hopeless in himself, and that only God can meet his need. That qualification is of paramount importance and no evangelist can be successful until he has it.

On the one side, there is the utter bankruptcy of the human race, but on the other, a salvation adequate to meet the need. In other words, God has a remedy. God has a cure. He has made adequate provision. God can quicken men from death into life. He has provided for the bankruptcy of the human race, for those who are dead in trespasses and in sins.

Over nineteen hundred years ago, through his only begotten Son, the Lord Jesus Christ, He made that provision. Hence, when you and I go out into our evangelistic work, realizing as we do that men are dead in trespasses and sins, that they are utterly helpless and hopeless in themselves, and that the human race is absolutely bankrupt, we know that we have a glorious gospel, a wonderful Saviour, a marvellous provision—all that is needed to meet man's desperate plight.

There is no other such message. With joy in our hearts and assurance in our souls, we can go with the gospel of the Lord Jesus Christ, knowing that it will work. The most desperate character, the man farthest away from God and deepest in sin, can be rescued through the power of the gospel of Jesus Christ. That is why Paul exclaimed, "I am not ashamed of the gospel of Christ: for it is the power of God unto salvation to every one that believeth . . ." (Rom. 1:16). The gospel is the remedy. There is no other. You and I must realize that and never turn to anything else. This only must be our message. Any other cure will be inadequate. God's gospel is man's only hope.

## 2. A Realization of the Adequacy of God's Salvation

The United Nations do not have the solution to the problem. No statesman has the solution. No politician can meet the need. No government is adequate. You and I are the only ones who have the solution, and our solution is the gospel. There is no other "Christ died for our sins" (1 Cor. 15:3).

The gospel solves all problems. The gospel is effective when nothing else is. The gospel meets all needs. Nothing else can. Therefore it is the gospel that we must preach. Thank God, we can preach it with the utmost assurance.

Now, my friends, unless you believe that the gospel is the solution and that there is no other, you will not get far in your evangelistic work. Unless you know that man in his helplessness and hopelessness is utterly bankrupt, and that apart from the gospel he is beyond recovery, you will not accomplish much. Unless you really believe that man is utterly depraved, that he is dead in trespasses and in sins, and that you have the one and only remedy, the gospel of the Lord Jesus Christ, and that this remedy can meet his direct need, hopeless though he may seem, you will have but little success as you seek to evangelize.

You remember that the Apostle Paul said, "This one thing I do." Paul was a man of one thing. The man who is going to be successful in evangelistic and soul-winning work is the man who has set everything else aside, who has become a man of one thing, one purpose, one aim in life. Any man with divided interests, any man with many schemes, plans and programmes, any man who is interested in other things, is not going to be successful as an evangelist. The one who is going to succeed is the one who has but one great purpose in his life.

## 3. A Life Given Over to One Great Purpose

When I was a student I never dreamed of getting married until I had graduated and had commenced my ministry. For a student to take upon him the responsibility of a wife and family is a tremendous financial burden. If his interests are thus divided, how can he concentrate on his studies and expect to succeed in his work? Would it not be better to wait until he is through with his schooling before taking such a step?

I never have been able to understand how some ministers can carry on their work as ministers and at the same time go into business on the side. If God calls a man to preach the gospel, he should live by the gospel. There is no reason why he should make a little money on the side. If he turns to business, he is going to become interested in business. He will give thought to it and he will not be a man of one thing. Part of his time will be spent in the ministry and part in business.

I have learned that the ministry demands all that there is of a man. It requires his entire attention—all his thought, all his study, both day and night. He must be completely wrapped up in his vocation. He must be given over absolutely to the one great work to which God has called him. If he is trying to make a little money on the side, if he is interested in business of one kind and another, he is not going to be able to concentrate on the one great work to which God has ordained him.

The monks had the right idea. They felt that they should withdraw from the world to lock themselves up in a monastery so as to devote their entire time to God. They felt that they should give up all other interests and have nothing more to do with the world so that they might serve God perfectly. I say, their aim was right, their purpose was right, although their method was wrong. God's plan is that we should mingle with our fellow men and yet be utterly devoted to him.

Can a wife be a successful wife if she is interested in another man? Can a husband be a successful husband if he is interested in another woman? You know the answer. How then can any man called of God be a successful evangelist if he has other irons in the fire? It is simply impossible. The evangelist must be a man of one great purpose in life. He must be able to say with the Apostle Paul, "This one thing I do."

My friend, have you a number of different interests? Are you trying to do several things instead of devoting yourself to the one great work to which God has called you? Do you want to be a success? Are you anxious to win souls to the Lord Jesus Christ and to know something of the glory of revival? Then, I say again, concentrate on one thing. Give yourself wholly to God and to the work of evangelism.

Do you remember the words of the Apostle Paul: "No man that warreth entangleth himself with the affairs of this life; that he may please him who hath chosen him to be a soldier" (2 Tim. 2:4)? Timothy was to be a man of one thing. Paul made it clear to him that no man that allows himself to be entangled in worldly affairs could ever be a successful soldier. So it is with the evangelist. If he is going to serve God as God wants him to serve, he must free himself from every other interest.

You want God to use you? Well, then, are you willing to pay the price? Are you prepared to let everything else go and become a man of one thing? Will you devote your entire life to this one thing, to see to it that nothing else absorbs your attention? Are you prepared to concentrate, to give yourself wholly to God's service, to become a man of one great purpose in life?

If you are, God will use you for his glory and honour, and your evangelism will be successful.

### 4. A Life from Which Every Hindrance Has Been Removed

Do you remember that statement in Psalm 66:18: "If I regard iniquity in my heart, the LORD will not hear me"? He will not even bend down and listen to what I say, if I harbour, if I regard, iniquity—sin—in my heart. All sin must be put away.

My friend, this may be the reason that God is not using you. It may be that you have an idol in your life, that there is an Achan in the camp. Perhaps you are burdened by a weight of some kind, or a habit that you are unwilling to give up. You may not even recognize it as a sin, but it comes between you and God, and it makes it impossible for God to use you.

Day by day, you try to go forward, but something drags you back, a weight of some kind holds you down and makes it impossible for you to run the race that God wants you to run. A habit, harmless in itself, is keeping God's power from your life; and because you will not forsake your sin, because you refuse to renounce it utterly, God is unable to use you.

Sin is bound to retard your progress. It grieves the Holy Spirit, and you will never know the blessing and power of God on your life and your ministry until you are ready to renounce it forever, to turn from it utterly and never to indulge in it again.

You will have to face that Achan in the camp, that idol in your heart, that habit in your life, whatever it may be. There must be a clean break. As long as you go on doing what you are now doing, God will withhold his power. His anointing you will never know, his blessing you cannot experience. If you want to succeed as evangelist, if you want to see revival in your ministry, then break with sin.

Why not do it now while you are young? Why wait until it gets a hold on you, until it becomes a confirmed habit? Why not deal with it before the chains have wrapped themselves around you so tightly that it is next to impossible to break them? Now is the time to deal with sin. You have your whole life before you. If you want God to use you, then be definite, be emphatic.

### 5. A Life Placed Absolutely at God's Disposal

Thus far we have been dealing with the negative side. Now we come to the positive. God's great purpose is that our lives should be placed completely and absolutely at his disposal. That is why we have the statement again and again: "Yield yourselves unto God."

No potter can do anything whatever with clay that continually resists the potter's attempt to shape it. If the potter cannot make the kind of vessel he wants to make, the reason is that there is something in the clay that resists his touch. Just as soon as that hindrance has been removed and the clay yields itself absolutely to him, the potter can make any kind of vessel he desires to make. So it is with your life and mine. If God is going to use us for his honour and glory, if his power is going to rest upon us, if he is going to bless our evangelistic and soul-winning ministry, then our lives must be placed absolutely at his disposal.

As long as we have any will of our own, God can do little with us. His will must become our will, and as soon as his will does become our will, then he can begin to bless us. We should be able to say with the Lord Jesus, "I delight to do Thy will, O my God."

God never acts as a taskmaster. He never compels us to do something that we do not want to do. First of all he makes us willing, and then we delight in obeying him. In other words, his will, as I have already stated, becomes our will and then there is only one will to obey. We have placed ourselves absolutely at God's disposal.

What could a doctor do for a patient as long as the patient refused his remedy? The patient must place himself absolutely in the hands of the doctor and must be perfectly willing to accept the prescription given him by the doctor. Only then is there any hope of recovery. As long as the patient goes his own way, takes his own medicine and refuses the prescriptions the doctor gives, little can be done for him. He must place himself in the hands of the doctor.

So it is with you and with me. Until we place ourselves absolutely at the disposal of God, God can do little for us. God wants your yielded life, and he will never be satisfied with you until, like a slave, a willing slave, you place yourself entirely at his disposal. Then he can use you for his glory.

### 6. A Ministry of Prevailing Prayer

There is nothing more important than this. Jacob, you remember, wrestled with God in prayer. We do little wrestling today. We get up in the morning, fall down beside our bed, mumble off a few words of prayer and then hurry off to our work. Then at night, when we are weary, tired and exhausted, we do the same again, and climb into bed. That, for the most part, is all that prayer means to us.

But that was not the way Jacob prayed. He wrestled all night and then he exclaimed, "I will not let thee go except thou bless me." Some have never learned how to wrestle in prayer. Therefore they do not know how to prevail. Not until we prevail with God will we prevail with men, and to prevail with men we must learn how to travail.

Jesus knew what it was to travail in prayer. He spent, you remember, whole nights in prayer. Again and again his disciples found him alone with God in some solitary place, pouring out his soul in agonizing prayer. You and I know but little of that kind of praying; but until we have learned how to get alone with God and travail in prayer, we will not be able to accomplish much. Not until then will he commence to use us, to answer our prayers and to glorify himself in our ministry.

Charles G. Finney had such a burden of prayer. Time after time he went out into the woods, or to some solitary place, and there agonized in the presence of God. Sometimes he was unable even to put his petitions into words. He tells us that he could only groan and weep, so tremendous was the burden that rested upon him. No wonder God used him. No wonder he became the greatest revivalist of all time. No wonder God glorified himself in his ministry. Finney knew how to agonize in prayer.

Every man used of God has been a man of prayer. If you have never learned how to pray, if you have never learned how to wrestle with God, if you have never learned how to agonize, if you know nothing about travail of soul, then you do not know what it means to get spiritual results. If you want to see God glorified in your ministry, you will have to become first and foremost a man of prayer.

### 7. A Ministry Saturated with the Word of God

I know ministers who never turn to the Word of God except to get sermons. Any man who does that will never get far in evangelistic work. You and I need to turn to the Word of God for the sake of our spiritual welfare. We ought to know the Book from cover to cover, and there is only one way to know it and that is to read it. Read it from Genesis to Revelation. Read it again and again. Meditate on it, mark it, study it, become saturated with it. Read it until it becomes a very part of you. Only then will God be able to use you as he wants to.

If you are not familiar with the weapon that you are going to use, you will find yourself at a disadvantage when you attempt to use it. Our weapon is the Word of God. Unless we are familiar with it, unless we know how to use it, we are not going to get far in our work of evangelism. God's Word must be both on our tongues and in our hearts. We must know it and meditate on it until it becomes a part of us. As we lie awake at night let us quote it again and again until we are saturated with it.

It is not our word, remember, that God uses; it is his Word. What we say may accomplish a little. What God says will accomplish much. Let us, then, use the Word, and in using it, know it. Therefore, again I say, let us read it until it becomes a part of us. There is no substitute for a knowledge of the Word.

## 8. A Ministry with a Vital Message for a Lost World

Why are you going to the foreign field? Why do you want to become a missionary? What do you expect to do "out there"? What have you for the heathen? Are you going to take them social service, or education? Is it your plan to raise their standard of living? Are you going to the foreign field to give them a little of our Western civilization? Is it your thought to concentrate on hospital and medical work?

My friend, if you are going to the foreign field for any of these reasons, then I would advise you to stay at home. There is no place for you in the regions beyond. Leave all nonevangelical work to the United Nations. They can do a much better job than you can. They have more money, skilled workers and resources than will ever be yours. They have the equipment that is needed. They can educate the heathen. They can carry on medical work. They can take care of social services. They can impart Western civilization and culture. These are the by-products of Christianity. The main work of the missionary is to preach the gospel.

Unless you are going out with but one message, you ought not to go. Your message should be John 3:16: "For God so loved the world, that he gave his only begotten Son, that whosoever believeth in him should not perish, but have everlasting life." Unless you are going with that message, the message of God's salvation for a lost and perishing world, unless you are going to proclaim eternal life to those in heathen darkness, you had better stay at home.

Why are you going into the ministry? What is your purpose in preaching the gospel of the Lord Jesus Christ? Do you want to entertain? Are you entering the ministry for the sake of a living? Are you interested in the money you can make? Are you doing it because it is the respectable thing to do and because it will give you prestige and influence? Is that your purpose?

Then, my friend, I say to you also, you had better seek another position. You had better look for something else, because God's blessing will never rest upon you, if these are your reasons. Unless you are going into the ministry with the message of God's salvation, unless you are going to present to those in sin and darkness a living Saviour and proclaim the message that "Christ died for our sins," unless you are going to say to the lost and perishing, "Behold the Lamb of God that taketh away the sin of the world," again I say, you had better turn to something else. The ministry is no place for you. It isn't worth while.

I am now thinking of a man in London, England. He visited two churches. In the morning he went to the City Temple, there in the heart of the great metropolis. He listened to one of the most eloquent sermons to which he had ever listened, and as he came out he was heard to exclaim, "What a wonderful sermon." At night, he went to Spurgeon's Tabernacle, that world-famous pulpit, that great auditorium with its two huge galleries made famous by Charles H. Spurgeon, the prince of preachers, and as he came out he was heard to exclaim, "What a wonderful Christ!"

If your purpose is to preach great sermons, then you had better give up. The world does not need sermons, it needs a message, and there is all the difference in the world between a sermon and a message. You can go to a seminary and learn how to preach sermons, but you will have to go to God to get messages. Sermons will never influence your congregation but messages will. Sermons appeal to the intellect, messages to the heart. What people need today are not great sermons but great messages. We must go out to present Christ, the living Saviour.

The world, I say, is waiting for God's messengers. If you are going into the pulpit to present Christ, a living Christ for a dying world, then God will bless you and use you for his glory. You will be engaged in the greatest of all vocations, that of the ministry, and you will never regret having responded to the call of God. At the end of life you will look back over your ministry and thank God for a life spent in the service of the Lord Jesus Christ.

### 9. A Ministry in the Anointing of the Holy Spirit

There are those today who are almost afraid to talk about the Holy Spirit. There has been so much cold conservatism and so much fanaticism regarding the Holy Spirit that they scarcely mention him. Yet he is the third Person of the Trinity, the Executor of the Godhead, the one who takes the leading place in the Book of Acts. It was the Holy Spirit who actually did the work. He it was who guided and directed the apostles. He it was who led. The Holy Spirit convicted of sin and started revivals. He—God, the Holy Ghost—was the one who founded the early church.

Today, to a large extent, he is ignored. We have an idea that we can get along without him, that education and training will take his place and somehow become a substitute for his power, and we have endeavoured to carry on our ministry in the energy of the flesh, apart from the Holy Spirit altogether. It is high time, I say, that we gave him his rightful place, for he is the one who must do the work. Unless you and I know something about the anointing of the Spirit of God we will not get far in the service of God.

Down through the years of my ministry I have studied the lives of those whom God has used, and I have discovered that every one was an anointed man. Each, evangelist or revivalist, knew something of a crisis experience in his life, when the Holy Ghost took over and began using him.

Evan Roberts knew that anointing. I will never forget the day I called on him, when I was in Wales. He was not home, but I saw the house in which he lived, and I felt that even the ground on which I stood was holy. Later, he wrote me a letter, in his own handwriting, and a few months later, passed on to be with his Lord. Evan Roberts, I say, knew the anointing of the Holy Spirit. Charles G. Finney knew that anointing. He knew what it was to be endued with power from on high. D. L. Moody knew it. John Wesley knew it. Every man whom God has used, all down through the centuries, has known what it means to be anointed by the Spirit of God.

Anointed men are not satisfied with education and training. They know that something more is needed and that God cannot use them until they have experienced the anointing. So they wait in the presence of God until they have been endued with power from on high. Then they go out and accomplish more in a few weeks or months in the demonstration and power of the Spirit than they could have accomplished in the energy of the flesh in years.

God wants anointed men today, and unless you and I know something of the anointing, we will not get far in the work of evangelism. So important have I considered it that I wrote a book on it—*The Enduement of Power.*

You do not have to go into fanaticism. There is a middle-of-the-road experience, a scriptural position that you can take, an experience set forth in the Word of God and recognized by men of God all down the centuries, an experience that may be yours. If you want to amount to anything in the service of God, you will see to it that it is yours and that you, too, are an anointed man.

I do not care whether you go to the foreign field, or whether you work among the heathen here at home, whether you do missionary work abroad, or whether you hold evangelistic campaigns in your own country, you must know the anointing of the Holy Spirit. Otherwise, there will be a lack of power in your ministry and you will accomplish little. If you want to see God use you, if you want souls to be convicted and saved under your ministry, you will tarry until you have been endued with power from on high. You will become an anointed man.

## 10. A Ministry Characterized by the Expectancy of Faith

One time Charles H. Spurgeon sent his students out to hold open-air meetings on the streets of London. Day after day they came back to report.

Some were successful, others were not. One day a young man with few gifts or talents approached Mr. Spurgeon with a downcast expression on his face. "Mr. Spurgeon," he said, "I cannot understand why it is I am not able to win souls to the Lord Jesus Christ. I am taking part in these open-air meetings, I have faithfully preached the gospel and I am doing my dead level best, but there seems to be little or no response to my appeals." Spurgeon looked at the young man for a few minutes and then he said this: "Do you mean to tell me that you expect God Almighty to save souls every time you preach?" The young man was taken aback. "Why no," he said, "I guess not. Of course not. I could hardly expect that. I haven't completed my training yet, and I haven't as many gifts and talents as others. No, I see, I am wrong, I shouldn't expect it." "Then," Mr. Spurgeon exclaimed, "that is why you do not see results." The young man did not have the expectancy of faith, and God's Word is, "According to your faith, be it unto you." If you do not expect results, you will not get them.

My friend, if you do not expect to see results, you will not see them. I quote again, "According to your faith, be it unto you." You are to step into the pulpit to preach the gospel with the expectancy of faith. You ought to be just as certain of results when you commence to preach as you are when you actually see men and women walking down the aisles to accept Jesus Christ as Saviour.

All through the years of my ministry, I have extended the invitation. I cannot understand how any minister can be satisfied to preach the gospel, pronounce the benediction and then go home without having seen anything happen. It seems to me that after I have spread the food on the table, I ought to give the people a chance to come forward and partake of it, and if I do not, I am leaving something vital out of my ministry.

Sunday after Sunday I have invited lost men and women as well as backsliders to come forward and accept Christ, and I can hardly remember a Sunday night through all the years of my ministry when I have not seen results. Night after night, I have seen them walk down the aisles, stand at the front and then go with the personal workers into the inquiry rooms, there to be dealt with individually. I am surprised when nothing happens. If I were to preach a gospel message, give an invitation and see no one respond, I would be amazed. I expect to see results.

I do not mean to say that all those who have come have been saved, but I have reason to believe that some at least have found Jesus Christ and are now God's children. When I step into the pulpit God seems to give me that expectancy of faith of which I have been speaking, so that I know perfectly well that when I have concluded my message and extended the invitation, there will be those who will respond. I think I would get out of the ministry if I could not see results.

Does not a lawyer expect a verdict? He does not speak to entertain. He talks to the jury in order to get a conviction; and unless he secures a conviction, his appeal has failed. So, too, should it be with the gospel preacher, with the evangelist. He should expect a verdict. He should get results. If he doesn't, there is something wrong. His ministry, I say, should be characterized by the expectancy of faith.

## 11. A Ministry Wholly Devoted to the Glory of God

My friend, if you are carrying on your ministry for any other purpose than the glory of God, it will not amount to much. If you are an evangelist for what you can get out of it, if you are preaching to exalt self, if you want an easy living, if you are after money or fame, you may see something of outward success, but you will never know the blessing of God. If you have any other motive save the glory of God, you cannot expect the kind of results that God wants to give. Your ministry must be for God's glory.

If that is not your purpose, then if I were you, I would get down before God and humble myself until all of self had been eliminated. I would ask God to break me so that I might glorify him. For unless you put the glory of God first, you will be a dismal failure. You will never accomplish anything really worth while. If you are out to please yourself, God will not honour your ministry. You must be broken if he is to use you. Otherwise, sooner or later, there will be disaster.

I have tried to bring you face to face with the eleven qualifications that God has revealed to me. May I suggest that you go back over them, one by one, and then ask God to search your heart. I am sure that you want him to use you, that you want to be a successful evangelist, and that you long for revival. Then face the prerequisites as I have outlined them and let God speak to you. He wants to use you. He longs to bless your ministry. But if there are hindrances in the way, he cannot; and it is for you to remove them, that is, if you want to be *The Man God Uses.*

*20*

# Vance Havner

*1901-1986*

Born in the Blue Ridge Mountains of North Carolina, Vance Havner was converted to Christ when he was ten years old, began preaching when he was twelve, and was ordained when he was sixteen. Identified with the Southern Baptists all his life, he never completed any formal education for ministry but he had a profound knowledge of Scripture, read widely, observed life carefully, and had an extra supply of old-fashioned common sense. He was also gifted with a penetrating sense of humor and the ability to say things in a unique and unforgettable way. He started writing books in 1934 and became the most quotable preacher in America, but not every preacher who quotes him gives him the credit.

The year 1940 was very special for Havner. He married Sara Allred and he launched an itinerant ministry that took him to churches and conferences all over North America. A champion of the "old-time religion," Havner sought to stir God's people to seek revival and he never ceased to remind congregations that "God's last word to the church isn't the Great Commission. It's Revelation 2 and 3—'Repent or else!'" It is claimed that he preached more than thirteen thousand times during his life. He wrote out his sermons, but you couldn't tell he had a manuscript in the pulpit, and occasionally he would extemporize and apply the truth to some contemporary event.

His beloved wife, Sara, died in 1973 and from that experience came one of his best books, *Though I Walk through the Valley* (Revell, 1974). He wrote many books of sermons and devotionals, and the closest thing he ever wrote to an autobiography is *Threescore and Ten* (Revell, 1973). Fortunately, there are many taped messages available so that new generations can hear this unique preacher deliver his messages as only he could do.

# Like Him in This World

As He is, so are we in this world.
1 John 4:17

Of all the New Testament writers, John stated the greatest truths in simplest terms. He clothed profundity with simplicity. As it stands in our King James Version, he spoke mainly in monosyllables. Our text is a fair sample. "As He is, so are we in this world." You cannot say that in shorter words. You cannot say a greater truth in any words!

I am aware of the diverse expositions of this text. It deals with love and judgment, and identification with Christ. If He abides in us and we in Him, we need not be afraid at the last great day. His perfect love in us casts out fear. One well-known writer was much puzzled as to the meaning of the verse, until he read it to mean, "As He is with regard to judgment . . . He will never come into judgment and since He and I are identified, neither will I." The applications of it stretch out in all directions, but I am going to take the text just as it stands in its simplest form, and just as it appears to the ordinary reader. "As He is, so are we in this world."

Here are nine little words that fall apart into three sets of three words each. *"As He is—so are we—in this world."*

*"As He is,"* not, mind you, "As He *was.*" There are those who see only the Christ of Galilee centuries ago as our example, and vainly try lifting themselves by their own bootstraps to be like Him. He is indeed our example, and if we are to walk as He walked we must know how He walked when He was among us.

230

But He is infinitely more than an example out of the past. So much has happened since the days of His flesh. He died and rose and ascended and is glorified, He stands at the Father's right hand and in all His glory will return one day. As He *is*, so are we; not of course in degree, but in kind. If we trust Him we are partakers of His nature, and what is His, is ours. All that He is *today* we share. Our experience is limited by our faith, understanding, and capacity but we are not pale copies of a model furnished nineteen centuries ago. As He *is*, so are we.

Then, "As He is, *so ARE we*. . . ." Again, it does not say merely "so should we be." Indeed we ought, but that is not what it says. Nor do we read, "As He is, so may we be." Indeed we may and can be as He is, but that is not the text, nor does it say, "As He is, so shall we be." We shall indeed be like Him one day for we shall see Him as He is, but that glorious prospect is not in mind here. "So *are* we" here and now. What He is up there, we are down here. If we have been born again He lives in us. We are the projection of Him into this day and age. In a Christian, Christ lives again. We are becoming saints but we also *are* saints. A Christian is a being and a becoming. We are far from perfection, but in so far as we let Him fill and control our lives, "as He is, so are we in this world."

Finally, we are as He is *in this world;* not just in church where it is not too difficult to look pious on Sunday morning; not in some favored spot in holy seclusion "far from the madding crowd's ignoble strife—" *"in this world—"* this wicked, foul, polluted and perverted Sodom and Gomorrah; in the old rat race, the old salt mines, every day of the week. I wouldn't give a nickel for a Christianity that cannot be lived out in the kitchen, on a pagan college campus, on the job in a shop full of cursing sinners, or in an office where Jesus Christ is only a byword. This world is no friend of grace to help us on to God. Although Christians are not *of* it, they are *in* it, and it is a good training ground for soldiers of the cross. We are the light of the world and light is needed in dark places. We are not saved to outdazzle each other at church and in religious conventions. Our Saviour said, "As Thou hast sent me into the world, even so have I also sent them into the world" (John 17:18). "As He is, so are we *in this world*."

This throws a lot of light on what a Christian really is. "So *are* we. . . ." What we believe is important, but a man may believe correctly with his head without anything happening in his heart. What we do is important, but a man may do things a Christian ought to do and still be an unconverted Pharisee. Creed and conduct have their places but we are dealing here with character; not what we believe and do but what we are. A Christian is not the sum total of what he believes in his head and does with his hands, but of what he is in his heart. He must be a partaker of the Divine nature of Jesus Christ by the miracle of the new birth. Only then can he have boldness in the day of judgment. Christians are not just nice people; they are new creatures. Old things have passed away and all things have become new. If one is what he has always been, he is not a Christian, for a Christian is something new.

Nowadays we ask people to "accept Christ." That is not a New Testament term. We are told to believe on the Lord Jesus Christ, trust Him with the heart (Acts 16:31) and receive Him (John 1:12). "Accept" gives the impression that our Lord is standing hat-in-hand, awaiting our verdict on Him. After all, He invites us to come to Him and what matters most is whether He accepts us. We hear about "taking Christ as Saviour." The Scriptures do not tell us to take Him *as* anything. We are to receive *Him,* period. If that were better understood today there would be none of this idea that we can take Christ as Saviour now, and maybe years later take Him as Lord as though these were two separate experiences—something not taught in the New Testament at all.

However, there is a sense, if properly understood, when we do take Christ as a wife takes a husband. In the New Testament, marriage is used to illustrate the relationship of Christ and the church (Ephesians 5:32). A Christian is married to Christ (Romans 7:4). Paul espoused the Corinthian Christians to one husband (2 Corinthians 11:2). When a woman marries a man she takes him for all that he is. She may not know all that he is and may discover more later that she did not know when she said, "I do," but for better or worse she took him as he was, became identified with him, and they became one. In a very real sense, from then on as he is so is she in this world. His joys and sorrows are hers; his successes and failures are hers; his past, present and future are hers. In this divorce-ridden generation, too many accept the privileges but not the responsibilities of marriage. By the same token, our church rolls are filled with members who accepted the privileges of church membership, but refuse to assume its obligations. They accepted the Saviourhood of Christ but not His Lordship. Some of them are what James called adulterers and adulteresses, untrue to their marriage vows to Jesus Christ, friends of the world and enemies of God.

When a believer receives Christ he takes Him for all that He is, both Saviour and Lord. All that Christ has becomes ours, and all that we have becomes His. It is about time we discovered the magnitude of this transaction in this day when people equate becoming a Christian with joining a church—pretty much as one joins a secret order or a civic club. This is a contract for time and eternity between a sinner and the Son of God. This is free salvation, but it is not cheap. It cost the Son of God His life to purchase it and it costs us all we are and have when we receive it, for thenceforth we belong to Jesus Christ; we are not our own; we are bought with a price. We do not pay for our salvation for "Jesus paid it all," as we sing sometimes, but "all to Him we owe," as the next line declares. This is not bondage; it is the glorious liberty of the sons of God. We are one with Him in the family of our Father, and we shall not fear in the day of judgment for perfect love casts out fear. We bear the family resemblance and "as He is, so are we in this world." Think what would happen in our churches if we ever woke up to this!

When we become Christians, Christ's life becomes our life. He did not come to earth to teach us a better way to live. He came that we might have *life*. Paul did not say, "To me, to live is to live like Christ or for Christ." He said, ". . . To me to live *is* Christ" (Philippians 1:21). We cannot live the Christian life until we have the Christian life to live. Every Christian is an extension of Christ's life. Paul did not say, "I'm living for Christ." He said, ". . . Christ liveth in me . . ." (Galatians 2:20).

When we receive Christ, *His joys become our joys.* What makes Him glad, makes us rejoice. How about that? What do you rejoice about? I am not speaking of mere happiness which depends on what happens. Do you rejoice in God's will in your life and in the lives of others? His joys are ours because His joy is our joy. He said, "These things have I spoken unto you, that my joy might remain in you, and that your joy might be full" (John 15:11). When we see the things most church members enjoy today, we wonder whether they have ever known anything about His joy!

Furthermore, *his sorrows become our sorrows.* We can grieve the Holy Spirit. Our Lord wept over Jerusalem, and He is burdened over a luke-warm church and a lost world. Any Christian who can take it easy and not be saddened over the state of the church and the world today is out of fellowship with His Lord. The Saviour even got angry on occasion and we need to share His indignation at the devil and all the works of the devil, instead of boasting broad-mindedness about the things that God condemns. We smile today at what breaks the heart of the Saviour in this generation that makes comedy out of tragedy.

When we are joined to Christ, *His friends become our friends.* He said, "Ye are my friends, if ye do whatsoever I command you" (John 15:14). A friend of Jesus is one who obeys Him. That leaves a lot of church members out in the cold! Christians should be friendly to everybody, but there is a higher friendship known only to those who love our Lord. What we call fellowship when we gossip over our coffee at some church suppers is often just sociability under religious auspices, and not necessarily the communion of saints. "We know that we have passed from death unto life because we love the brethren" (1 John 3:14), and we love the brethren because our Lord's friends are our friends and "as He is, so are we in this world."

From this it follows that when we take Christ, *His enemies are our enemies*. Paul writes of ". . . enemies of the cross of Christ" (Philippians 3:18). James says that the friend of the world is the enemy of God. Christians have no business hobnobbing with men who deny the blood of Christ or church worldlings, whom James calls adulterers, because they are untrue to their Christian vows. A wife who is eighty-five percent faithful to her husband is not faithful at all. There is no such thing as part-time loyalty to Jesus Christ. It is all or nothing. The man who plays with the enemies of Christ is a traitor to his Lord. We cannot be popular with a world that crucified our Lord. We cannot be popular with a world that crucified our Lord for "as the Master, so shall the servant be" and "as He is, so are we in this world."

When we are united to Christ, *His cross becomes our cross*. This cross is not ordinary trouble, for everybody has trouble. It is not chastisement, for that is not voluntary. The cross of Christ we choose ourselves. "If any man will come after me, let him deny himself, and take up his cross, and follow me" (Matthew 16:24). His cross is the trouble, the persecution, the reproach we suffer because of our identification with Him—because we are Christians. It is what we sing about:

> To the old rugged cross I will ever be true,
> Its shame and reproach gladly bear.

This kind of cross-bearing Christian is not popular with this world and never will be. Simeon said that our Lord would be "spoken against" and the Jews in Rome told Paul that everywhere his religion was "spoken against." I am not thinking now of run-of-the-mill church members. It is fashionable to be a church member these days. It is a status symbol. It helps business and looks good in an obituary. A great world church is shaping up before our eyes in these last days, having a form of godliness but denying the power thereof. It will be stylish to belong to this church but the despised sect of the Nazarenes—the followers of the Way, true New Testament Christians—will be called the scum of the earth and will be a spectacle to the world for the scandal of the cross.

There is one thing more. When we become Christ's and He becomes ours, *His future is our future!* And what a future! "If we suffer, we shall also reign with Him" (2 Timothy 2:12). He is coming back; the meek shall inherit the earth and the saints shall judge the world. We may not look like it now but our day is coming. All kinds of groups are trying to take over this old world. They are marching and demonstrating and shouting and waving their banners around the earth. The newsreels are loaded with them, but you never see the real future rulers for we do not demonstrate that way. We are not organized on that pattern. There are no statistics available. You will find some of us in all the churches. We are waiting for our King to return and when He does, everybody will know who we are and how many, for we will come into our own. The kingdoms of this world will become the kingdoms of our Lord and His Christ, Who shall reign until all His enemies are put under His feet, and where'er the sun doth his successive journeys run.

Are you married to this Heavenly Bridegroom? We are accustomed to brides walking down aisles to church altars to say, "I take this man. . . ." I invite you to a far greater altar to say, "I take Jesus Christ to be my Saviour and Lord. All I am and have is henceforth His, not 'until death do us part,' as we say in the wedding ceremony, for death will not part us. This is for time and eternity." Some have never received Him. Others have received Him but have been unfaithful and need to renew their vows, saying:

> O Jesus, I have promised
> To serve Thee to the end;
> Be Thou forever near me,
> My Master and my Friend:
> I shall not fear the battle
> If Thou art by my side,
> Nor wander from the pathway
> If Thou wilt be my Guide.

*21*

# John R. Rice

*1895-1989*

Born in Gainesville, Texas, John R. Rice was converted at the age of nine. He graduated from Decatur Baptist College in 1931 with further studies at Baylor University and Southwestern Baptist Theological Seminary. Gifted as a Bible-teaching evangelist and exhorter, he founded the Galilean Baptist Church in Dallas in 1932 and pastored there for eight years.

In 1934 Rice started publishing *The Sword of the Lord,* a tabloid-size weekly newspaper that emphasized personal soul-winning, evangelistic crusades, biblical preaching, and separation from theological liberalism. It grew to have a circulation of three hundred thousand and became an effective tool for promoting conferences on soul winning sponsored by *The Sword of the Lord.*

In 1940 Rice moved the ministry to Wheaton, Illinois, where he also founded the Calvary Baptist Church. In 1963 he relocated to Murfreesboro, Tennessee, where his brother Bill Rice, also an evangelist, conducted a Christian conference center. Rice was in great demand as a preacher and evangelist and helped to encourage revival crusades at a time in America when such ministries were neglected and even opposed by many churches. Not content merely to do the work himself, Rice worked strenuously to challenge and teach others to witness for Christ.

It is estimated that more than 60 million copies of his more than two hundred books and booklets have been distributed, particularly *What Must I Do to Be Saved?* which is available in forty languages. His biography, *A Man Sent from God,* was written by Robert Sumner (Eerdmans, 1959), and Howard Edgar Moore wrote his doctoral thesis at George Washington University on *The Emergence of Moderate Fundamentalism: John R. Rice and "The Sword of the Lord"* (1990).

# And God Remembered . . .

Genesis 8:1

No man on earth was ever more helpless than Noah. He was on an ocean-liner of a boat, but without chart or compass or sail or rudder. There was no land to reach if he could have reached it. As he looked through the window of the ark unto a boiling sea, the drenching cloudburst of rain, which continued for forty days and nights, hid from his vision anything more than a few feet away. Surging up from the depths came floods of water from the fountains of the great deep within the earth. About him was his little family; they were only eight souls in all. The ship was filled with animals, wild beasts into whose heart God had put the instinct to walk into the man-made home. Noah still felt, no doubt, the horror of the death of millions of human beings in the flood. Doubtless he had seen or heard, clawing at the side of the ark, the anguished, drowning remnants of a violent race. Noah had said good-by to the whole unbelieving, violent and blasphemous God-despising horde. Brothers, sisters, kinsmen, neighbors, friends, acquaintances, and strangers—all had chosen to go their way without God, and Noah, without any rebellion against God or any complaint at God's justice, must have felt the pain of separation and the tragedy of their death to the depth of his soul.

What would become of Noah and his little family? Not a piece of ground on which they could put their feet! Not an island, even, where they could unlade the ark's burden of beasts and fowls and creeping things! Nowhere to plant seed, to grow wheat, to start vineyards. Nowhere to build a house. Only this restless raging sea that covered the mountaintops and blotted from sight every well-known landmark, every familiar scene and place. Noah had faith in God, but it would not be surprising if stark fear clutched with icy fingers at his heart, while the ark floated he knew not where, and the future held he knew not what!

Noah was utterly helpless—but "God remembered Noah, and every living thing, and all the cattle that was with him in the ark; and God made a wind to pass over the earth, and the waters assuaged: The fountains also of the deep and the windows of heaven were stopped, and the rain from heaven was restrained; And the waters returned from off the earth continually: and after the end of the hundred and fifty days the waters were abated. And the ark rested in the seventh month, on the seventeenth day of the month, upon the mountains of Ararat" (Gen. 8:1–4). When Noah had no one else to depend upon, he could depend upon God. *God remembered!*

We have a God who remembers. It is one of the things said again and again throughout the Bible, that God remembers.

"And God remembered Noah" (Gen. 8:1).

"And God remembered Abraham" (Gen. 19:29).

"And God remembered Rachel" (Gen. 30:22).

And Hannah, too, "The LORD remembered her" (1 Sam. 1:19).

Yes, God remembered Abraham also! "And it came to pass, when God destroyed the cities of the plain, that God remembered Abraham, and sent Lot out of the midst of the overthrow, when he overthrew the cities in the land which Lot dwelt" (Gen. 19:29). God knew the heart of Abraham, tender with love toward his nephew, Lot. God called to mind the tender pleading of Abraham when he asked that if there were fifty righteous the city of Sodom be spared, or if there were not fifty, then if there were forty-five, or forty, or thirty, or twenty, or even ten righteous! And God had agreed that if there were ten righteous the city would be spared. But a careful check of the hearts, such as only God could give, revealed that there was only one person in the city who could in God's sight be called righteous, and that one was Lot, Lot, who had lost his testimony! Lot, who called the vile wretches of Sodom "brethren"! Lot, whose wife had grown worldly, whose children had grown up unsaved; Lot, who offered to give his daughters into the hands of the lewd Sodomites for night revelry; Lot, who to his own sons-in-law was as one that mocked when he warned of God's judgment! To our minds Lot would not have been righteous. But he had put his faith in God and had been counted righteous, and, according to the New Testament, Lot was a just man, a righteous man, who vexed his righteous soul day by day with their unlawful deeds (2 Peter 2:7–8).

But God was not thinking so much of Lot; He was remembering Abraham. He remembered the love of Abraham for Lot, the tender pleading.

And as God often does, He remembered the sense and heart of the prayer more than the words. He had agreed to spare the city if there were ten righteous. Now that He found only one, God still remembered Abraham and his prayers and tears and anxiety, and the love of this heart for his kinsman, Lot, his dead brother's son.

So God, remembering Abraham, brought Lot out of the wicked city, Sodom. He brought Lot out, though his wife was turned to a pillar of salt; brought Lot out, though his children were left behind to burn since they would not come; brought Lot out, though he was as one that mocked to his sons-in-law; brought Lot out, though Lot still clung to his wine and later ruined the only two daughters left alive. Knowing all the facts, God remembered Abraham, and for Abraham's sake did the thing that his trusting heart desired!

On and on, so it is throughout the Bible. God is always remembering His own. God remembered Rachel, the barren wife, when her heart was eaten out with longing for a son. Supplanted somewhat by her elder sister, Leah, whom Jacob married only by mistake and trickery, and then sore and troubled in spirit by the taunting of Leah because for years Leah's children had comforted the heart of Jacob and she, Rachel, the beloved and chosen wife, was barren still. How many times she had wept in the night! How many times she had prayed to God and cried out for help on this matter! With some sense of defeat, and yet with the self-forgetting love of a wife, she had given her handmaid to her husband that the husband might have the joy of children.

No doubt Rachel thought many times, "God has forgotten me! God does not know or care about the heart cry of a barren woman!" No doubt many a time she thought, "Nobody knows the longing of my arms for a baby! Nobody knows what I would give just to hold in my lap my own child and feel his baby fingers around my finger. Nobody knows and nobody cares!" That would be the natural thing for a poor, tried, troubled, barren woman to think. But if Rachel ever thought that, she was mistaken, for God did care. God did know. And God did remember! In Genesis 30:22–23, the Scripture says: "*And God remembered Rachel,* and God hearkened to her, and opened her womb. And she conceived, and bare a son; and said, God hath taken away my reproach."

It was another barren and heartbroken woman, Hannah, who in bitterness of soul prayed unto the Lord and wept sore and promised God that if He would give her a child, the child should be lent to the Lord forever! The old priest thought she was drunken, and her husband, who loved her so much, was vexed, and her "adversary" taunted her unceasingly. But in the poor, troubled, unsatisfied mother-heart of Hannah, God looked every minute of the time, and God never did forget. In 1 Samuel 1:19, we are told what happened after the brokenhearted prayer of Hannah: "And they rose up in the morning early, and worshipped before the Lord, and returned, and came to their house to Ramah: and Elkanah knew Hannah his wife; AND THE LORD REMEMBERED HER."

## God Remembers His Own Word

It is a wonderful thing how much God remembers. Your heart will be blessed if you take a good complete concordance and follow through the Bible and find all the places where it is said that God remembers or where He brings things to remembrance. And repeatedly and blessedly you will find that it is said in the holy Book of God, "And God remembered his covenant," and other words of like meaning. For example, read the comforting passage in Exodus 2:23–25 as follows: "And it came to pass in process of time, that the king of Egypt died; and the children of Israel sighed by reason of the bondage, and they cried, and their cry came up unto God by reason of the bondage. And God heard their groaning, AND GOD REMEMBERED HIS COVENANT WITH ABRAHAM, WITH ISAAC, AND WITH JACOB. And God looked upon the children of Israel, and God had respect unto them."

The bondage of the Egyptian taskmasters grew heavy on the Israelites and they cried and wept and they groaned. Perhaps they did not feel that God heard their groanings or cared about their sorrows. But God *did* hear, and God *did* care. And God's tender heart stirred, and He remembered His covenant and made His plans to bring out of bondage those who were so dear to Him and who loomed so large in His plans. Again God remembered.

So God sent Moses to tell the people, according to Exodus 6:5: "And I have also heard the groaning of the children of Israel, whom the Egyptians keep in bondage; AND I HAVE REMEMBERED MY COVENANT."

In Psalm 105:8 we are told about God: "He hath remembered his covenant for ever, the word which he commanded to a thousand generations." When God makes a covenant, it is good for a thousand generations, literally for tens of thousands of years. What God promises, He always remembers to do.

God's blessed promises and covenant to Israel held good even after they were in the land and carried again to captivity in Babylon because of their sins. Psalm 106:45 tells us again: "And he remembered for them his covenant, and repented according to the multitude of his mercies." Man's sin cannot make God forget His holy intentions, His tender proposals, His faithful promises! We are told in Romans 11:29: "For the gifts and calling of God are without repentance," which means that when God makes a promise He never goes back on it. When God gives a holy calling, He never forgets His obligation.

Another verse of Scripture which mentions the good memory of God concerning His word is Psalm 105:41–42, where we are told: "He opened the rock and the waters gushed out; they ran in the dry places like a river. For HE REMEMBERED HIS HOLY PROMISE, and Abraham his servant." A quarreling, doubting and unworthy people were the children of Israel gathered in the wilderness, complaining of their thirst. They said to Moses, "Would God we had stayed in Egypt." They said, "Have you brought us here to die in the wilderness because there were not enough graves in Egypt?" But in all this God remembered His holy promise. God acted, not so much on what He saw in the lives of His people, but on what He kept ever before Him, His own holy promise. God "remembered his holy promise, and Abraham his servant."

Surely it is apparent to even the most casual reader, that to God His Word is a most solemn thing, never to be forgotten. No wonder we are told: "For ever, O LORD, thy word is settled in heaven" (Ps. 119:89). God promises that "the grass withereth, the flower fadeth; but the word of our God shall stand forever" (Isa. 40:8). So holy, so eternally remembered, so everlasting is God's Word! God Himself through eternity can never forget His precious promises.

That means that when we talk to God we are in the certain place of blessing when we can call to God's remembrance His own Word. It was thus that David prayed when he said, "Remember the word unto thy servant, upon which thou hast caused me to hope" (Ps. 119:49). That was what Jacob did when he returned to his own land to meet the angry Esau, but on the way he prayed and reminded God: "O God of my father Abraham, and God of my father Isaac, the LORD which saidst unto me, Return unto thy country, and to thy kindred, and I will deal well with thee: . . . Deliver me, I pray thee, from the hand of my brother, from the hand of Esau . . . and thou saidst, I will surely do thee good, and make thy seed as the sand of the sea, which cannot be numbered for multitude" (Gen. 32:9–12). He who asks God anything on the basis of His own promise is on sure ground for God Himself cannot, will not, deny His Word. He never forgets His covenant, His holy promise. Thank God that He remembers His Word.

### God Remembers His People, His Own

I called your attention to the Scriptures which said: "And God remembered Noah," "And God remembered Abraham," "And God remembered Rachel," and concerning Hannah, "And the LORD remembered her." So now I want to remind you that God remembers all His people, every one.

We are told that perfect memory depends upon perfect knowledge. When I was a teacher, many times pupils, in answer to my question, said, "I can't remember." But I soon learned that those who could not remember were usually those who never knew the facts in order to remember them. Clear-cut, accurate, exact knowledge, powerfully felt and clearly apprehended, is not easy to forget. So it is about God's memory of His own. He knows all about us and therefore He cannot forget us.

Do you realize in what infinite detail God cares about you, dear sinning, doubting, and perhaps troubled reader? Well, you are worth to Him far more than you have ever realized. Jesus said, "Consider the lilies of the field, how they grow; they toil not, neither do they spin: and yet I say unto you, That even Solomon in all his glory was not arrayed like one of these." Then He gives us the plain and impressive admonition, "Wherefore, if God so clothe the grass of the field, which today is, and tomorrow is cast into the oven, shall he not much more clothe you, O ye of little faith?" (Matt. 6:28–30). And God so cares for the fowls that though they neither sow nor reap nor gather into barns, yet our heavenly Father feeds them all. And aren't we better than birds? And not a sparrow falls to the ground without our Father. How much more are we precious in His sight!

God knows so much about us that He tells us plainly, "The very hairs of your head are all numbered" (Matt. 10:30). You do not know how many hairs there are in your head, but God knows. If one of them comes out in the comb tomorrow morning, then that record is meticulously kept in Heaven. God has an account of every hair of your head and with such intimate knowledge of you, He will never forget you, you may be sure. God remembers His own.

And do you think that God would ever forget your work for Him? Once when I was brokenhearted and it seemed that God had forgotten me, I went aside to pray in my grief. The church building over which we had labored for years was burned and gone. Hundreds of dollars worth of tracts and booklets, of which I was giving away as many as I could, were destroyed. My library and my office equipment were ruined. Out of a burdened heart I cried out to God, begging Him that if He could not love me any more, then for His own sake He would some way keep the work going and let it not suffer and some way would take the message of salvation to sinners through my messages in print and my public ministry. But that was an unworthy prayer and not true to the plan of God. God did not forget for a moment His own beloved. It is not only that God wants His own work to prosper but God never will forget any good deed done in His name. Did He not promise us plainly that not even one cup of cold water would be given a disciple in His name without its reward (Matt. 10:42)? And do you remember how pleased He was with the widow who gave the two mites and how He had the incident written down so that it should be imperishably brought to the attention of the millions of believers in after years? And recall again that when Mary anointed Him with the precious ointment of spikenard a little while before His death He plainly promised that that deed of love which she had done should be known wherever the gospel was preached (Matt. 26:13). How anxious the Lord is that nothing good shall ever be forgotten!

The writer of the book of Hebrews, calling to mind the sorrows and patience and labors of the saints that are addressed in that epistle, said, "For God is not unrighteous to forget your work and labour of love, which ye have shewed toward his name, in that ye have ministered to the saints, and do minister" (Heb. 6:10). "God is not unrighteous to forget!" Blessed be God for such a memory as He has! God will never forget our work.

And after all, the memory of God goes deeper than that of man. Men so soon forget those that they laud to the skies. Today a man may be as famous and loved and lionized as was Woodrow Wilson when he went to Paris to dictate the treaties that closed the World War, and a few months later he may be like the same man, rejected by his own people, even by his own party, and evaded by his own friends, dying with a broken heart. Men so soon forget, but God never forgets. Best of all God sees not the spectacular, not the outward service, but the inward heart. God knew the heart of the widow who gave all she had, only two mites, and He said that she gave more than all. God sees the love, the faith, the suffering, the self-denial, the sacrifice of those whose good deeds are never known to men. That is the reason that Jesus has promised that many of the last shall be first and the first last (Luke 13:30). God remembers! And God remembers the facts just as they are, unseen or unappraised and unweighed by human eyes and mind.

No, God never forgets good deeds. The Scripture says, "He that hath pity upon the poor lendeth unto the LORD; and that which he hath given will he pay him again" (Prov. 19:17). And when God borrows, He puts it down in His book so He may safely pay it back and with interest, and one good day He will return many fold every penny that is given in His name to the poor. Do you remember that when Cornelius, the Roman centurion, prayed to God earnestly and so longed to know God and His salvation, how that the angel of God appeared to him to tell him where he might find a preacher and through him learn how to be saved? In Acts 10:4 we are told how the angel of God came to him in a vision and said, "Thy prayers and thine alms are come up for a memorial before God." And in Acts 10:31 the words are given as follows: "Cornelius, thy prayer is heard, and thine alms are had in remembrance in the sight of God." God never did forget a penny that Cornelius gave to a poor man or to any work of God. God kept a record and God remembered and in due time called it to remembrance and rewarded it!

And here, dear friend, is the sweetest comfort of all. God remembers the heart itself. As brokenhearted Peter beside the Sea of Galilee cried out to Jesus the third time, "Lord, thou knowest all things; thou knowest that I love thee," so we may think the same when we have sinned against God, when we have failed in our purpose, when we have lived unworthily, and when men may ascribe to us only the basest of motives. Then we can say, "Oh, Lord, thou knowest all things; thou knowest that I love thee." God will remember the intents and the motives of the heart.

Oh, yes, we have failures enough, sins enough. Perhaps you are wishing that God would forget. But I remind you now that even the frailty of your nature is known to Him and that is one of the things that the Bible expressly says that He does not forget. In Psalm 103:14 we are told: "For he knoweth our frame; he remembereth that we are dust." It is awfully hard for us to remember that the men with whom we deal are poor, frail creatures who even when they would do good often do wrong—people who, when, they do their very best, are tempted and tried and stressed and blinded and defeated by things we do not know and cannot understand. But while we cannot judge correctly and cannot remember men's frailties, nor even our own, thank God He does just that. "He remembereth that we are dust." When He was dying on the cross and prayed God to forgive His tormentors, He remembered to put in the simple word of explanation, reminding the Father, "for they know not what they do." God remembers our frailties, He remembers our bent to sinning, and He remembers the dust from which we are born and the sins of the race that tainted the blood. His tender heart understands, and our failures, our sins, the grievings, the disappointing, unworthy things He sees in us, He can properly evaluate, knowing from the beginning and never forgetting that we, His own beloved, are only dust! Oh, the dear memory of God who never fails to remember all the things that are in our favor and to judge us with the tenderness of One who sees even the excuses that we could not make and the explanations of our own shortcomings that we do not understand. No wonder that the Psalmist could cry out to God, "Thou knowest my down-sitting and mine uprising, thou understandest my thought afar off" (Ps. 139:2). None of our sins, none of our inborn taint, none of our blindness to the right, which we inherited as people conceived in sin and brought forth in iniquity, are hid from the face of our tender God who remembers us! God never forgets us and He never forgets that we are only dust.

### God's Aids to Memory: Bottles and Books

But again, God remembers our tears. All of us, God knows, are too quick to forget the sorrows of others. But God Himself has made especially careful provision so that He can never forget the tears of His own. David knew this, and in Psalm 56:8, he cried out, "Thou tellest my wanderings: put thou my tears into thy bottle: are they not in thy book?" This Psalm was written, we are told, when the Philistines took David in Gath. He was in the sorest danger and his heart was troubled, so he cried out to God, "Lord, you keep an account, a record of all my journeyings. Lord, put my tears in your bottle, are they not written down in thy book?" We said awhile ago that God's perfect understanding of all things makes sure His memory. But God has aids to memory also.

If accurate knowledge helps memory, another important factor in a good memory is good records. If we want to be sure of accurately remembering things, we put them down on paper. So God, who could never forget anyway, tells us in words that we can understand, that He put our tears in His bottle and writes them in His book!

There are times when the groanings of a nation seem to go unheard, as of Israel in Egypt. But God does hear and God does remember. It seems sometimes that men of Israel, now scattered over the whole earth and oppressed by wicked men in many nations, are forgotten in their grief and sorrow, but they are not. God remembers. And so it has seemed to many a saint of God, like Joseph in Potiphar's jail, or Jeremiah in the slime pit, or Paul and Barnabas imprisoned at Philippi, or widows forsaken, or poor people wronged and oppressed—it has seemed to many such, no doubt, that God had forgotten and that though tears fell down all the night long, no one kept any record, no one knew or no one cared. Perhaps some reader of these lines has often felt that there was no one to keep account of his sorrows, but he may be sure now, and be comforted by the fact that God puts all his tears in His bottle. God will one day comfort all that mourn. He will some day fill all those who hunger and thirst after righteousness. He will one day avenge all those whose adversaries oppress them unrighteously. God has a bottle for the tears of His own afflicted. God has a book for the record of their sorrows. God cannot, will not, must not forget.

And is your prayer unanswered?

Yes, God does hear and answer prayer. The prayers of the saints are to Him the sweet delight of His memory. Lest He should ever forget, the prayers of the saints are kept in golden vials in Heaven, and when those vials are opened, all Heaven is sweetened with the fragrance of the prayers of the saints of God!

In Revelation 5:8 we are told how twenty-four elders fell down before the Lamb, having every one of them harps, and golden vials full of odours, which are the prayers of saints. God does keep all the prayers that come up to Him in faith and truth! The same matter is mentioned again in Revelation 8:3–4. We are told: "And another angel came and stood at the altar, having a golden censer; and there was given unto him much incense, that he should offer it with the prayers of all saints upon the golden altar which was before the throne. And the smoke of the incense, which came with the prayers of the saints, ascended up before God out of the angel's hand."

Do you see how God regards the prayers of His own beloved? To Him they are sweeter than the attar of roses. Honeysuckles or carnations or Cape jasmines or heliotrope or delicate violets do not have an odor as sweet or strong as the odor of the prayers of the saints which God keeps, like jewels, in golden vials, to be opened before Him when His tender heart is ready to answer for His own glory and to the sweet satisfaction of His beloved who pray! Oh, how gladly we ought to pray, and how meekly and patiently we ought to wait on God for the answer since He regards our prayers as so precious, since to Him they are so fragrant, and since by His never-forgetting but always-remembering heart, prayers are always remembered and brought to the right answer when the prayers are such as can please His righteousness and honor His holy name.

God keeps records in Heaven, as I have said. In Malachi 3:16–17 we learn of some of God's bookkeeping: "Then they that feared the LORD spake often one to another; and the LORD hearkened, and heard it, AND A BOOK OF REMEMBRANCE WAS WRITTEN BEFORE HIM for them that feared the LORD, and that thought upon his name. And they shall be mine, saith the LORD of hosts, in that day when I make up my jewels; and I will spare them, as a man spareth his own son that serveth him."

Blessed book of remembrance, written and kept before God! Every saint who fears the Lord and speaks of Him one to another, would find, if he could but look up into Heaven, that God's ear was held down here, for the Lord hearkens and the Lord writes it all down in a book of remembrance. I am sure that we would talk about the Lord more often and that we would fear Him and walk so circumspectly before Him to please Him, if we could be ever conscious of the fact that God writes all such people in His blessed book of remembrance and counts them as jewels that He will gladly gather one day!

There are other books that we will mention, too, a little later; the Book of Life for those who are truly saved, and the record books, including all the deeds of the wicked, which records they sometime must face as they stand before God.

248

### God Remembers the Sins of the Impenitent

We have said much of the tender memory of God toward His own loved ones, those who please Him and seek Him and know Him. But here is a sad fact that we must mention along with the glad facts; God remembers sin and God bides His time but is certain to bring sin to judgment. God cannot forget unforgiven, unrepented, and unlamented sin.

Do you not remember how many, many times God has warned that sin must come to judgment? He has said that "the way of transgressors is hard" (Prov. 13:15). It would not be hard if God did not remember sin and bring it to its proper judgment.

God has said, "Be sure your sin will find you out" (Num. 32:23). Sin could not find us out if God did not remember our sin. And it has been rung into the ears of every one of us, "Be not deceived; God is not mocked: for whatsoever a man soweth, that shall he also reap" (Gal. 6:7). How could men reap what they sowed if God did not remember their sowing? And why could sinners not mock God if God did not keep accurate records and punish every sin?

And even our Saviour Himself said, "Every idle word that men shall speak, they shall give account thereof in the day of judgment" (Matt. 12:36). God must remember sin. God keeps a record of it.

For all the wicked and rebellious and impenitent, then, God's sharp, clear memory holds forever before Him their sins.

Concerning the Israelites, who went far away from God, Hosea 9:9 tells us: "They have deeply corrupted themselves, as in the days of Gibeah; therefore he will remember their iniquity, he will visit their sins."

God "will remember their iniquity."

How carefully God keeps account of sin as it piles up and piles up against the sinner! For instance, God watched carefully the Amorite nations in the land of Canaan, and He said to Abraham, "The iniquity of the Amorites is not yet full" (Gen. 15:16). But in due time, the cup of iniquity of the Amorites was filled so that God must in righteousness bring judgment, and He utterly destroyed the Amorites out of the land. God remembered their sins!

So it will be with other nations and people. For example, in Revelation, the restoration of the Roman empire is pictured, and God speaks of the great city that will be the center of this wickedness and the seat of the Antichrist, as "Babylon." Revelation 16:19 tells us: "And the great city was divided into three parts, and the cities of the nations fell: and great Babylon CAME IN REMEMBRANCE BEFORE GOD; to give unto her the cup of the wine of the fierceness of his wrath."

Sin, unrepented sin, sin unlamented, sin not put under the blood comes in remembrance before God, and God must pour out His wrath in judgment and punishment.

And that in fact must be the fate of every unrepentant sinner in all this universe. In Revelation 20:11–15 we have the tragic story of the Great White Throne judgment when every condemned sinner is dragged out of Hell and given his resurrected body in order that every knee shall bow and every tongue shall confess before God. And there we are told that the books will be opened, and that the dead shall be "judged out of those things which were written in the books, according to their works." The keen memory of God is unfailing, and day by day every detail, even to words and thoughts and impulses of the heart, is written down in the books of God. Sinner, God sees and God knows your heart. Unrepentant sinner, as certain as God is just and truthful, God must bring your sin to remembrance, and to judgment!

Oh, the memory of God, how long, and how true it is! How sweet is the memory of God when it is a memory of mercy, but how terrible is the memory of God when it is the memory of justice and judgment! Unsaved man, our sins pile up in the face of an angry God, and He never forgets. Psalm 7:11 tells us that "God is angry with the wicked every day." That is because He never forgets their sins. John 3:36 tells us that "he that believeth on the Son hath everlasting life: and he that believeth not the Son shall not see life; but the wrath of God ABIDETH ON HIM." God's anger stays, lives, dwells continually on unrepentant sinners! God never forgets, neither day nor night, the sins of the wicked who reject His Son, and who will not be saved. Such sinners go on in sin, and God keeps an account of their sins and holds them in mind until His anger must burn hot and His holy indignation must be like fire against them.

And one day the books will be opened and they will bow the knee before the Christ they have rejected and they will be judged every one according to their own works, according to the things written down in the books of God. Oh, the fateful and terrible memory of God concerning man's sin! Let no sinner think that he can get by. God never forgets, and God will have His say one day when all the witnesses are present, and when every man must tell the truth, and when no one will gainsay the verdict of guilty.

### God Remembers but, Praise His Name, He Also Forgets!

I have been saying to you over and over again that God remembers, *God remembers,* GOD REMEMBERS! And now I must say that there are some things that God forgets. God forgets sins when they are forgiven and covered by the blood of Christ!

In Isaiah 43:25 is this precious verse: "I, even I, am he that blotteth out thy transgressions for mine own sake, and will NOT remember thy sins." There we have it plainly stated; God will not remember sins that are blotted out for His own name's sake.

In Jeremiah 31:33–34, we are told of the happy time when the nation Israel will be saved and brought back to their own land. Then God will write the law in their hearts and no one will need to say to his neighbor, "Know the LORD." "For they shall all know me, from the least of them unto the greatest of them, saith the LORD, for I will forgive their iniquity, and *I will remember their sin no more.*"

God will remember the sins of Israel NO MORE. Oh, the sharp memory of God! What a mercy it is that sins can be so settled, so atoned for, so forgiven, that God will no more remember them!

This same teaching is given repeatedly. Hebrews 8:12 says: "For I will be merciful to their unrighteousness, and *their sins and their iniquities will I remember no more.*" And Hebrews 10:17 says: *"And their sins and iniquities will I remember no more."*

Does it not seem strange that God should remember so well all about us and that such an infinitely accurate and full record of our sins should be made and written down in Heaven's books and that even through thousands of years God should preserve the records of unconverted people, and bring them out at the judgment time when they are brought from Hell, with a resurrected body to bow the knee before Him? Does it not seem strange with such a terrible divine exactness and justice, clearly remembered, that elsewhere we are told of those against whom God will remember their sins and their iniquities no more? But that seeming strangeness and paradox is in fact a part of the holy memory of God.

This is what I mean. There are some things that God cannot forget. For one thing, He cannot forget His mercy. Concerning Israel, Psalm 98:3 says: "He hath remembered his mercy and his truth toward the house of Israel." God remembers His mercy. There is something in the nature of God Himself, something as much a divine attribute as His infinite memory, and that is His mercy. God cannot gainsay His own mercy. Mercy when applied to sin blots it out. Let us say it in other words that are clearer. God cannot forget His Son. We had better always remember this, that the Lord Jesus Christ is the dearest thing in all the universe of God to our Father. God has given all judgment to the Son. God has decreed that to Him every knee shall bow and every tongue shall confess. The Lord Jesus Christ is the express image of the Father's person. And God cannot forget the sacrifice of His Son and all the payment that Jesus Christ made on Calvary for man's sins.

So when a sinner comes to Christ and depends upon Him and loves Him and trusts Him for salvation from sin, his sins are blotted out. One who realizes his helplessness and his wickedness and knows that he has no claim on a basis of righteousness but comes asking for mercy, such a one gets forgiveness on the basis of the shed blood of Jesus Christ which paid for sin. First Corinthians 15:3 says: "Christ died for our sins according to the Scriptures." Isaiah 53:6 tells us that "all we like sheep have gone astray; we have turned every one to his own way; and the LORD hath laid on him the iniquity of us all." Jesus Christ has paid once for all the sins of the whole world. Now when a sinner comes to God and is willing to lay his sins on Jesus, those sins are counted paid.

In truth and in fact they ARE paid. Every bit of the debt, every stain of the sin is covered by the perfect and holy blood of Jesus Christ, who was offered as a Lamb without spot or blemish. The righteousness of God is appeased. God's holiness cannot be offended in the offering that Jesus made. God Himself cannot require more than Jesus has paid for every sinner. All that a sinner needs to do, then, to have his sins forever blotted out is to lay them on Jesus by faith, to count Jesus his Sin-bearer, his Offering, his atoning Lamb!

Here is the sweet meaning of John 3:16: "For God so loved the world, that he gave his only begotten Son, that whosoever believeth in him should not perish, but have everlasting life." And no wonder that Romans 4:7–8, says: "Blessed are they whose iniquities are forgiven, and whose sins are covered. Blessed is the man to whom the Lord will not impute sin."

There it is in a nutshell. God cannot remember sin against the sinner who is forgiven, because his sins are not even charged up to him. They are charged against Jesus and paid. God is just who must require sin to be paid for, but God is so just that He cannot require that it be paid for *twice*.

Thus the way is made so that God in righteousness can forget every sin that is put under the blood of Jesus Christ by faith. And so God can say with holy gentleness to every saved soul that "their iniquities and their sins will I remember no more."

In a revival service in a big furniture building in Dallas, Texas, several years ago, I noticed a woman before me as I preached. The tears again and again welled in her eyes, and her face was sad, sad! It is a horrible thing what sin does to the face of a woman, through the years. When the invitation was given and I urged sinners to come to Christ and depend on Him alone as Savior, this woman stood and sobbed and cried but would not come. Finally I felt led to leave the pulpit and walk down to her and ask her why she did not come to take Christ as her Savior. "Oh, I cannot forget the things I have done, I can never forget the things I have done!" But I explained to her that God would forget it every bit and that He would remember it against her no more forever. I told her how God would carry her sins as far away as the east is from the west (Ps. 103:12), how He would bury her sins in the depth of the sea (Micah 7:19), how He would remember them no more against her forever (Heb. 10:17). Light came into her face and she took my hand and came forward to claim boldly the Savior who can forget, thank God, as well as remember. God, remembering the price His Son paid for sin, can forget the sin which is covered forever from His sight by the blood.

Memory is sometimes a horrible thing for men. To the rich man in Hell Abraham said, "Son, remember!" He did not want to remember, but I am sure that the poor tortured soul now for these thousands of years has remembered, *remembered*, REMEMBERED! every day in Hell. Hell is a place of memory, and memory brings torment.

When Joseph was hated by his brethren and sold into slavery, he later rose by the hand of God to be the chief ruler under Pharaoh in all of Egypt. Then his brethren, after years, came to Egypt to buy corn and came face to face with Joseph, whom they did not know. When these brothers were faced with the prospect of imprisonment, they talked among themselves saying, "We are verily guilty concerning our brother, in that we saw the anguish of his soul when he besought us and we would not hear; therefore is this distress come upon us." The memory of an evil conscience tormented them years afterward. The memory of sin, I say, may be a horrible thing, a taunting thing, an irritation, a burning, a shame, like the tormenting of a demon from Hell.

I read that in a hospital a man lay sick and slowly dying. A visiting friend said to him again and again, "Is there anything I can do for you?" But always he received the same answer, that there was nothing he could do. One day as the man lay near death, the visiting friend said, again, "Is there anything I can do for you?" This time the man answered back, "No, there is nothing you can *do*, nothing that anybody can *do*. But, oh, I want to know, is there anybody who can UN-DO?" The anguish of memory, the memory of sin and wasted life no doubt haunted this dying man. He did not want what somebody could do; he wanted somebody to *un-do* the deeds of the past, the days that were wasted, the sin whose memory tormented him.

And to the sinner, I want to say that we have One who can un-do. We have One who can forget as well as One who remembers. If your sins are piled as high as the clouds of Heaven; if they are as black as the bottomless pit of Hell, if they are as wicked as those of Judas Iscariot himself, I say to you that Jesus Christ will forgive them and that they will then be carried away, hidden from the face of God forever and forgotten. God says, "And their sins and their iniquities will I remember no more."

Perhaps your heart has been stirred to love the God with such infinite care for His creatures that He remembers every need, the God that remembered Noah in the flood, and remembered Abraham when He destroyed

Sodom, and remembered Rachel the barren wife and Hannah, the God who remembered His covenant with His people, and keeps all His promises—what a wonderful God! Your heart surely has been moved to love Him better as you see the richness of His infinite love for us. And you can see the justice and righteousness of God in that He remembers sin and keeps a record and calls sinners themselves to repent and when they do not repent brings them to judgment and condemnation and ruin. God remembers sin! But how sweet it is for us to know that God can forget sin, can blot out the memory of it forever, can hold it against us no more but forgive it and blot it out from His sight. I hope that today you will trust Him for mercy and forgiveness, have all your sins so blotted out that they will never be remembered against your soul again.

Every saint of God should be comforted that God puts his tears in a bottle. Every praying child will surely rejoice that God has golden vials where He keeps the treasured prayers of His saints like sweet odors and incense, and opens them up to perfume all Heaven when the time comes for the answer to be given. Then surely you will be glad that God has a book of remembrance written for those who fear His name and speak often concerning Him. And best of all, those who trusted in Jesus Christ are written in the book of life and can never be blotted out. God remembers His own, and God keeps books over every one. If you, dear sinner, will today trust in Jesus Christ and His blood shed for you, then you will have your sins blotted out and forgotten, but you yourself will be written in the Lamb's book of life, ever to be remembered and held near the heart of God. Will you do that? Will you trust Jesus Christ today and take His forgiveness and mercy that He offers so that with iniquities and sins forgiven and forgotten, you will be the ever-remembered child of our heavenly Father?

# Norman Vincent Peale

*1898–1996*

*N*orman Vincent Peale was born in Bowersville, Ohio, the son of a Methodist preacher whom he idealized all his life. As a boy, Peale was very shy and not at all athletic like his younger brother, and this made him feel inferior. His mother encouraged both boys to be what God called them to be, to love life, and to be interested in everything good. She encouraged them to read widely and cultivate their imagination.

Peale graduated from Ohio Wesleyan University in 1920 and Boston University in 1924 and he pastored churches in Rhode Island, Brooklyn, and Syracuse before accepting the call to Marble Collegiate Reformed Church in New York City in 1932, where he remained until his retirement in 1984. It was the oldest church in New York City, chartered in 1696, but it had fallen on difficult days. Under Peale's leadership, the membership grew from six hundred to more than five thousand.

An effective communicator of spiritual truth in marketplace vocabulary, Peale's ministry began to reach around the world. His radio program *The Art of Living* was broadcast over NBC for fifty-four years. He was the author of more than thirty books. *The Power of Positive Thinking* was translated into forty-two languages and has sold more than fifteen million copies. He and his wife founded *Guideposts* magazine, which has a circulation of more than four million.

Early in his ministry Peale determined not to cloud spiritual truth with confusing theological language and to deal with the real problems that people face and that only Christ can solve. At times in his pulpit ministry, he invited people to come forward to trust Christ or to bow and pray to the Lord right at the pew or to come to an after-meeting to discuss personal commitment to Christ. He considered himself a theological conservative whose calling was to make Jesus Christ attractive and the gospel clear to people who don't understand theology.

Peale's autobiography, *The True Joy of Positive Living* (Morrow, 1984), recounts the effects of "positive thinking" in his own life and ministry, while *This Incredible Century* (Tyndale, 1991) reviews the twentieth century and Peale's responses to events and changes. *Minister to Millions* by Arthur Gordon is an early biography (Prentice-Hall, 1958), and *He Speaks the Word of God* by Allan R. Broadhurst (Prentice-Hall, 1963) is a study of Peale's sermons and philosophy of preaching.

# The Amazing Power of Prayer

James 5:16

Have you ever considered this proposition? What would happen to you and, through you, to the world if you were to make the practice of prayer a central program of your life? What do you think would happen if you saturate your mind with the Bible; if you study and practice the principles of prayer which it contains? I realize that we all pray to one extent or another, but I think most of us will admit that, really, we only dabble at it. Suppose you went all out in a thoroughgoing prayer program. What do you think would happen?

I believe it would be the most revolutionary, life-changing, tremendous experience you ever had. I believe that problems which now baffle you would be made clear; burdens which overwhelm would become lighter; sickness which cripples and hampers would be handled with power. Tremendous things would happen. Tennyson said, "More things are wrought by prayer than this world dreams of." The Bible says, "The effectual fervent prayer of a righteous man"—that could be "good" or "right-minded"—"availeth much."

I was led to a discussion of this subject by a man who told me of his personal experience with such a program. He had been having a lot of trouble with himself and he was advised to try for a solution through Bible reading and prayer. He smiled in disbelief, but finally was convinced that he ought to try.

So, he started to read the Bible. Having no previous familiarity with it, he found it hard going. Prayer, too, was a problem; he could not keep his mind from wandering.

"I found a solution to that," he told me. "When I started to pray and my mind wandered, I followed the diversion along and discovered that God had something to say to me at the end of that unexpected path."

You and I realize, of course, that this manner of praying might be no more than an excuse for intellectual indolence. But, also, you might come on a spiritual pot of gold in such prayer meandering.

At any rate, this man learned to pray. And after a while he loved to pray. Reading the Bible, he discovered, was for him like hacking his way into a gold mine. He had to work through many passages that were hard for him, but in the end he discovered glories and riches. And he developed some remarkable techniques. Every time he wrote a letter he put his hand on it and prayed that the words would convey the Grace of God to the recipient. What a wonderful habit to form, that of praying about every letter we send! When he made a telephone call, he prayed that it might be to God's glory. As he drove in his car, he prayed for other drivers. He confessed that he had formerly used similar language, but now he used it in a very different way.

He was doing what the Bible suggests; praying without ceasing. And he says the process revolutionized his life. It opened up solutions to problems which had bewildered him. He was better physically. And I want to tell you that I go along with him. To one degree or another, I have tried this myself. And I believe it to be one of the greatest spiritual techniques anybody can employ. As that man said to me, "I now realize the amazing power there is in prayer."

First of all, the thing we must do, and do well, is to be as nearly right as we can. It is very easy to make mistakes, for the error tendency is in all of us. But there is up atop our shoulders an instrument known as a head. I never see anybody without one. It is a wonderful mechanism, the head. Nobody but God could make it and nobody but you can use it. In that head is another instrument, the brain, which is the seat of the mind; and the mind is for thought.

We are human and our knowledge is limited, our senses often dull, and so we make mistakes. God is never wrong; He never makes mistakes; God is always right. Therefore, if your mind is in harmony with the mind of God, you will step up your percentage of rightness and you will live more effectively. And the only way you can get into this close harmony with God is through prayer.

I went South to make some speeches and traveled on a beautiful train called the *Silver Meteor,* surely one of the finest trains in the country, a gleaming thing of the most modern design, operated by the Seaboard Railroad. I was invited by the engineer to ride with him in the cab; I had never done that before. I have flown with the pilot in the cockpit of an airplane and experienced a tremendous thrill, but, believe me, riding in the cab of the *Silver Meteor* was even more thrilling. We traveled at eighty-five miles an hour, the track stretching ahead like a ribbon. Then I saw a trestle coming up. It looked exactly like a tight-rope over which we were going to ride in that cab.

The engineer is a great Christian and so is his fireman. They explained the signal system, and I got so I could read the signals. He would say, "What do we do here?" I would tell him and most of the time I was right. (No, I wasn't endangering the lives of anybody. He had his hand on the throttle and his eyes on the signals.)

"Who directs your activity?" I asked when we were near Palm Beach.

"The dispatcher in Jacksonville," he said.

"Does he know where you are right now?" Jacksonville seemed a long way off to me.

"He knows where I am every moment of this trip," the engineer assured me. "And he guides me all along the way."

"Doesn't that destroy your ability to think and make decisions on your own?" I asked. It was a foolish question, for, as I looked into his alert eyes, I knew that there was not a second of the hundred miles I rode with him that he didn't see everything.

"That dispatcher is running half a dozen other trains at the same time he is running ours," was his answer. "What keeps this train on schedule is my harmony with him."

The thought came to me, then, that we, driving down the rails of our own lives, would avoid many a crack-up and difficulty if we had the same contact with, and faith in, our Great Dispatcher. He, too, knows every minute of our lives, where we are and where we are headed. And only by prayer can we keep mentally and spiritually alert for His directions. He can keep us from mistakes. Keep in close touch with that Dispatcher who watches over us all the way.

When you come right down to it, the way to solve a problem isn't to become agitated and tense about it. Nobody believes in hard thinking more than I, but our hard thinking should be harmonious contact of our minds with the mind of God, so that our ideas are guided by His insight. When I make a lot of mistakes, it is always the result of getting cocky and thinking I, myself, have the answers. Only when you and I pray humbly and with a proper appraisal of our own wisdom do we get the right answers.

Out West a few years ago a woman asked to talk to me. I could see that she was nervous, her hands were so tightly clasped together.

"I just don't know what to do," she said. "I'm so baffled. My husband, after thirty years of happy married life, has become interested in another woman and has gone away with her several times. In fact, he is away with her right now."

"Does he want you to divorce him?" I asked.

"No, he doesn't, and that puzzles me," she said, and added, "I don't know what to do."

I tried to explain to her that the reason he did not want a legal separation was that she was not only his wife, but his psychological mother as well. When she objected to his behavior he got mad, like a child, like a small boy whose mother should permit him to do anything he wanted to do.

We struggled with this problem and the more we struggled the more difficult it seemed. Finally I said to her, "What do you say we stop discussing the problem and just think about God? What is God like to you?"

"When I was a girl I thought of Him as a Big Man with a kindly face," she said. "As I got older I substituted the picture of Jesus in the stained glass window of our church. In the Bible He had said, 'He that hath seen me hath seen the Father' (John 14:9). So I got to loving Jesus. God must be like Jesus."

I told her what I thought about God. Then we read the Bible and together we prayed.

"What do you think we ought to do about this matter now?" I asked her after that interval in which we had lifted our minds to the high level of God.

She said: "First, I must find out what is wrong with me. Then, I am going to lift that husband of mine up to God. And third, I am going to pray for that poor, misguided woman."

As she said this I knew she was beginning to solve her problem.

"I am going to be calm and peaceful," she continued, "and stay with this problem until I wash it out as Jesus would."

She did just that and finally, not without struggle, she solved her problem. She and her husband are together again and their marriage is on a higher spiritual level. No one can solve a problem by getting nervous or tense over it. You have to keep your mind on it, of course, but first, if you lift your mind to God, His insight will come into your thinking as in the case of the wife I have mentioned.

And, of course, you will not think of prayer as just a means of getting something you want. Prayer is the means by which we get what God wants us to have. What we want for ourselves may be wrong; what God wants for us is right. So, in prayer, it is always well to ask ourselves, "What is it that God wants for me?"

I remember talking once with a very rich man who was having trouble sleeping. "I believe if I can just get near to God everything will be all right," he said. "But I have been trying to find Him and I can't. Do you think I might, if I gave a lot of money to the Church?"

"How much are you willing to give?" I asked.

"I would give $100,000 if you can suggest how I can find God."

"You will have to give a good deal more than that," I replied. "You must give Him your whole self, your entire life. Your idea seems to be that all you need to do is to press a button and God will appear, like a glorified bellboy. There is only one way you can find God and that is to confess all your sins, tell the Lord that you are not asking Him to come to you, but you are giving yourself to Him. One hundred thousand dollars won't buy Him, but if you give yourself to Him, He will give Himself to you!"

He said, "Lord, I do not want to dictate to You. All I want is to have You and to serve You."

That is the way we get the power of God in our lives. We can tell Him what we want; that is perfectly proper. But we must always add, "If this isn't what You want for me, then I only want what You want to give me." When you achieve that kind of harmony with God, then things really begin to move in your life.

Finally, my friends, I believe that in order to bring prayer power into our lives we must face ourselves, analyze ourselves, be honest with ourselves, and get all the sin out of us. God can do tremendous things with a human being if that human being is a good transmitting instrument. If you do not know what sin is, read the Bible and you will find out. Sin has its grosser side, but it also has its subtle side. The gross side is adultery, drunkenness, riotous living, theft—you know all that. But its more sophisticated side is pride, hate, meanness, selfishness. These are harder to eliminate, but by the Grace of God even they can be taken from you; and then power comes.

I want to read a letter from Irwin W. Tucker who runs a gasoline station in Oklahoma. I have told you about him before. He has a chapel in his station for Jews, Catholics, and Protestants. It is a beautiful room. While he is filling your tank with gasoline, you can fill your spiritual tank with prayer. That is the idea.

His moving letter reads as follows:

> I have wanted for some time to tell you how you opened the door to Christianity and a partnership with our beloved Jesus.
>
> Perhaps you did not know I was a chronic alcoholic. I never did get on skid row, but that was because I had a family and friends to watch over me. But I had reached the point where I knew I faced death or deterioration, that I was destroying everything I valued in life.
>
> In a state of despair and hopelessness, I went to Alcoholics Anonymous. Of course, I recognize now that God came into my life at that time without my even knowing it. As time went on my life began straightening out. Wonderful things began to happen, and it began to soak into my mind that these things were coming from a Power greater than myself.

I went at this, though, like a crawling yellowbelly; reluctantly, shyly, hesitantly. As time went on I came to the full recognition that a Power which I could not visualize in my mind was giving me all my power and strength. I began to play with the idea, to recognize the tremendous possibilities of a full and complete turning of my life over to Him. I started to listen to you over the radio and, for the first time, I recognized the practical principles of Christianity. And then I could not satisfy my hunger and thirst for this knowledge.

About this time I got together with four other drunks like myself and organized a Bible study and prayer group. It is astonishing how ignorant we all were. (Imagine five defeated fellows getting together to read the Bible and pray! You have no idea what is going on all over this country.)

We started by reading and studying one of your sermons. Then, a member of a group in Oklahoma City suggested that we get Nelson's edition of the New Testament. And one night we decided we had better take our blessed Lord Jesus in as a member of the group and ask Him for wisdom and the ability to understand the principles He had given us. Of course, miracles began to happen from that minute.

I was approaching the realization of full and complete surrender of mind and body and I was frightened to death. But I also recognized the truth that, when God lays His hand on your shoulder, there is no turning back. I looked up my minister, a wonderful guy, and got down on my knees with him and committed myself to God and to serving Him.

My life has been a delightful, fascinating experience since that day. I began to realize that my spiritual life must be fed the same as my body. It was at the time of this recognition that I saw a television program which inspired my wife and me to put a prayer altar in our home. We knew that Jesus must become a member of our family, and He sure did. The change that came over our home absolutely astounded me: the joy, the happiness, the intense love and respect for each other, the attitude of our children toward our blessed Jesus as a member of the family and the loving Father to us all.

Irwin Tucker's prayer room in his gasoline station has inspired similar prayer rooms in a number of business houses in the Southwest. He was a rugged, two-fisted veteran of World War II and all mixed up until he got the answers from One whom he so touchingly calls, "the blessed Lord Jesus." It is the same "blessed Lord Jesus" who can revitalize the lives of every one of us if we turn to Him and surrender in prayer and in faith.

That is the way you can get greatness and the fullness and joy of life. That is the way you can solve your problems. Give yourself, as Irwin Tucker did, as I must, as we all must, to the "blessed Lord Jesus."

*Prayer:* Our Heavenly Father, help us now to face our lives and see them for what they are. Help us to want Thee so much that we will pay the great price of giving ourselves to Thee. Then, having Thy Grace, grant that we may give it to everyone everywhere. Through our blessed Lord Jesus. Amen.

# John Robert Walmsley Stott

*1921-*

From 1950 to 1975 John R. W. Stott was rector of All Souls Church, Langham Place, London, located next to the British Broadcasting Company building. Throughout his ministry, he has exemplified the best in the evangelical Anglican tradition, walking in the footsteps of such men as Charles Simeon, J. C. Ryle, Hendley Moule, and W. H. Griffith Thomas.

Stott trusted Christ at the age of sixteen while at Rugby, was educated at Cambridge, where he had a brilliant record, and was ordained deacon on December 21, 1945. He was assigned to All Souls as curate, but in March 1950 the rector died and Stott was appointed priest-in-charge. In June he was named rector-designate, and that was changed to rector by the end of September. That such a young man should be placed in this important pulpit disturbed some of the members, but Stott proved himself capable both as pastor and as preacher. He had a burden for evangelism as well as discipleship and wanted to see All Souls become a vibrant center for balanced biblical ministry. As his gifts became known, Stott was invited to speak at numerous conferences and university missions, and eventually he had a worldwide ministry, which continues to this day. Stott's sermons are based in solid exegesis and careful study and he has a remarkable gift for preparing outlines that explain the text clearly and concisely.

In 1959 Stott was named a royal chaplain. Frequently he gave the Bible readings at the InterVarsity triennial Urbana Conference, which draws thousands of students together to consider the claims of world missions.

After his resignation from All Souls Church in 1975, Stott founded the Institute for Contemporary Christianity. He was a key man in preparing the "Lausanne Covenant" that came out of the Lausanne World Congress in 1974, sponsored by the Billy Graham Evangelistic Association.

Stott's publications are too many to list. They include *Basic Christianity, Fundamentalism and Evangelism, God's New Society, Christ the Controversialist, The Cross of Christ,* and *I Believe in Preaching.*

Timothy Dudley-Smith is writing the official biography, and volume one has appeared—*John Stott: The Making of a Leader* (Inter-Varsity Press, 1999). It covers Stott's life and ministry through 1950.

# The What and How
# of the Christian Life

Wherefore laying aside all malice, and all guile, and hypocrisies, and envies, and all evil speakings, as newborn babes, desire the sincere milk of the word, that ye may grow thereby: if so be ye have tasted that the Lord is gracious. To whom coming, as unto a living stone, disallowed indeed of men, but chosen of God, and precious, ye also, as lively stones, are built up a spiritual house, an holy priesthood, to offer up spiritual sacrifices, acceptable to God by Jesus Christ. Wherefore also it is contained in the scripture, Behold, I lay in Sion a chief cornerstone, elect, precious: and he that believeth on him shall not be confounded. Unto you therefore which believe he is precious: but unto them which be disobedient, the stone which the builders disallowed, the same is made the head of the corner, and a stone of stumbling, and a rock of offense, even to them which stumble at the word, being disobedient: whereunto also they were appointed. But ye are a chosen generation, a royal priesthood, an holy nation, a peculiar people; that ye should show forth the praises of him who hath called you out of darkness into his marvelous light: which in time past were not a people, but are now the people of God: which had not obtained mercy, but now have obtained mercy. Dearly beloved, I beseech you as strangers and pilgrims, abstain from fleshly lusts, which war against the soul.

1 Peter 2:1–11

I hardly need to remind a company of Bible students such as are gathered here, that the Bible is rich with metaphors and similes, figures and images. We are well aware that our Lord Jesus Christ spoke often in parables and in allegories. We know, too, that the fertile mind and imagination of the great apostle Paul often resorted to the use of image and metaphor. The same is true of the apostle Peter, and I think no example is clearer than the passage we have before us.

In this passage, Peter employs a number of interesting secular images in order to illustrate and to enforce some vitally important spiritual truths. Each one of these metaphors, similes, or images indicates or describes a different aspect of what a Christian is, and we shall find that joined to every one of these metaphors is a corresponding obligation or responsibility. We shall learn again, as we find so often in Scripture, that we are in a position to learn how we ought to behave as Christians only when we have first discovered what we are as Christians. The "how" is governed by the "what." It is only when we have discovered the *character* of the Christian life that we shall be able to discover the *conduct* that is expected of a Christian.

When you stop to think about it, this is true, of course, in every sphere of life. The apostle Paul says in 1 Corinthians 13: "When I was a child, I behaved like a child," and he might have added, "because I was a child, and the fact of my childhood determined my childish behavior; but when I became a man I discarded my toys and I put away childish things, and I began to behave like a man because I was a man." If you are a lady, you behave like a lady. If you are an American, you behave like an American. I think you will agree that how we behave depends on what we are.

I have been greatly blessed by this passage in the Word of God because it describes the rich variety of the Christian life, and a number of different aspects of what it means to be a Christian. As we look at these metaphors we shall find that each one brings with it a significant Christian obligation.

Let's begin with verse 2, a verse I hope you have committed to memory. "As newborn babes"—the word *as* or *like* introduces the metaphor, or the simile if you prefer it. "Like newborn babes, desire the sincere milk of the word, that ye may grow thereby."

Now, the Christian, and particularly the new Christian, the one who has recently trusted Jesus Christ and committed his life to Christ as Saviour and Lord, is here described by the well-known simile of the newborn baby. The reason for that is found in 1 Peter 1:23. Peter says, "Being born again, not of corruptible seed, but of incorruptible, by the word of God, which liveth and abideth forever." The Word of God, the good news in Christ, had been dropped like a seed into their hearts, and it fructified, and a new birth was caused in the personality of these people to whom Peter wrote. Since they had been born again, since they had experienced their new birth, they are described in 2:2 as newborn babies.

I want to digress for a few minutes and consider a number of important matters connected with the doctrine of the new birth. As it's my privilege to move around and talk with Christians I find that many are very hazy about the Biblical doctrine of the new birth. Here are one or two things for us to consider about it.

First, the new birth is a deep inward revolutionary change wrought by the Spirit of God in the inner recesses of the human personality, so that it is called a birth from above, and a birth of the Spirit, and a birth of God. No man can force himself to be born again. No man can cause any other man or woman to be born again. It's an inward thing, and it's so radical that it is described in Scripture as receiving a new heart, undergoing a new creation, being made partaker of the divine nature and being born again.

One of the most dramatic verses in the whole New Testament is 2 Corinthians 5:17. In the Greek text there are no main verbs at all. The King James Version says: "If any man be in Christ, he is a new creation," which is a bit laborious and a bit pedestrian. The Greek phrase goes like this: "If any man in Christ—new creation." There isn't a verb in the whole sentence. So dramatic is this experience, "If any man in Christ—new creation." That is what the Bible begins to teach about the new birth.

Allow me to say a word or two about baptism. I realize we do not all belong to the same churches, and I hope that I shall not be guilty of treading on anybody's theological corns, but I simply want to make one point for the clarity of our own thinking. Whatever else baptism is, it is not the new birth. Baptism is an outward thing; the new birth is an inward thing. Baptism is a visible rite or ordinance instituted by Jesus; the new birth is an invisible thing. Baptism is a public ceremony; the new birth is a private, secret experience. The one is a counterpart of the other, and if you are confusing the two, I would suggest that you're making a mistake.

The second thing is that the new birth is an instantaneous experience. There is a great deal of discussion and confusion among Christians today about whether conversion is gradual or sudden. I don't want to be drawn into any lengthy debate on that subject, but when we are speaking of the new birth, which is the work of God the Holy Spirit in the soul, I would say that if words have meaning, it is instantaneous. For we are very well aware that there are months of preparation before a birth, and there are years of growth after a birth, but birth, if words have meaning, is a dramatic crisis. Oh, yes, there may be many months in which we consider whether we are going to turn to Christ. We may take many months in repenting and beginning to get interested in Jesus Christ. We may begin to come to church; we may begin to read the Bible, even to pray. But when eventually we have turned to Christ in repentance and faith, the work of the new birth by the Holy Spirit in our hearts is instantaneous. I did not say that we emerge from the new birth a fully developed Christian adult; I did not say that we emerge from the conversion experience with the fully grown wings of an angel. I said that the actual new birth was instantaneous, and then begins the process of growth from Christian babyhood through to Christian manhood and womanhood and maturity.

I want to suggest to you further that the new birth is an indispensable thing; there is no substitute for it at all.

Being a Christian is neither believing certain dogmas, nor is it accepting a certain moral code, nor is it undergoing certain external ceremonies, although all those things have their place. To become a Christian one needs to be born again.

It is an interesting thing that Jesus taught the indispensable necessity of the new birth to Nicodemus. Have you ever contrasted in your mind the third and fourth chapters of the Gospel of John? Jesus speaks in chapter 3 to Nicodemus and in chapter 4 to the Samaritan woman, and you could not find two more different people. In the one case, Nicodemus was righteous, and the woman was unrighteous. For another thing, he was a Jew; she was a Samaritan. For another thing, he was probably of noble birth, and she was a poor woman, because she brought her water pitcher to the well—she had nobody to take it for her. For another thing, he was educated, and she was probably uneducated. Yet it was to Nicodemus, the moral, educated, religious, righteous, upright man, and not to the Samaritan woman, that Jesus said, "Ye must be born again"; "Except a man be born again, he cannot see the kingdom of God," let alone enter into it. It is an indispensable thing.

The fourth thing, which brings us back to our text, is that it is an initial thing, it is only a beginning.

Do you remember the famous speech Sir Winston Churchill made, in 1941 or '42, at the conclusion of the battle of Egypt? He was invited to what is now a historic meeting in the Mansion House in London, given by the Lord Mayor of London. In his speech he said, "Gentlemen, this is not the end; it is not even the beginning of the end; it may perhaps be the end of the beginning." What is true of the battle of Egypt is certainly true of the new birth. It is not the end of Christian experience; it isn't even the beginning of the end; it may perhaps be the end of the beginning. But it's only a beginning, and then comes the beauty of growth.

"As newborn babes, desire the sincere milk of the word, that ye may grow thereby." I ask myself, and I want you to ask yourself, "Am I growing?" So many Christians, yes, truly born-again Christians, are retarded in their growth. There are too many Christians in the church today who are suffering from a spiritual infantile regression; they've never grown up. Just as it's tragic to meet people who've never developed physically or mentally or emotionally and who are still children in those ways, it is tragic to meet Christians who have never grown up spiritually and morally.

I find that in the New Testament there is a great deal said about this gradual progression that we call sanctification. You cannot grow until you've been born, but once you've been born, you must grow. The Bible talks about growing in faith. "O ye of little faith," said Jesus. You've only a little faith. So the disciples came to Him and said, "Lord, increase our faith; we want more." Paul spoke in Thessalonians about their faith growing exceedingly. Is your faith growing?

Then the Bible talks about growing in love. Oh, brethren, we need that more than anything else today in evangelical circles. I believe that God has been teaching me this in recent days, and I've been learning in my study of the New Testament that love is the greatest thing in the universe. The Bible says that love is greater than knowledge. You read 1 Corinthians 8:1–3 and you will find that we are there told that knowledge puffs up, whereas love builds up, and we are told a number of other distinctions. In that sense you can only know things, doctrines, dogmas; but you can love people, and people are greater than things and greater than doctrines. For another thing, knowledge is one-sided. I know a doctrine but it doesn't know me. But if I love a person, a person can love me. The fourth difference between love and knowledge is that when you know a doctrine, you know it and you've got it and it's finished. But when you love a person, it's a growing thing, and you can never say, "I love somebody as much as I can ever love him. It's finished." It's a reciprocal thing, it's a growing thing, it's a personal thing; it's greater than knowledge. Some of us are taking pride in our orthodoxy, in our evangelical, Biblical orthodoxy; I tell you, charity is greater than orthodoxy according to the Bible.

Not only is love greater than knowledge, it's greater than faith. We pride ourselves on the life of faith that we talk about. The life of love is greater than the life of faith. And it's greater than hope. We talk a lot about the return of Jesus Christ, and we're looking for His return; but love is greater than hope. Love is the greatest thing in the universe. Are we growing in love? I don't mind how narrow your mind is as long as your heart is big. Paul said to the Corinthians, "Our heart is enlarged," and I hope God will enlarge our hearts until they embrace the whole world, and until we specially love people we don't agree with. How we need that love today! Didn't Jesus say, "By this shall all men know that ye are my disciples, if ye have love one to another"?

We need to grow in faith, we need to grow in love, we need to grow in holiness. The Bible speaks of a progression in holiness. Paul wrote to the Thessalonians: "We beseech you . . . that as ye have received of us how ye ought to walk and to please God, so ye would abound more and more" (1 Thess. 4:1). Look up the references in a concordance for "more and more." You'll find verses for more and more faith, more and more love, more and more holiness; yes, and more and more knowledge. We need to grow in understanding, increasing in the knowledge of God. "Grow in grace, and in the knowledge of our Lord and Saviour Jesus Christ." Are we growing in these things? I trust we are.

How can we grow? "As newborn babes, desire the sincere milk (the pure, unadulterated milk) of the word, that ye may grow thereby." You know that the most important secret of a baby's growth is the regularity of a right diet.

I was recently reading an interesting little book written in 1859 by that great pioneer nurse of the Crimean War, Florence Nightingale. In this book, titled *Notes of Nursing,* the last chapter is called "Minding Baby," and was written for the benefit of the eldest daughter in the family who might be left in charge of the baby when mother was out. In this final chapter Florence Nightingale begins:

"And now, girls, I have a word for you," and she gives seven conditions of the growth of a healthy baby. The fourth condition is feeding it with proper food at regular times, and she explains, "You must be very careful about its food, about being strict to the minute for feeding it, not giving it too much at a time. If baby is sick after its food, you have given it too much. Neither must baby be underfed. Above all, never give it any unwholesome food. Baby when it is weaned requires to be fed often, regularly, and not too much at a time. I know a mother whose baby was in great danger one day from convulsions. It was about a year old. She said that she wished to go to church and so before going she had given it its three meals in one. Was it any wonder that the poor little thing had convulsions!"

There are many Christians with spiritual convulsions because they have not learned this elementary lesson about taking food regularly and not too much at a time.

The food here described, is the milk of the Word which is God's revelation of Himself in Scripture. It is very often likened to food of different kinds: it's honey because it is sweet to the taste; it's milk, it's meat, it's solid food.

Now what about the daily, dogged discipline of the Christian life? How is it going with you? The Christian life is one of discipline, and one of the important things in the discipline of the Christian life is carving out time from your busy schedule in order to meet God every day in Bible reading and prayer. I have never met a Christian who is growing, who doesn't do that. If you want to grow in faith and love and holiness and knowledge, then you must meditate on God's Word day by day.

You'll notice that Peter says "desire."

One of the most recent commentators on the Greek text of 1 Peter says that the Greek word there indicates "the ardor of a suckled child." You know, the ardor with which the baby takes its milk, thirsting after it. Peter says you are newborn babies. Thirst after the milk of the Word, "if so be you have tasted that the Lord is gracious." You've had a taste; then thirst after Him and His Word.

I've spent a long time on that metaphor, deliberately so. We'll look now at verse 4: "To whom coming," that is, when you come to the gracious Lord Jesus, "as unto a living stone, rejected indeed of men, but chosen of God, and precious, ye also, as" or like—and here he introduces the second metaphor—"living stones, are built up a spiritual house."

Now the metaphor changes. We leave the nursery with a lot of babies in it, and coming out into the open air, we see a building that is growing. It's a stone structure, and with the eye of faith, we recognize that it is the Church, the blessed company of all believers. Every Christian is a member of that Church, whatever his nation or denomination or social rank or income group. Since the Church is likened to a building, then every Christian in the Church is likened to a stone in the building; and since every stone is a person, Peter uses the astonishing contradiction in terms—a living stone. Of course no stone has ever been alive, but Peter uses this expression.

The beauty of newborn babies is growth, and the beauty of living stones in the building is fellowship. Every stone in a building is cemented and mortared into the stone above it and below it and on the left of it and on the right of it, and it cannot get away from the building.

Was it not John Wesley who said, "To turn Christianity into a solitary religion is to destroy it." Now, Christianity has its solitary aspects. In the Sermon on the Mount Jesus said, "When thou prayest, enter into thy closet, and when thou hast shut thy door, pray to thy Father . . ."—that's solitary. A few verses later on we read, "When ye pray, say, Our Father." Yes, there is a personal and there is a corporate aspect; there is a solitary and there is a fellowship aspect of the Christian life.

Every Christian's place is in a church. I do hope and pray that every Christian here is in the fellowship of a local worshiping, witnessing community. I don't mind what community it is, as long as it's a Christian community of fellowship. I hope you're not a fringe member. I hope you're not an ecclesiastical gypsy, with no fixed abode, wandering from one to another. I hope you're in the building. I've never seen a stone slipping out of its place and wandering along to another place. You get into your place and stay there. There is the duty of fellowship.

The third metaphor is found in verse 5, and I think you'll agree it's a surprising one: "an holy priesthood, to offer up spiritual sacrifices, acceptable to God by Jesus Christ." Christians are newborn babies. Christians are living stones in the building. Christians, all Christians, are holy priests. I did not say they are ordained ministers of the gospel or of the church, but they are holy priests. Here is my authority for it, as well as at least one other passage, in Revelation 1:5–6.

What does that mean? This is a phrase lifted out of the Old Testament, in Exodus 19. The Old Testament makes a rigid distinction between the priests and the Levites, on the one hand, and the people, on the other.

The priests in the Old Testament had two particular privileges. Their first privilege was the enjoyment of access to God. The priests were permitted into the tabernacle, into the temple, into the court of the priests. The high priest was allowed into the holy of holies on the day of atonement. Here the visible symbol of the divine presence was manifested. The priests were allowed near in a way that the people were not allowed near. Their second privilege was the offering of sacrifices. It was the priests who killed the victims and offered the sacrifices, and not the people.

That rigid distinction is done away in Christ, and the two privileges that the priests had in the Old Testament have now devolved on the whole Christian Church. All Christians are holy priests, and those two privileges belong to every Christian. Thus we enjoy intimate access to Christ, and an ordained minister does not enjoy a closer access to God than those we like to call the laymen. Through Christ we have the same access.

What about sacrifices? The whole Church and every Christian in the Church has the privilege of offering sacrifices to God. And what are these sacrifices? They're different from the Old Testament sacrifices in two ways. First, in their nature; second, in their purpose. As to their nature, they're not material sacrifices; they are called here spiritual sacrifices. What are they? They are the sacrifices of our worship and our praise and our thanksgiving and our adoration. The whole Church ought to be offering up these songs of praises all day long, and especially on the Lord's Day when they gather together for worship.

And then the purpose of the sacrifices is different. Some of the sacrifices of the Old Testament were sin offerings to make atonement. But mark this—there is no sacrifice the Church offers today that is a sin offering for atonement or for the sins of men. All our offerings are thank offerings. The only sin offering that the Church recognizes is the offering of the Lamb of God on the altar of Calvary all those years ago, and through that sin offering we have atonement and can come into the presence of God. If anybody seeks to offer a sin offering today, he is insulting the offering of Jesus Christ. It was a one-offering, a unique offering, offered once and for all upon the cross, and the offerings of the Church are the spiritual offerings, thank offerings of worship.

The duty of the holy priesthood is worship—access in order to worship. Is your life and mine a life of worship? Do we come to church on the Lord's Day with the Lord's people to worship, or do we come only to hear the Word preached? The purpose of the preaching of the Word in the congregation is to arouse worship. Do we come to church to worship God? In our own periods of prayer, do we spend time just gazing upon God? A humble believer one day was worshiping at the Lord's table and somebody asked him, "What are you doing?" The humble worshiper replied, "I look at Him and He looks at me." Isn't that a wonderful description of a quiet time of Bible reading and prayer? I look at Him in His Word, and He looks at me, and we just love each other. I spend time in worshiping Him as He spends time manifesting Himself to me. Oh, I hope our Christian life is a life of worship. I'm increasingly sure that sin is fundamentally self-centeredness, and that we get imprisoned in our own little world. There is nothing that will liberate a person from his self-centeredness more than learning how to worship God, just to turn his eyes away from himself and gaze and gaze upon God. That's what we are doing as holy priests offering up spiritual sacrifices.

One of the places that we do it especially is at the Lord's Supper. This is a time of thanksgiving, when we remember and commemorate Christ's precious death for our sins. It's all part of worship. So newborn babes have a duty of growth; living stones have a duty of fellowship; holy priests have a duty of worship.

Now look at verse 9: "Ye are a chosen generation, a royal priesthood, an holy nation, a peculiar people." Of course we all know what that means, not a lot of odd folks, but a people for God's own possession. Why? "That ye should show forth the praises of him who hath called you out of darkness into his marvelous light."

To my mind this is fascinating. These expressions, a royal priesthood, a holy nation, a people for God's possession, are lifted by Simon Peter out of Exodus 19:4–6. In that passage God through mercy described the Old Testament Israel as a kingdom of priests, a holy nation, a people for His possession; "my people," said God. Peter lifts these expressions out of Exodus and transfers them to his own epistle, and he lifts these expressions from the *old* Israel and he transfers them to the *new* Israel. He says, "You are a chosen generation." Who are God's chosen people today? Not the Jews, but the Christians, the Israel of God, the true circumcision. We are descended from Abraham by faith, according to the New Testament.

If that is true, what was the great purpose that God had in choosing His people? Surely it was that He might reveal Himself to them, and that they might be the recipients of His revelation, and that receiving His revelation they might guard it, and that guarding it they might dispense it to the rest of the world. Light to lighten the nations, and Israel miserably failed. Oh, they received it, they guarded it, but they didn't spread it abroad. Now Peter says, you are God's people, in order that you should spread abroad the excellencies of Him who hath called you out of darkness into His marvelous light.

Here is the next duty of the Christian. We are God's people by faith in Jesus Christ. We belong to God, we belong to this holy nation; and if so, we have this duty resting upon each of us to spread abroad these excellencies. Every Christian is called to be a witness. The Christian life is not only a life of growth, and a life of fellowship with one another, it's a life of witness to the outside world.

I want to give you a bit of practical advice. I believe that many Christians make the mistake of spreading their net too wide and trying to win too many people. Some Christians are called to that ministry, but I believe the majority are not. I suggest that you might find it a good idea to pray that God will give you a burden for just one or two people; then spend the next year or two years or three years praying for those people—maybe your brother or sister, or your best friend, or your business associate or colleague at work, or your wife or husband.

I don't like this expression, "a love for souls," because I don't know what it means to love somebody's soul. A man once said to an evangelist who was trying to win him to Christ, "If you love me as much as you love my soul, you would do better." Can't you learn to love people, and not just souls? Love the whole person and let the love be real. I read about a letter from a department store written to a disgruntled customer, but the letter came to grief in the typewriter. The letter went like this: "We assure you that we do our best to please every customer and we *fake* a personal interest in each." So much of our love is fake. May God give us a real love for people; then it may be that God will use us to win them for Christ.

The fifth metaphor is in verse 11: "Dearly beloved, I beseech you as [like] strangers and pilgrims, abstain from fleshly lusts, which war against the soul." In 1 Peter 1:1 you will see that Peter, an apostle of Jesus Christ, is writing to "the strangers scattered throughout Pontius, Galatia, Cappadocia, Asia, and Bithynia"—five of the Roman provinces, or what we call Turkey, Asia Minor. They were literally scattered abroad, they were literally strangers away from home; but Peter takes their literal status as an illustration of their spiritual status, and he says that we as Christians are to behave as strangers and pilgrims.

The Greek word means alien and exile. The alien is somebody who has no rights where he lives, and the exile is somebody who has no home where he lives. Has it ever occurred to you that the Christian is like that on this earth? We're aliens and exiles on earth; we have no rights, we have no home down here. Why is that? Because if we've been born again into the kingdom of heaven and we are citizens of heaven, then as soon as we gained a heavenly citizenship we became aliens and exiles down here.

Don't misunderstand that, because Peter goes on immediately to speak about duties as earthly citizens. We have to pay our taxes, we have to submit to the powers that be, we have to submit to every ordinance of man for the Lord's sake. Peter talks about our earthly citizenship. But the Christian never forgets that his primary citizenship is heavenly and he's an alien and an exile down here.

Now, if we laid hold of that, it would affect our whole life; it would revolutionize our Christian behavior; it would affect our attitude to sin—we would abstain from fleshly lusts which war against the soul, that is, a pilgrim traveling heavenward. It would affect our attitude to property and to possessions. We would learn to sit lightly in the saddle of this earth; we would not set our affections on things on this earth. We would not want to lay up treasure on earth; we would want to lay up treasure in heaven, because we're exiles down here, we belong in heaven. It would affect our attitude to suffering, and pain, and sorrow and bereavement if we once laid hold of the fact that we're aliens down here.

Do you know what it is to feel a bit homesick? Do you know what it is to feel a tug at your heart because you want to go home to God? Every Christian ought to be longing to go home. Every Christian ought to know what Paul meant when he said, "I have a desire to depart." Oh, yes, we're not going to neglect our duties down here, but at the same time we're aliens and exiles. Do we behave like it? So many of us are engrossed in the affairs of this world.

I've read somewhere of a young man who found a five dollar bill on the street. After that great discovery, he never lifted his eyes when walking. In the course of years he accumulated 29,516 buttons and 54,172 pins, 12 cents, a bent back and a miserly disposition. And think what he lost! He lost the sheen of the stars and the glory of the sunlight, and the smile of his friends, because his eyes were in the gutter.

There are so many Christians like that. Let your eyes look up for the first glimmer of light behind the clouds when Christ shall come again. Let's remember we're aliens and exiles, traveling home.

So I recapitulate and summarize these lessons: as newborn babes, the duty is growth; as living stones, the duty is fellowship; as holy priests, the duty is worship; as a chosen nation or people, the duty is witness; and as aliens and exiles, the duty is holiness.

# Charles R. "Chuck" Swindoll

*1934–*

Born in El Campo, Texas, Charles R. Swindoll responded to a call to ministry while serving in the United States Marine Corps. He graduated from Dallas Theological Seminary in 1963 and pastored churches in Massachusetts and Texas before going to First Evangelical Free Church in Fullerton, California, in 1961. There he honed his gift for meaningful expository preaching, founded the *Insight for Living* radio program, began publishing award-winning books, and has been invited to minister the Word in conferences and conventions around the world. Swindoll's clarity and transparency in preaching have made him one of America's most respected and beloved radio preachers. He was named president of Dallas Theological Seminary in 1993.

Some of Swindoll's numerous titles include: *Hand Me Another Brick, Living on the Ragged Edge, Dropping Your Guard, Improving Your Serve, Rise and Shine, The Grace Awakening,* and *Laugh Again.* He has won several Gold Medallions from the Evangelical Christian Publishers Association.

# Faith and Hurting People

Most of us are acquainted with the little booklet entitled "The Four Spiritual Laws." It's been published to help non-Christians understand the gospel. Someday I would like to work up the courage to write a similar booklet with a similar name, but a different emphasis. It would be a booklet to help non-Christians understand Christians, and I would like to call it "The Four Spiritual Flaws" rather than "The Four Spiritual Laws." In that booklet, I would try to put to bed forever the fallacious ideas that non-Christians have about those of us who are born again. Let me share with you these "four flaws," the four mistaken ideas unconverted people have about those of us who belong to Jesus Christ.

Flaw number one—"They are followers of Jesus, so they are meek, mild, passive and wimpy." People have the weird idea that Jesus was sort of "the living doormat for the world." It's true that He is the classic illustration of submission to the Father's will, but there were courageous times when He stood absolutely alone, and the greatest of those times was when He died on the cross on our behalf.

Some sincere religious people have the idea that Christians are supposed to be constantly passive, but even some of those people have their breaking point. I smiled when I heard about a Quaker farmer who owned a rather ornery milk cow. Each morning at milking time, no matter how positive the Quaker's attitude was when he began to milk the cow, his passivity was put to the test.

One morning as the Quaker had an almost full pail of milk, the cow kicked the pail and the milk spilled on him. The farmer

276

patiently put the pail back in place and continued to milk. The cow looked back at him, and suddenly with one great sweep of her hind leg, she knocked the fellow back about fifteen feet.

The Quaker brushed off his overalls, walked around in front of the cow and said, "Thou dost know that I am a Quaker, and thou dost know that I cannot strike thee back, but I can sell thee to a Baptist." There are times that not even the passive can successfully remain passive.

The second spiritual flaw that I would include is: "They are people of faith and therefore they never doubt." People who think that way have not spent much time around real Christians. It has been my observation that we sometimes struggle with the very things we say we believe. There are occasions when we're put to the test, and if the truth were known, we prove that we don't believe those things. That's hard for us to admit, but there has never been a generation without its defectors. I wish it could be true— I wish it were true—that we are always people of faith, but we're not. Hence, there is the need to be bolstered up in the Word of God so that we might stand firmer in faith.

There's a third flaw: "They are Christians, therefore they must be perfect, free from imperfection." Perhaps this is the most popular of all four of the flaws. I love the little bumper sticker that reads, "Christians aren't perfect, just forgiven." It's usually on the back of a speeding car that's going around you about seventy miles an hour in a fifty mile zone.

People have the erroneous idea that Christians always drive the speed limit, that we are always courteous and kind, and that we always think of others. We always pay our bills early and play fair in ball games. We always claim the promises of God, we always turn the other cheek, we never cheat on exams, and we never get discouraged. Because we're saints, we never bad-mouth our employer, never consider retaliating, never eat too much— what a joke—never pad the expense account, and never act hypocritical.

My good friend Joe Bayly says it straight in his book *Psalms of My Life*. He wrote in the "Psalm in the Hotel Room":

I'm alone Lord, alone, a thousand miles from home.

There's no one here who knows my name except the clerk, and he spelled it wrong. No one to eat dinner with, laugh at my jokes, listen to my gripes, be happy with me about what happened today and say, "That's great."

No one cares. There's just this lousy bed and slush in the street outside between the buildings. I feel sorry for myself, and I have plenty of reason to. Maybe I ought to say I'm on top of it and "Praise the Lord," and "Things are great," but they're not. Tonight it's all gray slush.

That's true stuff. There *are* those days and nights that are all gray slush, and there are some days when, in the gray slush of it all, we're not even near being perfect.

The fourth spiritual flaw leads into my thoughts from Hebrews 11. It says, "These Christians know God so they are protected from hardship, calamity, suffering, and tragedy." What fallacious thinking!

A Christian man I know was finishing the floor in a bowling alley and was applying the last layer of that volatile solution that turns into a hardened surface. Someone had spilled a glass of water behind him and it had left a wet spot. Not thinking, one of the helpers lit a blow torch to dry that spot. And boom! The place went up in flames and my friend raced out of that area on fire, with something like 60 to 70 percent of his body covered with third-degree burns.

Bad things do happen to forgiven people, tragic things, hurting things. Christians can and do experience financial disaster. Christians can become victims of rape and murder. Christian wives can be battered by their husbands or children by their parents. Christians can go through the deepest valleys imaginable; they can experience divorce against their wishes, they can be robbed, assaulted, put in jail for illegal acts. Christians can even be called on to die for their faith.

It was the old song that Satan sang to God about Job: "You've put a protective hedge about him. Take away that hedge and Job will curse you to your face." Unbelievers often think that God has a special hedge about His people, but it's been my observation that it rains on the just, just as it does on the unjust. And perhaps you have been in a rainstorm lately. Hebrews 11:32–40 is written for people who, from the human point of view, have had bad things happen to them.

It's been my observation, that in the school of life, suffering is a required course in the curriculum. It is never an elective. And we never graduate out of this course either. When we read this list of people in Hebrews 11:32–40, we're not reading *Aesop's Fables* or *Alice in Wonderland*. We're reading about real people who played prominent roles in God's work in this world.

"What more shall I say? For time will fail me if I tell of Gideon, Barak, Samson, Jephthah, of David and Samuel and the prophets." We have a long, black marble memorial in Washington, D.C., in honor of the Vietnam veterans. We have numbered the names—57,939—and every name is etched in that stone. But when God begins to write the names of His people, the writer says that "time would fail me" to put them all down. They are more than could be numbered. History is filled with many great men and women.

Look at the list—we have a judge or two, we have a king, we have a prophet. And if we would bring the list up-to-date, we would have to add homemakers and teenagers and retired folks, coaches and athletic teams, ball players and businessmen and businesswomen, pastors and trustees and elders and deacons—but time would fail us.

Perfect people? Not one of them. Protected people? Not one of them. Just people, all of whom qualify for the list because they had gone through hurt. I love the words of Ben Franklin who wrote, "Those things that hurt, instruct." Our tendency is to find an escape from the hurts so that we can somehow feel better, and we'll do anything to feel better rather than let the hurt run its course.

Karl Jung, Swiss psychiatrist now dead, wrote "Neurosis is always the substitute for legitimate suffering." Isn't that an insightful statement? By circumventing, by attempting to escape, by getting away from the pain of the hurt, we build the neuroses of our lives, and they often take the place of legitimate suffering. Not one of these people in Hebrews escaped the pain in God's classroom, nor will you, nor will I.

We have come to a eulogy in Scripture. I hope that the pastors and young preachers listening will learn from my mistake. Let me share it with you. Years ago in my earlier days of ministry, I would analyze every verse and with meticulous concern give attention to each phrase and each part of speech and what modifies what. I would do my best to exhaust it, and then I would exhaust the congregation as I gave back from the pulpit all the information I had gathered in my study. Even if I was studying a Bible prayer or a psalm, I analyzed it. I didn't realize that some parts of Scripture are meant to be sung, not analyzed.

Friends, we don't take a clipboard to a graveyard so we can take notes. We walk quietly through the graveyard and we reminisce. We let the memories wash over us. My imagination floods me when I walk through cemeteries and I feel the names that come out of those stones. It's one of my favorite places to be when I'm alone. I sound like a ghoul when I say that, but it's true. It ministers to me, for those "being dead still speak." I don't speak to the dead, but they have a marvelous way in that silence of speaking to me, saying things like "Keep going," "Don't quit," "Don't stop."

Now when I come to this passage, I confess to you that I have no plans to exhaust it or even attempt to analyze it. I want you to hear the names of triumphant and tragic men and women, not just names but events, events that marked their lives; and I want you to feel with me and identify with these heroes. Don't be afraid of the feelings that come to you when you read a passage like this. Those of us who minister at funerals, at weddings, at various celebrations and dedications, are not untrue to the text of Scripture if we use a little imagination. As a matter of fact, you will endear yourself to people as you help them feel the emotion of a passage like Hebrews 11. I only ask that you read it with feeling.

Let's give silent praise for a few moments to those who triumphed. Verse 33 . . . "by faith [they] conquered kingdoms, [by faith] they performed acts of righteousness, [they] obtained promises, shut the mouths of lions, quenched the power of fire, escaped the edge of the sword, from weakness were made strong, became mighty in war, put foreign armies to flight." There were even "women [who] received back their dead."

What a list! How we ought to praise our great God for such triumphs! Again, we don't spend enough time remembering the triumphs. How is it that young David, not yet twenty years of age, could face that arrogant Philistine across the valley of Elah. Saul didn't understand it and tried to put his armor on that young man. Did you ever try to picture that scene? The breastplate, the helmet, the leggings just don't fit, and David said, "I can't fight like this." So he took it all off, and Saul wondered, "What manner of man is this?"

David said, "King Saul, when I was keeping my father's sheep [and I take it that there wasn't anybody else around] I slew a lion and I killed a bear." If you want to try something on for size, start with a lion, or take on a bear. When you've killed a lion and a bear, a nine-foot eight-inch giant is zilch. David remembered the grace of God in his past, and he said, "In light of that, Saul, who is that uncircumcised Philistine that defies the army of the living God?"

Remember the victories, remember the triumphs. Remember those sleepless nights, mothers, when you watched God break the fever of your child. Remember the recovery, dads, when you lost your boy, and God gave you a tomorrow. Weeping endured for the night, but joy came in the morning. Remember, pastors, what God did for you through that difficult pastorate of years gone by—you survived. The faith of God's people, the grace and the power of God saw you through. Call to mind those great days, those days of triumph.

But there is a connecting link in verse 35, and it changes the scene to tragedy—I mean tragedy from the human point of view. It says, "And others were tortured, not accepting release in order that they might obtain a better resurrection; and others experienced mockings and scourgings, chains and imprisonments. They were stoned, they were sawn in two, they were tempted, they were put to death with the sword; they went about in sheepskins, in goatskins, being destitute, afflicted, ill-treated . . . wandering in deserts and mountains and caves and holes in the ground." You think you've got it rough? Ever lived in a cave? Ever made your home in a hole in the ground?

It reminds me of the writings of John Foxe, sixteenth-century saint, which have been recorded in a book entitled *Foxe's Book of Martyrs*.

It has been said that the lives of the early Christians consisted of persecution above ground and prayer below ground. Their lives are expressed by the Colisseum and the catacombs. Beneath Rome are the excavations called the catacombs which were once temples and tombs. The early church of Rome might well be called the Church of the Catacombs. There are some sixty catacombs near Rome in which some 600 miles of galleries have been traced, and these are not all. These galleries are about eight feet high, from three to five feet wide, containing on either side several rows of long, low horizontal recesses, one above another, like berths in a ship. In these, the dead bodies were placed, and the front closed either by a single marble slab or several great tiles laid in mortar. On these slabs or tiles, epitaphs or symbols are engraved or painted. Pagans and Christians buried their dead in these catacombs. When the Christian graves had been opened, the skeletons tell their own terrible tales. Heads are found severed from bodies, ribs and shoulder blades are broken, bones are often calcined from fire; but despite the awful story of persecution that we read here, the inscriptions read toward peace and joy. Here are a few. "Here lies Marsha put to rest in a dream of peace. Lawrence to his sweetest son borne away of angels. Victorious in peace and in Christ. Being called away, he went in peace."

The stories tell of persecution, torture and fire, but the full force of these epitaphs is seen when we contrast them with the pagan epitaphs which read . . . "Live for the present hour since we're sure of nothing else," "I lift my hands against the gods who took me away at the age of 20, though I had done no harm," "Once I was not, now I am not, I know nothing about it and it is no concern of mine," "Traveler curse me not as you pass, for I am in darkness, and I cannot answer." The most frequent Christian symbols on the walls of the catacombs are the Good Shepherd, the lamb on His shoulder, a ship under full sail, hearts, anchors, crowns, vines, and above all, the fish.

If you read through Hebrews 11 and do not feel the anguish, you have missed it all. Just as there is joy and delight in the *triumphs* of the faithful, so there is anguish connected with the *suffering* of the faithful. And it was all so alone. We're surrounded by thousands in this place, and we feel so together, but one week from this moment tragedy may strike, and we will be so alone. You'll feel like Coleridge who wrote in "The Rime of the Ancient Mariner":

> Alone, alone, all, all alone,
> Alone on a wide, wide sea!
> And never a saint took pity on
> My soul in agony.

You'll have times like that. You'll feel like there isn't anyone else around, and you'll wrestle with disillusionment.

When our oldest daughter was very young, she was diagnosed with having an eye that wasn't muscularly correct, and so it "wandered." Lovely child then, beautiful young woman today, but back then it was so tough. The pregnancy had been difficult. Cynthia spent long months hemorrhaging and could not get up from the bed, and we didn't know what kind of baby would be born to us.

So when this precious gift came, Caressa was just a unique person. She had all of her equipment and everything was in the right spot and looked the right way, except this little eye we had to deal with. Our Christian ophthalmologist did the first surgery, and he made no promises. He said, "Now you folks need to realize this eye may not be corrected in just one surgery." But in my heart I knew that we deserved at least one surgery from God, and that would be His affirmation. And when the child came out of surgery, the eye had now moved to the outside.

In the providence of God we were moved from Texas to California, and this little eye of hers still troubled us. She was by now wearing very thick glasses, so we sought the finest ophthalmologist. We heard similar words, only now more intense. "You must understand that there's now scar tissue that complicates the surgical process."

I canceled all that out because I had given God one of the surgeries, and He was going to give me the right one this time, and He and I had a little bargain. *You* never do that, but I do that on occasion. I remember when she went into surgery, it was going to come out perfect. The surgeon had warned us ahead of time, but I was relying on my own strength, my plans, my purpose, and I had it all put together. When Caressa came out of surgery, I'll never forget standing right over her, looking down into her eyes. One was bruised and had little blood marks around the lid, and blood was running down the side of her face, and I said, "Honey, open your eyes for Daddy. Let me see your eye. Let Daddy look at your eye." And Cynthia kept saying, "Take it easy. Take it easy." I said, "Wait a minute, I want to see this eye!" And finally when she was able to open it, it was totally white, and the eyeball was looking directly at the bridge of the nose. I felt so ripped off, so alone. I stood back, and I said to my wife, "I'm gone." She said, "Where do you intend to go?" And I said, "I don't know, but I'm getting out of here."

I got in my car and I drove to the only wild place I knew, my study. I opened the door, went inside, turned on all the lights, locked the door, told the secretary to take off, and I hung "Keep Out" signs on both of the doors, and I took the phone off the hook. A friend of mine came by the hospital and found out about this disappointment that I had had, and he wouldn't leave me alone. He knocked on my door, and I wouldn't answer. You have friends like that? I thought, "He will tear the door down if I don't open the door." And I opened the door, and I said, "What do you want?"

He says, "I want you." We got in his car, and we took a drive. What a wonderful ministry. I'm so grateful he didn't say, "Here Chuck, listen to one of your tapes when you talked about suffering." He did not preach, he did not even force me to pray, he didn't share with me twelve verses out of Job. He just loved me in silence, and took time to listen to me cry, because he, too, had also lost things. Hurting people know how to minister to other hurting people.

We went back to the hospital that afternoon. The following morning I looked at the eye, and it had begun to change. And the next morning, and the next morning, and in two weeks time it was straight. And in two months time, she was no longer wearing glasses. And in the meantime, an artist friend of mine came by with a little picture that he had painted. It was supposed to represent Martin Luther—monk, long robe, big feet, big toe sticking out of the sandal, and the words from Luther's hymn "A Mighty Fortress Is Our God."

> Did we in our own strength confide,
>     our striving would be losing.
> Were not the right man on our side,
>     the Man of God's own choosing.
> Dost ask who this may be? Christ Jesus, it is He.
> Lord Sabaoth His name, from age to age the same,
> And He must win the battle.

I am forever indebted to those two friends who didn't leave me alone when I felt so left alone, so abandoned. You may be a friend of someone who has begun to experience mockings and verbal scourgings and chains and imprisonment—don't forget them! Pastors, don't leave them out of your life. Take time for them. Let them cry on your shoulder. Let them break your heart. I don't want to hear you preach if you don't take time for people. I don't want to hear your message, I want to hear your heart. And I can tell—and do you know something? So can everybody else.

You wonder what kind of people these Hebrews 11 folks were? I purposely left out the parenthesis. They were people "of whom the world was not worthy." And why does he say it like this? Well, because of the effect on us today. I love verses 39 and 40. They may not be as dramatic, but what they say is a perfect transition to our lives today. "And all these, having gained approval through their faith, did not receive the promise." [I take this to mean the promised Messiah. They all kept believing, they all kept looking, they kept dying for the promise, and they died having never seen Him.] "Because God had provided something better for us, so that without us, they are not complete." That's the thought of this last section—not made perfect, but completed.

The whole story isn't complete without our generation. Isn't that exciting? We're still writing the book of Hebrews, chapter 11, just as we're still writing the book of Acts. This story isn't complete unless they have the last part of the sentence, which refers to our input. New names are still being added into God's book, and the psalmist says, "He numbers our tears, He keeps them in a bottle." For some it will be jugs of tears. But without us there, the story and investment of their lives could not be complete.

I close with three very important statements that I have tried to put down with the right words—as Solomon says in Ecclesiastes, "Well-driven nails so as to cinch out the truth."

First, undeserving and sinful Christians often rejoice in unexpected triumphs. That's an answer I would like to give the unsaved world. Undeserving and sinful Christians often rejoice in unexpected triumphs.

Here's the second: Godly and great Christians often suffer through unexplainable tragedies.

Now the clincher: Both extremes link God's family to an uninterrupted history.

To me, those three statements are exciting. All of us are just part of the train of His triumph and the story of tragedy. Sometimes those tragic stories are enough to turn lives around. I think of five martyred missionaries that attempted to reach the Aucas. I never knew one of them. I was just a disillusioned and discouraged young man, lonely on a bus on a rainy day, going from Pasadena, California, back to Camp Pendleton where I was about to go overseas with the Marine Corps. My older brother—God bless him—pushed into my hand a book, *Through Gates of Splendor*. He said, "Charles, read this."

I started reading and couldn't put it down. Nate Saint, Roger Youderian, Jim Elliot, Peter Fleming, Ed McCully, men of whom the world isn't worthy, turned my life around. I couldn't wait to get to the Orient with all of its loneliness to see what God was going to do in my life. And that book and those lives rearranged my whole future. Without them, the story is incomplete.

I was at the Christian Bookseller's Association gathering at Anaheim, California. I was to be the speaker at the final banquet, and I was scared. I looked out in the audience and I saw two dozen people who could have done a far better job than I, and I wondered, "What in the world am I doing here?" Do you ever wonder what people think of when they sit on the platform waiting to minister? They think, "Why in the world did I say yes? Who am I kidding? Why would I come to this place and say these things when I feel so alien in life to many of them?"

So while wrestling with that, I'm pleased to say the spotlight turned from the front table over to the side. Sitting on the platform on the other side was a woman who caused my mind to go back to the summer of 1967 and Chesapeake Bay. She had dived off a barge, and from that moment on, never had feeling below her shoulders. She loved to laugh and ride horses and run and play and dance and swim. Joni Eareckson Tada would never do any of those things again. What a tragedy. In that chair the rest of her life.

But that night she was not to speak. Oh, I hoped that she would have spoken, and that would have been the message of the evening and we could have all gone home, but she said, "I'm here to sing." And someone fixed a mike in front of her, and she said, "Now when I get to the higher notes, I want you to help me because I haven't the muscles in my diaphragm that I need to get up there. So if you see me kind of straining, hum along with me." And she began . . .

> When peace like a river attendeth my way,
> When sorrows like sea billows roll;
> Whatever my lot, Thou hast taught me to say,
> "It is well, it is well with my soul."

There wasn't a dry eye in the banquet hall. I had such renewed strength from that experience that I could have preached all night. I only preached half the night I'm glad to say.

Do you need courage and strength to go on? You've got it. The secret is faith, and the Person to trust is Jesus Christ. By God's grace, let's be among those people of God "of whom the world is not worthy."

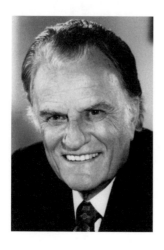

# William Franklin "Billy" Graham

*1918–*

The best-known evangelist of the twentieth century, Billy Graham has preached the gospel of Jesus Christ personally to more people than any preacher who has ever lived. He was converted at age sixteen in an evangelistic crusade conducted by Mordecai Ham. He studied at Florida Bible Institute and graduated in 1940, the same year he was ordained into the Southern Baptist ministry. He did further work at Wheaton College, graduating in 1943. While a student at Wheaton, he conducted evangelistic campaigns and also pastored the Wheaton Tabernacle. For the next two years, he served the Village Church in Western Springs, Illinois, a suburb of Chicago, and spoke weekly over the *Songs in the Night* radio program.

Graham's frequent absences from the church to conduct evangelistic campaigns disturbed some of his church leaders, and after resigning the pastorate, in 1945 he joined the staff of Youth for Christ International as their staff evangelist. His ministry became nationally known when the Los Angeles tent crusade in 1949 hit the headlines. The next year Graham founded the Billy Graham Evangelistic Association and Worldwide Pictures and began the *Hour of Decision* radio broadcast as well as television specials.

Graham's crusades have taken him to more than eighty countries and he has been the recipient of many awards and honors. His evangelistic crusades have long been multiracial and interdenominational, but his philosophy of "cooperative evangelism" has alienated some more conservative leaders. He is probably the most visible preacher of the gospel in this century and has been the confidant of many world leaders.

Graham has authored more than twenty books, which have been translated into numerous languages. He has been the subject of many biographies; his autobiography, *Just As I Am* (HarperCollins/Zondervan, 1997), has been a best-seller.

# Building on the Rock

I want to take an old obscure sermon that Moody preached. I do not know where it's found but I think it was in one of Wilbur Smith's books on Moody. I made notes from it and made my own little outline and preached it one time years ago in North Carolina. And this text is found in Deuteronomy the 32nd chapter and the 31st verse: "For their rock is not as our Rock." And then switching over to the 7th chapter of Matthew beginning with verse 21 these words:

> Not every one that saith unto me Lord, Lord, shall enter into the kingdom of heaven, but he that doeth the will of my Father, who is in heaven. Many will say to me in that day, Lord, Lord, have we not prophesied in thy name? And in thy name have cast out devils? And in thy name done many wonderful works? And then will I profess unto them, I never knew you; depart from me, ye that work iniquity. Therefore, whosoever heareth these sayings of mine, and doeth them, I will liken him unto a wise man, who built his house upon a rock. And the rain descended, and the floods came, and the winds blew and beat upon that house, and it fell not; for it was founded upon a rock. And every one that heareth these sayings of mine and doeth them not, shall be likened unto a foolish man, who built his house upon the sand. And the rain descended, and the floods came, and the winds blew and beat upon that house, and it fell; and great was the fall of it.

There have been only relatively few men in the history of the church that have had such a profound impact as Dwight L. Moody. Directly, he touched thousands in his day. Indirectly, through all things that he started, he has touched millions. His example in his single-minded zeal to preach the gospel has influenced my own life tremendously.

There have been few institutions in the history of the church which have so broadly touched the world for Christ as the Moody Bible Institute during these past one hundred years. It has been my privilege to preach the gospel in sixty-two countries and on every continent, and virtually everywhere we have gone we have found alumni of the Moody Bible Institute proclaiming the gospel and working for the gospel in all those places.

Toward the end of his life Moody said, "I have started some streams which will flow into eternity." And look at the streams he has started. Certainly the work of the Moody Bible Institute has produced results in abundance which will flow on into eternity. It is an eloquent testimony to your commitment to world evangelization that one out of every fifteen Protestant missionaries from North America is a graduate of the Moody Bible Institute. Over 70 percent of the pilots serving on the mission field are graduates of Moody's aviation program. (It is just across the mountain from where my son lives. He is in full-time Christian work. He has his airplane and he flies it over there to get it fixed from time to time.) And every four minutes somewhere in the world a Moody-trained missionary pilot is taking off. Every day a half million people see one of your science films and millions read the books and the literature, and hundreds of thousands read *Moody Monthly* and listen to the radio programs produced at Moody. Many of the greatest missionary and evangelistic outreaches of this generation were founded by people who studied at Moody. And I could go on and on, for God has greatly blessed and used this institution during the past one hundred years. Several members of my own team are graduates of Moody.

In thinking about what I should say today, I thought of this rather obscure passage that I had preached years ago not knowing quite where I found it. "For their rock is not our Rock." And Jesus, I am sure, had this passage in mind when He spoke the words of the second text from Matthew that I read.

As we think of the last one hundred years of the Moody Bible Institute, we cannot help but ask, "Why, why, why has God blessed it and used it so greatly, and how could it apply to our lives here today?" I think part of the answer lies in the Board of Trustees through these years and the six Presidents that Moody has had. It is quite remarkable that there have only been six presidents in one hundred years—D. L. Moody, R. A. Torrey, James Gray, Will Houghton, William Culbertson, and George Sweeting. God has used the Moody Bible Institute because it has always sought to build its ministry upon the rock of God's truth. It has sought above all to be faithful to the Word of God and God has rewarded that faithfulness. In an age in which we have seen powerful waves of secularization engulf most educational institutions, Moody Bible Institute has been willing to go against the trend and remain faithful to its original vision. It said with Moses, "For their rock is not our Rock."

These words were spoken by Moses in his farewell address to the people of Israel. He had been their leader for forty years and he had been with them day and night. He had shared their burden, lifted their vision, ached when they turned away from God from time to time. He had been their king, their president, their judge, their father—all wrapped in one. Now he is an old man getting ready to depart to heaven, and the people are going to go into the Promised Land. Only two people will go in with them that had started, Joshua and Caleb. And now with his long white hair and his long white beard he reminds them of God's faithfulness of the past.

Then he warns them of nations round about who do not believe in a living God. And he warns the people within Israel who had strayed from God's path and he warns that judgment will come. He said, "Their rock, their foundation—these nations round about you—their rocks, their foundations are not your ways. The places and ways in which they look for stability and security are not yours. The way they live and the goals they have are not yours. You have a different Rock, a different set of values, a different set of ethics, a different message."

Let's look at some of the rocks on which people build their lives today. In Moses' time as in the time of Jesus and today, people built their lives on different rocks. Some of them look very attractive and stable—but they are not. Jesus' parable at the end of the Sermon on the Mount warned that those foundations will wash away when the storms of life come. The foundations will be destroyed. What are some of these rocks?

Well first, there is materialism. There are people today that think if they only had more money, more income, they'd be set. (And by the way, being debt free one hundred years . . . I wish that the Board of Trustees of Moody Bible Institute had been running this country.) In Deuteronomy 32:15 we read that Jeshurun had waxed fat, and he was covered with fatness. He forsook God, which made him, and he lightly esteemed the Rock of his salvation.

Many people are under the impression that more money will make them happy. If I can just live on a higher standard of living, I'll be happy.

We have been in places where the average income was $300 a year. In Bangladesh $150 a year. We have seen people who live under those conditions find a happiness and a peace and a joy in Christ that people who live on millionaires' row would give anything in the world to find. Some of the most miserable people in the world I have ever met are wealthy people. Film stars and show folk go to Beverly Hills. They have more psychiatrists in Beverly Hills than any other place in the whole world and yet it has the highest standard of living in America. Many people are under the impression that if they could just get more, that would take care of their longings and needs.

Just a few weeks ago, a poll was taken in the country asking people, "If your office had a copy machine that would copy money and it wouldn't look counterfeit, would you use it?" Twenty percent of the American people said yes. Jesus said, "You cannot serve God and mammon. Man's life does not consist in the abundance of the things he possesses."

A famous man said not long ago, "I am worth millions, and I can tell you: money is not where it is at!" Adolph Berle, in his study of power, points out that "riches make people solitary, lonely, and often afraid." And one of the great things about Dwight L. Moody was that he never had a love for money. He had a number of wealthy friends both here in Chicago, in Philadelphia, in New York, and London. And Moody could have been a wealthy man. But R. A. Torrey said about him, "Money had no charms for him." He loved to gather money for God's work. He refused to accumulate money for himself.

He would have loved the way the collection was taken today because Moody didn't mind asking people for money. Now Hudson Taylor did. George Mueller did. Some of these other great men did. But Moody would look you right in the eye and say, "Look here, you have promised $5,000; make it 10." If you said 10, he said, "make it 20." He would ask people for a half million dollars. He didn't mind that. God had given him that gift of faith to believe.

Somebody said, "Well, George Mueller lived by faith and he never asked people for money." Moody said, "You show me a man with $10,000 for God and I've got faith enough to ask him for it." But he never let any stick to his fingers. A biographer wrote that "millions passed through his hands, but he never kept it for himself." The love of money has been the ruination of many a Christian believer.

And then, secondly, people are building their lives on the rock of self-ish pleasure. We are a satiated society, looking for new kinds of new thrills. Sex and violence fill our television screens. Billions of dollars of drugs are used by old and young alike to take "trips" that often destroy the mind and the body.

John Belushi was born and reared out here in Wheaton. Before his tragic death at thirty-three, he is quoted as having asked his psychoanalyst, "Why is it that I give so much pleasure to the world through *Saturday Night Live* and all the films I have acted in, and yet I have so little pleasure myself?"

Sexual deviation has become a way of life. As it was in ancient Greece and Rome it is being presented to us as an alternate lifestyle. And what a price we are already beginning to pay for it. It may be the biggest problem and the greatest plague that our nation has ever known.

Our world seems to be on a wild roller coaster ride frantically seeking new pleasures. But King Solomon tried them all. He tried education, he tried money, he tried the whole works, and at the end he said, "I've said in my heart, go to now. I will prove thee with mirth, therefore, enjoy pleasure: and, behold, this also is vanity." At the end of each one of those he said, "It's all vanity. Remember now thy creator in the days of thy youth."

I've learned that none of these things satisfy. Only God satisfies. Only Christ can give us the lasting happiness and true pleasure. "In thy presence is fulness of joy; at thy right hand there are pleasures for ever more." When troubles come, or you stare death in the face, the rock of pleasure turns out to be sand.

Someone asked me at one of the universities—I spend a great deal of time at universities and we have question and answer periods—and they asked, "At your age (I guess they thought I was a real old man), what is the greatest surprise in your life?"

I said, "The greatest surprise of life to me at my age is the brevity of life. How quick it is all over."

And then there is the rock of false religiosity. Jesus said, "This people draweth nigh unto me with their mouth, and honoreth me with their lips; but their heart is far from me."

There are many people that think that they can do good and that good works are going to save them. "You are saved by grace through faith; and that not of yourselves, it is the gift of God; not of works, lest any man should boast." So many famous people, especially in the jet set, socialites, give charity balls and charity events, and one of the most prominent of these ladies said to me, "Certainly God will count this toward me getting into heaven."

And I replied, "No ma'am. You could give a million of these affairs and it wouldn't get you one glimpse into heaven."

She looked at me very startled and said, "Well, what is the gospel all about then?"

I said, "The gospel is all about Jesus Christ dying on the cross and shedding His blood and rising from the dead and us repenting of our sins and receiving Him as Savior. There is nothing you can do about it. You could give all the charity balls and give all your money, but that is not going to save your soul."

A few months ago when that volcano blew its top in Colombia and the waves of mud engulfed whole towns, killing 22,000 people, those who were saved were those who were able to lodge themselves on the high rocks until they could be rescued. And as the mudflows of modern society threaten to devour us, we need, in the words of the old song, to "flee to the Rock that is higher than I!"

There are warning signals all about us today. Anybody that has ever been briefed by the Pentagon, anybody that has been briefed in the Soviet Union and seen them put before you all the weapons that we have and they have that could destroy the world 18 times over would agree. Remember the words of President Kennedy nearly a quarter of a century ago. He said, "Each day the crisis multiplies. Each day the solution grows more difficult. Each day we draw nearer the hour of maximum danger and time has not been our friend." President Kennedy was speaking prophetically. Time has not been our friend.

There is a little glimmer of hope at the moment in the world; a little sigh of relief when Mr. Gorbachev and Mr. Reagan met and talked and seemed to get along in their private sessions. There is a little glimmer of hope out of Geneva.

But when we know what man's heart is. . . . I'm not so sure that the Soviet Union and the United States will ever go to war, but what about those fifteen other little countries that have the atomic bomb? One of them with their back to the wall could start a chain reaction that could destroy a great deal of the human race. They are not going to destroy the whole human race in an atomic war because God has another plan. And God's plan is that when man stands at Armageddon ready to destroy himself, Christ is going to come back. He is the King of kings and Lord of lords.

But, whether we like it or not, we are engaged in warfare right now. There is a terrorist war that we do not know how to handle. If there was ever a time that we needed to "flee to the Rock that is higher than I," it is now.

The history of the Moody Bible Institute points us to the Rock that will stand, and on which we should build our lives. What are the rocks that we should build on? Throughout its century of ministry, the Moody Bible Institute has built its foundation on different rocks from the "rocks" of the world and pointed its students to build their lives on different rocks— "Their rock is not our Rock." What are these rocks? A rock speaks of unchanging strength like Gibraltar, or the Dome of the Rock in Jerusalem, or El Capitan at Yosemite.

First, there is the Rock of the Lord Jesus Christ. In Ephesians 2:20 Paul said, "And are built upon the foundation of the apostles and prophets, Jesus Christ himself being the chief cornerstone." In 1 Corinthians 3:11 the apostle Paul said, "For other foundation can no man lay than that is laid, which is Jesus Christ."

Across the decades, Moody Bible Institute has sought to exalt Christ. Moody Bible Institute's second president was R. A. Torrey, one of Moody's close associates. A brilliant graduate of Yale, he did post-graduate studies in Germany where he found himself surrounded by higher critics who scorned the Bible and its teachings. It was a time of tremendous struggle for him, but eventually he gave his life without reserve to Christ. In addition to being the second president of the Moody Bible Institute, Torrey conducted huge evangelistic campaigns around the world in the first decade of this century—whether in Sydney, London, Glasgow, Belfast, or Toronto. Last week I had the privilege of preaching the funeral service of Dr. Oswald J. Smith and he was converted under R. A. Torrey when he was preaching at Massey Hall in Toronto, and I thought about this text. Isaiah 32:2 was the favorite text of R. A. Torrey, "And a man shall be as an hiding place from the wind, and . . . as the shadow of a great rock in a weary land." And Torrey would thunder time after time, "That man—that great Rock in a weary land—is the Lord Jesus Christ."

That is the Rock that D. L. Moody has established this institution on. It is the Rock that all succeeding leaders of this institution have continued to build on. I have been thrilled at the progress of this institution under the leadership of Dr. George Sweeting. How he, too, had an evangelistic background and he has kept a steady course and built on that Rock all of these things that Moody stood for. And I thank God today that Moody is still there and making progress and Mr. Moody would be thrilled today. There have been many storms that have battered, but the institution stands stronger than ever because it stands on the Rock.

Secondly, there is the rock of the Bible, the Word of God. We are living in a period when there is a great discussion going on once again just like it did in the latter part of the last century and the early part of this century, and we thought perhaps the battle was over. But no, it's flared up again.

D. L. Moody had a simple childlike faith in the Bible as the inspired, infallible Word of God. He was not a student of psychology. He was not a student of the sciences. Many of the words that we take for granted today even in theology he would not have had the slightest idea what they meant. As Torrey said, "He was a profound and practical student of the one Book that is more worth studying than all the other books in the world put together." That Book was the Bible. Moody used to rise at 4 o'clock in the morning to study the Bible. He said, "If I am going to get in any study, I've got to get up before the other folks get up." And most of us merely play at Bible study. Moody took it seriously. How many of us cut off the TV to study the Word of God?

It was largely because of his tremendous knowledge of the Bible and his practical application of the Bible that Moody drew such immense crowds. People are hungry for the Word of God.

I found that in my small way throughout the world, in Eastern Europe especially. (We have been to all those countries in Eastern Europe except Bulgaria and we are going there probably next year.) And here in October we saw twenty and thirty thousand people a night in Romania jamming the streets with their tape recorders and everything to hear the Word of

God and they are hungry for Bibles. They don't want books about the Bible; they want the Bible. And I find in our generation that people are hungry for God's Word. They are not interested in what we have to say about so many other things.

In Moody's day, as in our day, there have been massive attacks on the authority and inspiration of the Bible as the infallible Word of God. But beyond question, one of the Moody Bible Institute's secrets is that it has never wavered in its conviction that the Bible is the inspired Word of the living God. And the Bible alone is God's infallible Word.

Moody's great assistant Ira Sankey once said, "One of the reasons for Moody's phenomenal success in bringing souls to God was that he believed absolutely, implicitly in the message that he preached. His faith was the faith of a little child. No doubts ever dimmed his faith in the Word of God. To him it was the truth and the whole truth." God has promised, "My word shall not return unto me void but it shall accomplish that which I please and it shall prosper the things where unto I sent it."

During the years when radical theology seemed to be predominant in this country, the Moody Bible Institute stood like a Rock of Gibraltar on the Word of God. It became a lighthouse to which Christians look throughout the world for guidance and leadership.

Thirdly, there is the rock of prayer. Moody was a man of prayer. Not pompous, not to impress others. But it flowed from a close and intimate daily walk with Christ.

When Oswald Smith prayed, and he was a great man of prayer, he paced back and forth. I do that a lot and wondered if I ever was sacrilegious or wrong. There is no certain position in the Bible where you are to be when you pray. I find myself praying all the time—in season, out of season. My subconscious is praying now, "Lord, help me to say the right things to these people," because there are some people here today I believe, and I felt it since a little while ago; there are some people here that do not really know Christ. You know about Him, you may be a professing believer, but deep in your heart you are not sure. And there are some people here today who need to rededicate their lives to Christ and rededicate themselves to the principles for which this institution stands and the rocks upon which it stands.

As one of Moody's friends said concerning him out of a very intimate acquaintance with him, "I wish to testify that he was a far greater pray-er than he was a preacher." Time after time he confronted problems that seemingly had no solution. He didn't know where to turn. He turned to God in prayer and God answered his prayer.

My first time to visit the Moody Bible Institute was in 1940 when I came to school at Wheaton. I came here. My mother had wanted me to come to the Moody Bible Institute. I could sense and feel God's presence in those halls just walking through the hall. And in 1943 I came here. I was pastor of a little church in Western Springs and I came in here to "steal" one of your men. (Now I do not mean that God is going to honor your stealing. Don't get me wrong, I didn't mean "steal." I meant "borrow.") And over a period of two years I was successful. George Beverly Shea came with me. Not for more money. I don't know why he came except God sent him. And then about a few weeks later came Cliff Barrows. T. W. Wilson and Grady Wilson were already with me. So we have been together all these years. And God has honored it and blessed it and part of it came from the Moody Bible Institute.

The Bible says, "Call unto me, and I will answer thee, and shew thee great and mighty things, which thou knowest not." Is there a failure in your prayer life? There is a failure in my prayer life. I sense it all the time. There is a failure in my study of the Word of God. Someone asked me at a seminary, If I had it to do over again, what would I change? I said, "I would study more, and pray more, and preach less." I believe that has been one of the great failures and mistakes of my life. I'll have to wait until the judgment seat of Christ to find out but I'm sure that is true. Someone has said, "If there are any tears in heaven, it will be over the fact that we prayed so little." Someone else has said that, "Heaven is filled with answers to prayer for which no one ever bothered to ask."

Moody Bible Institute has been built on the rock of prayer.

Fourthly, there is the rock of the Spirit-filled life. Moody had been filled with the Holy Spirit and his life showed it. If ever a man had the fruit of the Spirit produced in his life by the Holy Spirit, it was Moody.

Some years ago I heard of one great clergyman who said concerning another (both of whom are now in heaven or I wouldn't tell it) that he "is a fine preacher when he gets in the pulpit, but in his personal life he has everything but love, joy, peace, longsuffering, gentleness, goodness, faithfulness, meekness, and temperance." And if we don't have that, we don't have anything. You can be a great preacher and not produce the fruit of the Spirit, or the Holy Spirit producing it through you and in you; and you are nothing but sounding brass and tinkling cymbals. Our lives must match our lips. The apostle Paul said, "If we live in the Spirit, let us also walk in the Spirit." Moody lived in the Spirit, he walked in the Spirit.

Fifthly, there has been the rock of a missionary vision. Moody had a consuming passion, soon after his conversion, to win people to Christ. He made a resolution that he would never spend twenty-four hours without speaking to someone about their faith in Christ. Moody's personal commitment to winning people, not only here at home but throughout the world, has been one of the rocks upon which this institution has been born. In America, the YMCA would have never gotten off the ground had it not been for Moody. Many of the great evangelical movements of our day came from

Moody because of his tremendous vision. And when he sat down and talked to the people here in Chicago and some of them had a burden for a Bible school here, he joined right in. And he said, "I have a burden for the people of all the world. Not just America but the whole world." And it is difficult for us to envision and grasp what Moody started in his conferences at Mt. Hermon. Certainly he would be proud today of that part of his ministry that stands called the Moody Bible Institute. Moody never preached a social gospel sermon in his life, but his ministry led to some of the great social movements of our time.

For example, Kier Hardy, the founder of the British Labour Party, was influenced by Moody. He went to Mr. Moody and he said, "What can I do for God?"

Moody said, "Help the laboring people of Scotland."

Kier Hardy became an evangelist all of his life, but he also founded the British Labour Party to help the laboring people of that day who were in such dire straits. We could go on and on about the great social movements that he began. His great passion for souls and his passion for missions gathered momentum toward the end of his life. That was the passion that helped him start the Moody Bible Institute.

For the first time in the history of the human race you and I have the technology to reach the whole world with the message of Christ. Jesus said that one of the signs that would appear before His return would be, "And this gospel of the kingdom shall be preached in all the world . . . then shall the end come." And it is significant that Jesus began His final commission to His disciples with these words: "All power is given unto me both in heaven and on earth." How dare we disobey the command of our sovereign Lord to "Go ye into all the world and teach all nations."

One of the great missions that Moody held was at Cambridge University. (It has been my privilege to hold two eight-day missions at Cambridge University; one the year before last. And I sympathize with what he went through, especially in the early days of the mission.) They laughed and sneered and made fun. But in the second half of the mission, things turned around. Hundreds of students began to come to hear him. Other hundreds received Christ and out of his mission at Cambridge came the famous Cambridge Seven. One of those whom you have heard about many times was C. T. Studd.

C. T. Studd was captain of the prestigious Cambridge University Cricket Team and the son of a wealthy man. But he sensed the claim of Christ on his life and he offered himself for missionary service in China. At the age of twenty-five he inherited a fortune from his father's estate. He gave it all away to Christian work. At the age of fifty, and in poor health after missionary service in China and India, he felt that God had called him to take the gospel also to Africa.

As he prepared to leave for Africa, he wrote this: "Last June, at the mouth of the Congo, there awaited a thousand prospectors, traders, merchants, and gold seekers, waiting to rush into these regions as soon as the government opened the door to them—for rumor declared that there is an abundance of gold. If such men," Studd said, "hear so loudly the call of gold, and obey it, can it be that the ears of Christ's soldiers are deaf to the call of God and the cries of the dying souls of men? Are gamblers for gold so many, and gamblers for God so few?"

Today, I am asking you, will you rededicate your life on this hundredth anniversary of the Moody Bible Institute, to stand on the Rock on which Moody stood one hundred years ago? Not on the sinking sands, but on the rocks that we have mentioned here today.

There is another rock. The rock of the second coming of Christ. Moody believed it and he preached it. And when Jesus was ascending into heaven and those two men stood in white apparel and the disciples had tears coming down their cheeks because their Master and their Lord was leaving, they said, "Why are you weeping? Why do you stand gazing into heaven? This same Jesus shall so come in like manner as you have seen Him go into heaven." And they went out filled with the Holy Spirit after Pentecost and preached the resurrection and the coming again of Christ.

> My hope is built on nothing less
>   Than Jesus' blood and righteousness;
> I dare not trust the sweetest frame,
>   But wholly lean on Jesus' name.
> On Christ the solid Rock I stand;
>   All other ground is sinking sand,
>   All other ground is sinking sand.
>
> When He shall come with trumpet sound,
>   Oh, may I then in Him be found;
> Dressed in His righteousness alone,
>   Faultless to stand before the throne.
> On Christ the solid Rock I stand;
>   All other ground is sinking sand,
>   All other ground is sinking sand.
>
>                                   Edward Mote

Do you stand on the Rock, or do you stand on the sand? When the storms of life come, the disappointments come, death comes, are you ready? Are you sure? Are you certain? If you have a doubt in your heart this day that you know Christ, you really know Him, that you have repented of your sins and received Him into your heart by faith and you want to make sure and you want to be certain, I want you to be sure.

# Credits
## and Acknowledgments

The editor and publisher acknowledge the kindness and cooperation of publishers and individuals who granted permission for the use of copyrighted material. The editor especially thanks those individuals who helped locate sermons or get approval for their use: Dr. Wendell Hawley, Jim Jeffery, Roger Carswell, Kate McGinn, Read G. Burgan, Roger and Joy Martin, Sybil E. Light, John D. Hull, and Stephanie Wills.

**Donald Grey Barnhouse.** "Justification without a Cause" was taken from volume 3 of Barnhouse's commentary on Romans, *God's Remedy* (Eerdmans, 1954), 91–100. Used by permission. Photo courtesy of Tenth Presbyterian Church, Philadelphia, Pennsylvania.

**Frank William Boreham.** "Hudson Taylor's Text" was taken from F. W. Boreham, *Life Verses*, vol. 2 (Grand Rapids: Kregel, 1994), 102–12 (originally published by Judson Press, 1922, with the title *A Handful of Stars*). Used by permission of Dr. Geoff Pound.

**Harry Emerson Fosdick.** "The Essential Elements in a Vital Christian Experience" was taken from *Living under Tension*, by Harry Emerson Fosdick (Harper Brothers, 1941), 182–91. Used by permission. Photo courtesy of the Burke Library, Union Theological Seminary, New York.

**Charles Edward Fuller.** "Seven Marvels of God's Mercy" was transcribed and edited from the *Old-Fashioned Revival Hour* cassette

#162M for January 12, 1958. Used by permission of Dr. Daniel P. Fuller. Photo courtesy of the Billy Graham Center Museum, Wheaton, Illinois.

**William Franklin "Billy" Graham.** "Building on the Rock" was originally delivered at the 1986 Founder's Week Conference at the Moody Bible Institute in Chicago and was transcribed and published in the conference report, pp. 267–77. It is used by permission of The Billy Graham Evangelistic Association and the Moody Bible Institute. It has been slightly edited by the BGEA. Photo courtesy of the Billy Graham Center Archives, Wheaton, Illinois.

**Vance Havner.** "Like Him in This World" was taken from Vance Havner, *Living in Kingdom Come* (Grand Rapids: Revell, 1967), 58–65. Used by permission of the publisher.

**Henry Allan "Harry" Ironside.** "The Heart of the Gospel" was taken from H. A. Ironside, *Addresses on the Gospel of John* (Loizeaux Brothers, 1974), 102–16. Used by permission. Photo courtesy of the Billy Graham Center Museum, Wheaton, Illinois.

**Robert Greene Lee.** "Pay Day—Some Day" was taken from *25 of the Greatest Sermons Ever Preached,* Jerry Falwell, comp. and ed. (Grand Rapids: Baker, 1983), 234–54. Used by permission of Mrs. Bula King. Photo courtesy of Joy Martin.

**David Martyn Lloyd-Jones.** "The Christian Message to the World" was taken from D. Martyn Lloyd-Jones, *God's Way of Reconciliation: Studies in Ephesians Chapter 2* (Evangelical Press, 1972), 59–69. Used by permission of Lady Elizabeth Catherwood and the Banner of Truth Trust.

**Clarence Edward Noble Macartney.** "While He Is Near" was taken from Clarence Edward Macartney, *The Greatest Texts of the Bible* (Nashville: Abingdon-Cokesbury, 1947), 34–45. Used by permission of the American Tract Society. Photo courtesy of First Presbyterian Church, Pittsburgh, Pennsylvania.

**Aimee Semple McPherson.** "Come—If—But" was taken from Aimee Semple McPherson, *This Is That* (Los Angeles: Bridal Call Publishing House, 1919), 281–85 (reprint, New York: Garland Publishing House, 1985). Used by permission of the International Church of the Foursquare Gospel. Photo courtesy of the Billy Graham center Museum, Wheaton, Illinois.

**Walter Arthur Maier.** "Awake! Watch! Pray!" was taken from *Courage in Christ: Radio Messages Broadcast on the Eighth Lutheran Hour* (Concordia Publishing House, 1941), 265–78. Used by permission. Photo courtesy of the Billy Graham Center Museum, Wheaton, Illinois.

**Peter Marshall.** "The Rock That Moved" was taken from *Mr. Jones, Meet the Master,* Catherine Marshall, comp. (Grand Rapids: Revell, 1950), 77–88. Used by permission of the publisher.

**Dwight Lyman Moody.** "Excused." Mr. Moody frequently repeated his sermons but since he spoke extemporaneously, he never duplicated a sermon. Therefore, there are several printed versions of some sermons. This version was taken from *D. L. Moody* of the *Great Pulpit Masters* series (Grand Rapids: Revell, 1949; Baker reprint, 1972), 237–53. Used by permission of the publisher.

**George Campbell Morgan.** "Understanding, or Bit and Bridle" was taken from *The Westminster Pulpit: The Preaching of G. Campbell Morgan,* vol. 6 (London: Pickering and Inglis), 36–47. Used by permission. Photo courtesy of the Billy Graham Center Museum, Wheaton, Illinois.

**Norman Vincent Peale.** "The Amazing Power of Prayer" was originally published by the Foundation for Christian Living as booklet #25 of vol. 7. It was preached at the Marble Collegiate Church in New York City in 1956. Used by permission of the Foundation for Christian Living. Photo courtesy of the Billy Graham Center Museum, Wheaton, Illinois.

**John R. Rice.** "And God Remembered . . ." was taken from John R. Rice, *"And God Remembered . . ." and Other Favorite Messages* (Sword of the Lord Publishers, 1941), 7–28. Used by permission of the John R. Rice family. The original version was printed from a transcription of the author's actual delivery of the message. This version has been edited to make for smoother reading. Photo courtesy of Joy Martin.

**Fulton John Sheen.** "Life Is Worth Living?" was taken from Fulton J. Sheen, *Life Is Worth Living,* first and second series (Garden City, N.Y.: Garden City Books, 1953), 13–17. Used by permission of the Literary Estate of Fulton J. Sheen, Patricia A. Kossmann, Literary Representative. Photo courtesy of the Fulton Sheen Archives, Diocese of Rochester.

**Thomas Todhunter Shields.** "The Doctrine of Election" was taken from T. T. Shields, *The Doctrines of Grace* (Toronto: The Gospel Witness, n.d.), 29–44. Used by permission of the Jarvis Street Baptist Church, Toronto, Canada, and The Gospel Witness.

**Oswald Jeffrey Smith.** "The Man God Uses" was published in various books and booklets. This version appeared in *The People's Magazine* (spring 1986): 18–22. Used by permission of the O. J. Smith family and the People's Church, Toronto, Canada. Photo courtesy of the Billy Graham Center Museum, Wheaton, Illinois.

302

**John Robert Walmsley Stott.** "The What and How of the Christian Life" was delivered at the fifty-first Founder's Week Conference (1957) of the Moody Bible Institute in Chicago and was published in the conference report by the Moody Bible Institute, pp. 178–90. Used by permission of Dr. Stott and Moody Bible Institute.

**William Ashley "Billy" Sunday.** "Wonderful" was taken from Elijah P. Brown, *The Real Billy Sunday* (Grand Rapids: Revell, 1914), 272–85. Used by permission. Photo courtesy of the Billy Graham Center Museum, Wheaton, Illinois.

**Charles R. "Chuck" Swindoll.** "Faith and Hurting People" was delivered at the 1983 Founder's Week Conference of the Moody Bible Institute in Chicago and was published in their conference report. It is used by permission of Dr. Swindoll and the Moody Bible Institute. Photo courtesy of Dallas Theological Seminary. The original transcript has been edited to make for smoother reading.

**Reuben Archer Torrey.** "The Only Gospel That Has Saving Power" was taken from R. A. Torrey, *The Gospel for Today* (Grand Rapids: Revell, 1922), 62–76. Used by permission of the publisher. Photo courtesy of the Billy Graham Center Museum, Wheaton, Illinois.

**George Washington Truett.** "Trumpeting the Gospel" was taken from George W. Truett, *We Would See Jesus and Other Sermons* (New York: Revell, 1915), 54–75. Used by permission of the publisher. Photo courtesy of Joy Martin.

# Textual Index

Warren W. Wiersbe has pastored churches in Indiana, Kentucky, and Illinois (Chicago's historic Moody Memorial). He ministered with *Back to the Bible* broadcast from 1979–1989. He is the author or compiler of more than 150 books and now focuses his energies on writing, teaching, and conference ministry.